Black Theatre

Premise and Presentation

*"What the authors have done in this volume ...
is the foundation for the creative advancement
of our performing arts."*

**Molefi Kete Asante
Temple University**

Carlton W. and
Barbara J. Molette

SECOND EDITION
"Revised and Enlarged"

Wyndham Hall Press

BLACK THEATRE
Premise and Presentation

Carlton W. Molette and Barbara J. Molette

SECOND EDITION
"Revised and Enlarged"

Wyndham Hall Press is an imprint of the
Cloverdale Corporation.

Library of Congress Catalog Card Number
86-050584

ISBN 0-932269-94-X (paperback)
ISBN 1-55605-212-X (hardback)

Printed in the United States of America

Cloverdale Corporation
Wyndham Hall Press
Bristol, IN 46507-9460

TO

CARLA AND ANDREA

PREFACE

Our intention is to describe the nature of African-American theatre as an expression of culture and a medium for communicating values. We have divided this book into two sections. Part One, PREMISE, describes the terms and concepts needed to examine African-American theatre from an Afrocentric point of view. Essential to that discourse is an understanding of culture and values and their impact upon an individual's point of view and subsequent interpretation of what is seen and heard. We cite examples of historical interpretations and analyses to illustrate the differences in these statements of evaluation that result from variations in culture and values.

Aesthetics and standards for evaluating creative works are controlled by the evaluator's culture and values. Therefore, African-American theatre is controlled by African-American culture and values. Since assertions of universality and objectivity are often made by public evaluators of creative works and since their evaluations are controlled by the values of their culture, we have examined the myths of objectivity and universality and concluded that these phenomena do not exist.

Part Two, PRESENTATION, delineates values that influence theatrical presentations by and for African Americans and their impact upon style, form, and the performance environment. The values of specific cultures also control concepts such as space and time that are crucial to the way in which performance art is perceived. Both Afrocentric and Eurocentric concepts of time and space are described in order to contrast Afrocentric and Eurocentric conventions of theatrical presentation.

African-American rituals, religious and secular, are recounted from the point of view of dramatic theory. An examination of African-American rituals provides a foundation for understanding African-American heroic values, characterization, and the use of space and time in the performance environment. Several plays by, about, and for African Americans are depicted as exemplars of elements of traditional African-American ritual and the values that such rituals communicate. Visual images in African-American theatre are compared to images in film and television drama revealing differences in the way realities and truths are perceived and communicated.

Our understanding of the nature of African-American theatre has been augmented by several important African-American playwrights. We mention the work of some of these playwrights in the book while there are others whose work is not mentioned. The choices we have made in selecting plays to illuminate a generalization should not be taken to imply that there are not many other excellent examples of plays by African-American playwrights that could have been described. Many theatre professionals have encouraged us at times when their encouragement was very much needed. We are especially grateful to William Branch, Alice Childress, Abram Hill, and Douglas Turner Ward. To Baldwin Burroughs, S. Randolph Edmonds, and Hoyt Fuller, we wish this opportunity to say "thank you" had been available to us earlier. The insightful questions and comments of Richard Long, Molefi Asante, John Scott, Thomas Pawley, and Orlando Taylor provided valuable assistance with the articulation of especially complex ideas that we wished to express in the book. Also, we owe an indescribably large debt of gratitude to our professors at the historically Black colleges we attended as undergraduates.

Our sincere thanks to Samuel Andrews and Martha Walton of Texas Southern University and Oscar Brockett of the University of Texas, Austin for their thorough reading and understanding criticism at various stages of the development of the first edition of this manuscript. We also wish to thank Ron Collins and Eugenia Collier of Coppin State College for undertaking the task of reviewing the manuscript for the second edition.

Many persons have shared their ideas freely with both of us over a period of years. Often such exchanges of ideas took place in informal group settings. As a result of the nature of these discussions and the passage of time, we are unable to accurately document the origins of many of the ideas expressed herein. Alas, we can only beg the indulgence of those who should be individually acknowledged here or in the end notes, but are not.

--Barbara & Carlton Molette

TABLE OF CONTENTS

PART ONE

PREMISE

n. 1 Logic. a statement assumed to be true and used to draw a conclusion. **2** any assumption or presupposition; postulate.

v.t. 1 to set forth as an introduction or explanation; mention beforehand.[1]

The theatre of a specific time, place, and societal strata will be more effectively illuminated by a broadly based inquiry into the general characteristics of the society. The theatre arts vary from time to time, place to place, and social strata to social strata. These variations are more heavily influenced by the forces of time, place, and social strata than by any internal forces within the theatre itself. In some very important ways, the study of theatre cannot be limited to the study of theatre. Theatre is a reflection of the time, place, and social strata of those who present it and those for whom it is presented.

Insights into the artistic creations of a culture are more likely to be valid when they occur after exposure to the values and the dominant creative motifs of that culture. Cultural values determine the qualitative standards by which art is judged. In order to develop a thorough understanding of a particular play or group of plays, in script or in presentation, one must first acquire an understanding of the culture that produced the particular drama and theatre and the values upon which that culture is based. Most importantly, the aesthetic values of the culture must be understood before the art in general, or any specific work of art that grows out of that culture, may be understood. The PREMISE of Black theatre is predicated on a particular set of values and the culture that is informed by those values.

Black theatre is a thread of the fabric of African-American culture. Differences in culture generate differences in theatre and in the aesthetic standards by which a culture's theatre is evaluated. Mavor Moore, Chairman of the Canada Council, suggests that, when one responds to art from a different cultural context, the interpretations that follow are so inextricably connected to one's own cultural patterns that they are almost always wrong. Further, he expresses the notion that close proximity in terms of geographical location, language, history, tradition, and even family ties may cause the observer to "be beguiled by the obvious similarities into overlooking important differences."[2] Although Moore has the societal context of Canada in mind when he makes the above statement about a relationship to mainstream America, his statement is at least as applicable to the African-American societal context as it is to Canadian culture.

To say that Black people in the U.S.A. are different from American White people is NOT to say that they are different in all respects; there are probably more similarities than differences. These rather obvious similarities undoubtedly carry over into Black theatre and White theatre as well. With regard to inquiry into the nature of African-American theatre, those who are beguiled by the obvious similarities into overlooking important differences seem to be far more influential than those who are not. Often, when we venture a public statement about some of the important differences between African-American theatre and European-American theatre, one or more persons are moved to recite a litany of the obvious similarities as though it serves to refute our assertions regarding the important differences. We will try to refrain from reciting the obvious similarities simply because they are obvious, not because we want a one-sided argument. This is not a "comparative analysis." No attempt is made to treat non-African-American cultures on an equal basis. Other cultures are mentioned because any work of this kind must use the existing knowledge of the reader as a basis for adding to that knowledge.

We do not suggest that all Black theatre has all of the characteristics attributed to Black theatre and described herein and that none of these characteristics are recognizable in any form of White theatre. To isolate any one characteristic of African-American art and point to an example of that single characteristic among some group of Whites reduces the highly complex organic whole to a series of independent binary functions. Art cannot be reduced to a series of independent binary functions. We are describing a set of functions that are connected in a complex manner. The manner in which these things are connected may be of equal or greater importance than the combination of the things. But certainly no single thing may be disconnected from the organic whole and function as the determining factor in defining or identifying African-American theatre, or differentiating Black theatre from White theatre.

In 1980, Molefi Asante published a book entitled *Afrocentricity: The Theory of Social Change.* In the relatively brief period that has followed, "Afrocentricity" has provided a linguistic and conceptual mechanism for many Black people to expand their understanding of themselves and the world. We use the terms "Afrocentric" and "Eurocentric" to describe philosophical positions or ways of perceiving reality that place Africa and Europe, respectively, at the center. Asante believes, and we agree, that in a very broad sense, there are at least three views of cultural reality: Afrocentric, Eurocentric, and Asiocentric. He emphasizes that these three categories are much too restrictive of the human personality; they only address the general thrust of each of the three cultural entities; and they are possibly oversimplifications. Within this context Asante generalizes:

> The Afrocentric viewpoint holds that all modalities and realities are united and move in one grand manner. There can be no separation between material and spiritual, profane and sacred, form and substance. ... The human being, acting with personal power, can animate, activate, and galvanize the material or the spiritual. The continuity from material to spiritual is the reality of the Afrocentric viewpoint.

> Asiocentric viewpoints hold that the material is an illusion, that the real only comes from the spiritual. Therefore, Asian philosophical concepts are enamored with spirit-over-matter notions.

> The Eurocentric perspective on reality ... holds that the material, the experiential, is real and that the spiritual is an illusion. Everything that is not within sense experiences is nonsense.[3]

Asante explains that each of these ways of perceiving the world is constrained by the history, mythology, creative motif, and collective ethos of each of the three cultures. A person's view of himself is determined by the history, mythology, creative motif, and collective ethos of his own culture. Further, that person's ability to communicate with any and all external entities is constrained by that view of self. Afrocentricism seeks to reinforce a view of self for Black people that is appropriate for Black people--a view that

4

PREMISE

locates African people and their traditional, contemporary and evolving values at the center.[4]

To argue that there are White people who behave in a manner that is different from our characterization of a White behavioral ideal is to ignore a fundamental concept. We are not attempting to describe all White people, or any aspect of all White people. Likewise, we are not claiming to describe all Black people. We are attempting to describe the traditional and the prevalent in African-American theatre art and culture and values. In order to reduce that description to the realm of the comprehensible, we make some generalizations. In order to clarify those generalizations, we make similar generalizations about White theatre art, or culture, or values. The generalizations that we make about White values, culture, and theatre art are not intended to describe the popular, but rather the dominant and influential. We deliberately focus upon those Eurocentric ideas that have been articulated in a manner that can only grow out of endorsement by the influential and the powerful and that have also been of significant advantage in the process of mis-educating African-American people.

Throughout this book there are instances when the description of a Eurocentric phenomenon from an Afrocentric perspective may appear to some to be judgmental. Such descriptions herein do not seek to pass judgment on any aspect of Eurocentric culture as it relates to interaction among Caucasian people. Our sole concern with Eurocentric culture is its impacts upon persons of African heritage. By liberating the minds of African Americans from the notion that Eurocentric culture is universal, Afrocentricism also allows African Americans to recognize that Eurocentric people have a right to maintain their Eurocentric values and beliefs--so long as other people's civil and human rights are not violated as a result.

BLACK THEATRE

Carter G. Woodson, in his seminal work *The Mis-education of the Negro*, articulates several concepts that have been absorbed into the consciousness of many African Americans. One of those concepts is especially germane to this PREMISE.

> The same educational process which inspires and stimulates the oppressor with the thought that he is everything and has accomplished everything worth while, depresses and crushes at the same time the spark of genius in the Negro by making him feel that his race does not amount to much and never will measure up to the standards of other people.[5]

A case in point: One of us had an art teacher in college who regularly asserted "African art is ugly." This art teacher's physical appearance unmistakably proclaims his African ancestry; but he had been "well educated" by a system that he can now be trusted to perpetuate. The dissemination of information about the aesthetics of African-American theatre will not alleviate the notion that the aesthetic standards of African Americans are inferior to those of White people. This PREMISE of Black theatre asserts that aesthetic standards which grow out of African culture are legitimate, important, and valuable. Cognitive information about the characteristics of African-American theatre is useful only to the extent that it is acquired in concert with affective acceptance of the assertion that African-American aesthetic standards are legitimate, important, and valuable. A deeper appreciation of African-American theatre requires some knowledge of traditional African aesthetic standards. Cognitive knowledge of traditional African aesthetic standards may be extracted from a descriptive analysis such as this study. On the other hand, cognitive knowledge is no substitute for the traditional process of acquiring aesthetic sensibilities that are in harmony with African-American culture. Living within a culture as a part of that culture, and acquiring the values of that culture from birth through adulthood allows for the development of a depth of appreciation of the art of that culture. Sensitivity to art is at least as important as knowledge about it. Cognitive learning that begins in late adolescence or later does not provide an optimum potential for the development of sensibilities in response to the art of a second culture.

Afrocentric theatre involves the communication of ideas through presentation to an audience. Presentations can include actual rituals and ceremonies in addition to the imitations of actions. The performers can be dancers, storytellers, singers, instrumentalists, preachers, or orators, as well as actors. The ideas that are presented may be rituals, legends, myths, poems, sermons, spontaneous responses, or scripted interpretations of such presentations, or even Eurocentric realistic well-made plays. Audiences can be both passive and participatory. Presentations may take place in the opulence of a concert hall, or the paucity of an urban store front, or the unembellished spaciousness of an open field. African-American theatre transcends the traditional Eurocentric division into disciplines and encompasses artistic presentation of every form. These attributes comprise the quintessence of this PREMISE of Black theatre.

There are four attributes of Afrocentric theatre that were articulated by W.E.B. DuBois as early as 1926. He said that "our" theatre must be ". . . About us. . . . By us. . . . For us. . . . Near us."[6] Changes in transportation and housing patterns for African Americans demand a reassessment of the mandate for a theatre that is "near us." In cities such as Houston and Los Angeles, nearness is an attribute that is often unattainable. On the other hand, general agreement apparently prevails with regard to the notion that Afrocentric theatre must be for, by and about Black people. When either "for," "by," or "about" becomes "integrated," the PREMISE and PRESENTATION change. These changes occur because "others" bring different priorities and assumptions to the production. Since theatre is responsive to its audience, these different priorities and assumptions will force the nature of both the PREMISE and PRESENTATION of African-American theatre to adapt to its "integrated" audience. People who are concerned with theatre for, by, and about African Americans tend to agree that theatre done by African-American people for a general American audience often has other goals that take precedence over the reflection and perpetuation of African-American values.

A. Peter Bailey expresses this notion in a manner that suggests several of its most important ramifications:

> . . . the difference between the man who wrote 'Slaveship' and the man who wrote 'Dutchman' is the difference between those two names, Jones and Baraka. Baraka is talking directly to his people, whereas Jones is screaming: 'Acknowledge me! Hear me!' White critics have never given 'Slaveship' the praise that they gave 'Dutchman' most likely because 'Slaveship' talks more to black folks.[7]

We retain use of the terms "Negro" and "Negro theatre" for the specific purpose of describing an attitude that speaks primarily to White people and favors integration, leading to assimilation by African Americans into European-American culture. The use of the term "Negro" in this manner does not indicate that assimilation is necessarily wrong--or necessarily right either. We recognize that, among African Americans, integrationist and assimilationist ideas exist. The term "Negro theatre" seems to be the most appropriate way to label that phenomenon.

This "Black" versus "Negro" dichotomy does not neatly divide African-American individuals into two discreet groups.

PREMISE

W.E.B. DuBois wrote about a phenomenon that suggests the "Black" versus "Negro" dichotomy is not two different groups of African-American individuals, each with its separate set of values and priorities. Instead, there are two, often contradictory, sets of values and priorities at work within each African American. DuBois called this phenomenon "double consciousness." He further explained:

> It is a peculiar sensation, this double consciousness, the sense of always looking at one's self through the eyes of others, of measuring one's soul by the tape of a world that looks on in amused contempt and pity. One ever feels his twoness--an American, a Negro, two souls, two thoughts, two unreconciled strivings . . . longing to attain self-conscious manhood.[8]

This statement represents DuBois' thinking at a relatively early stage in his adult life. Further, DuBois describes a phenomenon as it existed in the very early 1900's in his *The Souls of Black Folk* which was first published in 1903. In spite of some evolutionary progress since 1903, the phenomenon of double consciousness remains a painfully persistent force in African-American reality and in the art that grows out of that reality.

One of the fundamental assumptions that we make in the treatment of this subject is that an introductory exposure to African-American theatre ought to place a primary emphasis upon values and concepts rather than upon a chronological cataloging of events. We contend that the major reason for cataloging events chronologically is that the practice sometimes leads to insights about what causes events to occur as they do and what it all means to mankind. If, however, one is to derive some valid meaning from the study of historical evidence, one must first be able to relate the events being analyzed to the values and concepts of the people who

9

participated in the events. The worth of historical evidence grows out of such things as the judgments that may be derived from it. These judgments are generally subject to much greater influence from the values that exist in the person reaching the conclusions than from the actual historical evidence upon which the conclusions are allegedly based.

The focus of this work is on the nature of Black theatre. We present historical information for the purpose of providing supporting evidence for some of the assertions that we make about the nature of Black theatre. On the other hand, there is a large body of significant historical data about Black theatre that is not mentioned in this work. By focusing on aesthetic characteristics and the values that control them, a foundation for further study and more appropriate interpretation of the extant body of historical data will be developed.

Our goal is to examine the nature of Black theatre from an Afrocentric point of view. However, a dilemma exists. Sometimes, "the" Black point of view, or even "a" Black point of view may not be so clearly definable or even recognizable. Some Black points of view may turn out to be very similar to some White points of view. Some Black points of view may even bear a greater similarity to some White points of view than to some other Black points of view. Or, to complicate matters even more, Black people often have been placed in a situation in which a forced choice between two White points of view has seemed to represent the only two viable options. White oppressors frequently get into debates as to the relative merits of heavy handed violent oppression as opposed to a style of oppression that is more paternalistic and less belligerent. Within that context, African Americans have often assumed that the point of view that is less objectionable to African Americans is "the" Black point of view. So, as we seek to describe the nature of Afrocentric theatre in a manner that reflects an Afrocentric point of view, we must recognize this dilemma.

Another set of terms needs to be clarified--terms used to describe the oppressor and the oppressee. The oppressee being discussed here, but certainly not the only such group, is people of African descent. All White people, or people of European descent, are not part of the oppressor class. When we use the terms "White," "European," "European-American," or "Eurocentric," we recognize that many people who may be classified as one or more of those terms are, themselves, victims of what we call "White oppression." The problem is that, while a term like "Anglo-Saxon or Teutonic, Upper to Upper-Middle Class Male Chauvinist Imperialist Elitist Oppression" is more specific than "White oppression," it is also considerably more cumbersome. Further, it should not be necessary to point out, after every reference to the oppression of Black people, that Semitic people and Native American people, and other racial groups, and the poor and uneducated generally, have been oppressed by the same or similar people to those who oppress Black people. So, when we mention White oppressors, or White imperialists, we mean those Whites who are oppressors, or imperialists, or both. Such a statement does not and is not meant to imply that all White people are oppressors or imperialists. There are several major tribal groups of Europe who would contend that they do not contribute to the racial oppression of Black people. These groups may legitimately assert that they are not a part of this problem; but they do not appear to be a part of its solution, either.

We have made a choice with regard to the capitalization of the word "Black." The word "Black" is capitalized whenever the term is used to describe people of African descent or their culture. This stylistic device allows us to differentiate between people of African descent, the visual sense perception

11

black, and the negative connotations of that word in Eurocentric culture such as "black humor." This stylistic choice enables us to differentiate between, for example, Black comedy (a comedy that grows out of Black culture), and black comedy (comedy that has negative or sinister overtones). The word "white" has been dealt with in the same manner. Although we alternate the terms "Black," "African-American," and "Afrocentric," we recognize certain subtle differences in the meanings of these terms.

Black people are people of African descent wherever they may be located now. African-American people are people of African descent who are geographically, and in part culturally, located in the Americas. African people are people who reside on the continent of Africa. Most African people are Black. Most European people are White. Although there are Black people who live in Europe and White people who live in Africa, we generalize to the extent that we refer to Black people when we use the term "Africans" and White people when we use the term "Europeans." The term "an African people" has been used by others to describe any group of people who are descended from African people. Although we find "an African people" to be an acceptable term, we do not use it when writing because of the likelihood that its distinction from the term "African people" will be blurred.

We further recognize that such terms as "Black," "White," "European," and "African" may appear to suggest that racial purity is prevalent in reality. We do not seek to lend credence to the concept of racial purity by classifying individuals by race in the manner of the laws of several states in the U.S.A. and of South Africa. Further, we recognize that complex mixtures of various racial types have occurred in many parts of the world for thousands of years. Thus, we concede the use of racial and geographic descriptors, however vague and inadequate, as necessary to communicate the ideas herein.

PREMISE

Afrocentric values that exist in America today are a continuation of African culture as it has passed down through the generations of people who are descendants of Africans who were brought to this hemisphere as a part of the slave trade, and Africans who came earlier on their own. Slavery did not destroy all vestiges of African culture among the people who were subjected to its cruelties. There are scholarly works that support the existence of African cultural continuity in the Americas. Examples of these cultural continuities in the visual and performing arts have been documented. We recognize and accept the work of those scholars who have provided ample evidence in rebuttal of the popular notion of a few decades ago that African Americans have no real African cultural heritage. We will seek to build upon the extant foundation rather than to replicate it.

In our view, African Americans ought to analyze African-American culture from within the context of an Afrocentric value system and in a way that conforms to generally accepted standards of scholarship. Further, other Americans need to be exposed to such an analysis as well. None of us is free from the pervasive impact of the miseducation process. Miseducation that denies the existence of significant information because it is "pro-Black" is detrimental to White people as well as to Black people. Hopefully, exposure to the various cultures that exist in the United States will lead to the eventual possibility that these cultures can exist in an atmosphere of mutual respect. Our goal is to provide a basis for organized, reasonable, and analytical deliberations about the nature of African-American theatre by viewing it in the broader context of Afrocentric culture and values.

ENDNOTES

1.   *The World Book Dictionary*, edited by Clarence L. Barnhart and Robert K. Barnhart (Chicago: Doubleday and Company, 1979). All definitions cited herein are from *The World Book Dictionary*.

2.   Mavor Moore, address to the International Council of Fine Arts Deans, Washington, D.C., October 24, 1982. The Canada Council is similar to, but broader in scope than, the National Endowments for the Arts and Humanities in the U.S.A.

3.   Molefi Kete Asante, *Afrocentricity: The Theory of Social Change* (Buffalo: Amulefi Publishing Co., 1980). After the completion of the book, but before its actual publication, Dr. Asante presented a paper at the International Conference on Black Communication in Bellagio, Italy, in 1979. The paper "Intercultural Communication: An Afrocentric Inquiry into Encounter" was published in *International Conference on Black Communication* (New York: The Rockefeller Foundation, 1980). Because the paper is a later and more succinct statement of this concept, all quotes are from the conference paper, 5-6.

4.   For examples of this documentation see Robert Farris Thompson, "African Influence on the Art of the United States," in *Black Studies in the University*. ed. Armstead L. Robinson, Craig C. Foster, and Donald H. Ogilvie (New Haven: Yale University Press, 1969), 122-170; Ivan Van Sertima, *They Came Before Columbus* (New York: Random House, 1976); and for an overview of significant African cultural values as retained in Africa to use as a basis for comparison with African cultural retentions in the Americas,

see John S. Mbiti, *African Religion and Philosophy* (New York: Praeger, 1969).

5.   Carter G. Woodson, *The Mis-Education of the Negro* (Washington, D. C.: The Associated Publishers, Inc., 1933), xiii.

6.   [W.E.B. DuBois], "Krigwa Players Little Negro Theatre: The Story of a Little Theatre Movement," *The Crisis*, 32, No.3 (July, 1926), 134.

7.   A. Peter Bailey, "The Contemporary Black Theatre Movement," *The Crisis*, 90, No.2 (February, 1983), 22.

8.   W.E.B.DuBois, *The Souls of Black Folk* (1903; rpt. New York: New American Library, 1969), 45.

Chapter One

CULTURE AND VALUES

Art communicates the values of its culture. In addition, art is limited by the values of its culture to communication modes and messages that are acceptable to the values of that culture. This work examines the nature of African-American theatre art while recognizing that inquiry into aesthetics, culture, communication, and values are involved. When one inquires about the nature of African-American theatre, one cannot separate aesthetics from communication, culture, and values.

Eurocentric classification presumes that aesthetics or theory of the arts, rhetoric or the art of communication, and the social sciences are separate disciplines with separate modes of inquiry and ways of knowing. To suggest that one must choose to analyze theatre as either art or communication or social science to the exclusion of either of the other two is to create a false separation.[1] According to Eurocentric classification, the subject of theatre is categorized as one of the fine arts; therefore, from a Eurocentric point of view, a theoretical inquiry into the subject of theatre must adhere to the modes of inquiry and ways of knowing appropriate to the study of aesthetics. Eurocentric thought classifies the study of culture and values as an aspect of the social sciences; social science is regarded as a mode of inquiry that is inappropriate to the study of the arts. On the other hand, we contend that inquiry into the nature of Afrocentric theatre art cannot be effectively conducted without venturing into the territory of culture and values.

CULTURE AND VALUES

First, we will seek to articulate a working definition of the term "culture" from an Afrocentric point of view, while recognizing that the phenomenon of double consciousness mitigates against successfully achieving a totally Afrocentric point of view. African Americans and many others as well have been taught that culture is the set of things that we know that makes us civilized. The most "liberal" of those who accept this point of view stress the idea that culture is learned. These individuals may then seek to do good by helping the "culturally deprived." The "liberal" point of view seems to assume that certain Eurocentric things that White people learn to make them civilized must be learned by anyone and everyone who is to be considered civilized. This point of view further assumes that African-American people and other "culturally deprived" people have been deprived, not of what makes one culturally White, or European, or Anglo-Saxon, but rather of what makes one civilized. Therefore, if one of these "deprived" individuals can have large quantities of Eurocentric culture crammed into his or her brain, the individual will become more civilized. The "liberal" point of view stresses the notion that "cultural deprivation" is usually not the fault of the "culturally deprived." Therefore, they should not be blamed for the fact that they are less civilized. Instead, they should (and they CAN) be taught to be more White, more European, more Anglo-Saxon--therefore, more civilized.

The definition of culture espoused by the "liberal" position is also held by well-educated White racists who generally label themselves "conservative." Their elitist and exclusionist point of view only disagrees with the "liberal" point of view in that the "conservative" position tends to believe that: (1) the "culturally deprived" should be held responsible for their condition; (2) since the "culturally deprived" are responsible for their own plight, they should bear the responsibility for extricating themselves; and (3) life was better in the good old days when law and custom systematically excluded the assimilation of such unfortunates into the more genteel facets of Eurocentric society. This elitist, exclusionist position assumes that those African Americans who are illiterate, jobless, homeless, or underemployed are not willing to expend the energy necessary to alter their condition and, therefore, are responsible for their unfortunate plight. This position excludes those African Americans who do not acquire Eurocentric culture and values from full participation in the American economy while holding them responsible for their exclusion.

The question of what to do with or about people of African descent has permeated discourse about national policy in the U.S.A. since the arrival of Europeans on this continent. With regard to cultural issues, European-Americans have espoused two major responses to this question of what to do with or about people of African descent. The "liberal" response takes the position that all African Americans can and should learn to be European-Americans in all respects except skin color; whereas the "conservative" point of view takes the position that all African Americans cannot and should not be expected to assimilate fully into European-American society. Each of these points of view contains elements that, when taken out of context, many African Americans find attractive.

Most people of African descent in the U.S.A., when required to choose between these two major responses to the question of what to do with or about them, seem to select the "liberal" response since the "conservative" response appears to blame African Americans for simply being African American. Further, the "liberal" point of view recognizes that African-American people have the capacity to learn those things that White people have learned and have labeled "civilized." On the other hand, some African Americans seem to prefer the "conservative" response to this question. Elements of the

18

"conservative" point of view, such as the praise of individual African Americans for their apparent ability to pull themselves up by their own boot straps, are extremely attractive to many African Americans, especially to those who are the objects of such praise. Individual African Americans seem to have generally chosen to avoid what seems to be the more objectionable point of view in a two-option, forced-choice situation.

More than those two options exist from which to derive a model for a working definition of the term "culture." An example of an additional option may be developed by examining some of the fundamental principles of culture as articulated by the leaders of Nazi Germany. In general, those fundamental principles proclaimed that many of the generalized group characteristics that are often alleged to be learned behavior or adjustment to environmental conditions are, in fact, a result of biological (genetic) imprinting. In other words, Nazi thinking would insist that many of the significant differences in cultural identity are differences that are genetically passed on. When these notions were combined with the barbaric racism of Nazi Germany, the result was the Holocaust. The Nazis said that these genetic differences meant that one race was superior, rendering all others inferior to varying degrees. Their barbaric racism prevented them from even considering the question: Do genetic differences necessarily demand that there is superiority and inferiority?

The horrendous scope and magnitude of Hitler's crimes have left an ironic legacy. For more than a half-century, humanists have refused to consider seriously the possibility that many cultural differences might actually be genetic differences. There is an understandable reluctance among persons who regard themselves as humanists even to think something that is similar to what the Nazis thought. What is considered even worse, the articulation of those Nazi ideas could lead to another organized attempt at genocide. Many humanists would probably be willing to avoid open confrontation with a "truth" in order to avoid a genuine risk of genocide. While recognizing that the central ideas promoted by the Nazis are alive and well, both in Europe and the U.S.A., we hope we are far enough away in time from the Holocaust now to risk questioning some of these liberal notions about culture. Must we still insist that all of our differences that are not irrefutably physiological (skin color, hair texture, etc.) are learned, and therefore, constitute our culture? Or is it all right to ask whether some of those differences might not be biological and therefore passed on genetically?

Having presented this dilemma, we will now examine an Afrocentric point of view of what culture is while recognizing that this Afrocentric point of view is a synthesis of ideas articulated by African and African-American intellectuals who were heavily influenced by their very White liberal college professors. Many of the leading spokesmen for the Black arts movement of the 1960's and 1970's agree that there are seven elements that comprise a culture. These elements are mythology, history, social organization, political organization, economic organization, creative motif, and ethos. Maulana Karenga, one of the leading Black nationalist spokesmen and theorists of the 1960's, often said that "Culture is the basis of all ideas, images, and actions." We may, therefore, assume that, in this model, all art consciously or unconsciously represents and promotes the values of its culture.

Since an art grows out of a culture and reflects and perpetuates the values of the culture from which it emerges, the values of an art are inextricably connected to the cultural identities of the creators of the art. The thing that culture does, then, is to transmit a value system that makes one civilized according to the requirements of one's own culture. Culture transmits the system of values that influences our thoughts and behaviors and causes us to act in ways that members of our culture mutually agree are unique characteristics of civilization. The same culture and value system that creates a particular political system creates a mythology, a history, an ethos, and a creative motif to accompany the political, social, and economic systems. All seven elements in any viable culture and value system are compatible with each other. They are inseparable. This simply means that every culture is whole.

In order to gain an optimum understanding of a culture, it must be examined holistically. This analysis presents us with another dilemma. Our stated goal is to examine the theatre that grows out of African-American culture. Therefore, we need to focus upon this theatre of African-American culture. On the other hand, the previously outlined African-American working definition of culture suggests that African-American theatre cannot be well understood unless one also seeks to understand the mythology, the history, the politics, the economics, the social organization, the ethos, and the creative motif of African Americans. We will address this dilemma in two ways. First, we will discuss some things that are not "Theatre" in the Eurocentric American sense. Second, we will provide a bibliography that surveys various aspects of Afrocentric culture in America in far greater depth and detail than could possibly be included in a single volume.

A dictionary definition of the term "culture" will help to substantiate some of the notions about culture that have been mentioned earlier. We acknowledge that the dictionary definition is "correct" in that it accurately reflects the meanings of those Americans who are "important" enough to influence the compilers of the dictionary. The dictionary is not at fault for articulating the underlying assumptions of racial superiority and inferiority that motivate the use of the word "culture." The goal of the dictionary is to describe those meanings that are attributed to the word by "important" and influential people who write and publish in the English language.[2]

> **culture, -n.** 1 fineness of feelings, thoughts, tastes, or manners; refinement: . . . **syn**: breeding. . . .2 Anthropology. **a** the civilization of a given people or nation at a given time or over all time; its customs, its arts, and its conveniences: . . . **b** socially inherited artifacts. 3 the development of the mind or body by education or training: . . .

The first definition of culture suggests that there are criteria that determine the absence or presence of fineness or refinement equally well without regard to race, culture, or nationality. Our observations seem to indicate that variations in race, culture, and nationality are closely related to variations in what is generally agreed to represent fineness or refinement among people. The terms "fineness" and "refinement" imply purity; subtlety; the absence of coarseness; the presence of extreme care and accuracy; and superiority of quality, appearance, and conception. The dictionary definition seems to presuppose that Eurocentric criteria for determining what constitutes fineness are the only valid criteria. If one accepts this assumption, then one must conclude that any criteria that are significantly different from the Eurocentric elitist criteria must be inferior. The synonym "breeding" that is listed in the dictionary is even more blatantly racist in its assumptions. If the word "breeding" is used to indicate "fineness" and "refinement," the implication is that these highly complimentary traits are passed on genetically. Therefore, if one has not inherited some basis for the development of these traits by virtue of "breeding," they cannot possibly be acquired. This term "breeding" suggests

22

that the identity of one's parents determines membership, or the lack of it, in an elite group. Persons who do not have parents with "breeding" cannot possibly obtain "breeding" themselves. On the basis of parentage alone, persons may be declared incapable of achieving a high level of "refinement" or "culture."

The anthropological definition of the word "culture" was devised to avoid the underlying prejudices in the most commonly accepted meaning of the word "culture." On the other hand, there is a specific difficulty that this definition presents from an Afrocentric point of view. Eurocentric qualitative judgments often precede the use of the word "civilization" when used to describe the system of customs, arts, and conveniences of a given people or nation. *The World Book Dictionary* defines the word "civilize" as follows:

> **1** to change from being savage and ignorant to having good laws and customs and knowledge of the arts and sciences; train in culture, science, and art:...**syn**: enlighten, educate, humanize. **2** to improve in culture and good manners; refine. **syn**: polish.

So the word "civilization" serves as a reminder of the notions of racial superiority that are more obvious in the most widely accepted meaning of the word "culture."

A discussion of the term "culture" that seeks to reflect an Afrocentric perspective must scrutinize some of the most commonly held notions about anthropology. We do not mean to imply that these commonly held notions are necessarily the views of the leading contemporary authorities in the field of anthropology. Rather, these are the notions that trickle down to those literate Eurocentric Americans who comprise the "general public." The most important of these notions is that anthropology is a science. Further, the dictionary states that anthropology is a science, while defining science as "knowledge based on observed facts and tested truths arranged in an orderly system. . . ." To the contrary, an expert in the field of anthropology has recently stated:

> It is still tremendously difficult to understand a culture different from our own.
>
> Anthropology is highly individualistic. One person goes to a place and writes an account and then later another scientist will see things differently.
>
> There is no final interpretation of another culture.[3]

The general public assumes that the conclusions drawn by scientists using the scientific method are scientific, which means "systematic; accurate; exact. . . ."

Another commonly held notion is that societies evolve from simple to complex. This notion is now regarded by the general public as a scientifically established fact. Such a view enables racism to shift its vocabulary while claiming that the disappearance of the old vocabulary represents the disappearance of racism itself. The old racist terms such as "heathen" and "savage" are replaced by new pseudo-scientific terms such as "pre-literate."

There is still another factor in the anthropological definition of the word "culture" that must be addressed. That factor is an apparent absence of a clear distinction between the evidence that anthropologists use to validate their descriptions of a culture and the culture itself. Customs, arts, and artifacts provide evidence that may be used by anthropologists to validate a description of a culture. But the interpretation of that evidence is often "unscientific." The culture itself is the commonly accepted body of knowledge that the people of the group have that causes them to create, use and make qualitative judgments about the customs, arts, and artifacts that they have. But culture is also the manner in which customs, arts, and artifacts are used in order to transmit the values of the society. Our concern with African-American theatre as culture requires that we examine (1) African-American theatre to derive information about the body of knowledge that African-American people have in common that causes African-American theatre to have the particular set of characteristics that it has, and (2) the manner in which African-American theatre transmits the values of the society from which it emanates.

African-American values are inextricably connected to their African cultural heritage. These values are a continuation of the principles of Maat, which were the basis for ancient Egyptian moral behavior. Diop noted that "the African is dominated by his social relations, because they reinforce his equilibrium, his personality, and his being."[4] The essence of Maat may be summed up with the statement from Nefer-Seshem-Ra:

> I have spoken truly and done right. I spoke justly and repeated that which was just. ... I judged between two in such a way that would satisfy both of them. I rescued the weak from those who were stronger as much as was in my power. I gave bread to the hungry, clothes to the naked and brought the boatless to dry land. I buried those who had no children and built a boat for those were without one. I respected my father, pleased my mother and raised my sisters and brothers.[5]

The ancient African strove for truth, justice and righteousness. The following lines are indicative of the essence of a life not of struggle, but of harmony.

Do not terrorize people for if you do, God will punish you accordingly. If anyone lives by such means, God will take bread from his or her mouth. . . . If one says I will rob another, he will end up being robbed himself. . . . Therefore, one should live in peace with others and they will come and willingly give gifts which another would take from them through fear.[6]

In tune with the attitude expressed by Ptah-Hotep, the ancient Africans did not have a military aristocracy. Diop states "the soldiers play only an unobtrusive, if not nonexistent, political role."[7] In contrast, Eurocentric moral values are related to war and conflict and "Those who fall in battle or who died of their wounds were admitted to heaven, the dwelling-place of the gods. . . where lived the Valkyries and where Fricka. . . received the heroes and presented them with the drinking-horn."[8] These Eurocentric values were prevalent in early Greece and gave rise to the concept of conflict as an essential component of drama. Conversely, the values of the Egyptians generated drama that fostered harmony by celebrating the people and events that were considered deserving of veneration. Such celebration continues to be an important function of theatre among African Americans today.

We have expressed the opinion that a total grounding in and familiarity with a given culture should provide the opportunity for a better analysis of that culture. This opinion may presuppose that all things are equal and they generally are not. Nevertheless, the point seems worth postulating. It seems so because the question, "Can a White person analyze African-American culture as well as an African-American person can?" continues to be raised. The complexity of this issue is exacerbated if one adds the possibility of the genetic transfer of some aspects of cultural identity. We cannot provide words that will cause a general sense of agreement in response to this issue. However, we recognize the presence of the phenomenon of racism and assert that it is the pivotal factor in a complex set of factors. Whether or not African-American people can or should sing opera would hold little fascination as a question were it not for the presence of racism. We regularly hear expressions from Eurocentric people who consider themselves to be totally free from racial biases who seem to us to say:

> All the disadvantaged people of the world could learn to behave just like us Europhiles if only they would work at it. Some non-Whites are intelligent enough; nothing in their genetic makeup prevents them from doing so. If we simply expose them to our way of doing things, they will see the obvious error of their previous ways and learn to act like us. Then they will be civilized.

We regret to add that such views as those summarized above constitute one of the most insidious forms of Eurocentric racism. By the same token, the question of whether or not White people can or should analyze African-American culture is also a question of racism. The real issue is "Can White people respond to Afrocentric culture in a non-racist manner?"

One factor must be recognized even though it may seem to contradict a previously stated theme. American culture does exist. The "melting pot" myth of American culture, overrated though it may be, is not totally without validity. There has been some cultural diffusion in the United States. African culture has influenced European culture and European culture has influenced African culture. The myth of the "melting pot" implies that a single conglomerate culture has been produced. In reality, we have here in the United States several diverse cultures that are profoundly influencing each other. African culture in America has been profoundly influenced by European culture, Native American culture, Asian culture, and so forth. Consequently, many of the most cherished beliefs of European-Americans are also the most cherished beliefs of African Americans--even some beliefs that are not in our own best interest as a people. For instance, we do not control the schools that our children attend. Consequently, our children are taught that Greece is the "cradle of civilization." The Afrocentric truth is that the cradle of civilization is in Africa. Our children are taught to parrot phrases like "Columbus discovered America," as though there were no people here already when Columbus arrived. The essential point is that African Americans get their formal education in Eurocentric American schools. Much of their informal education is equally subject to Eurocentric American influences. The result is African-American culture--not American culture with brown skin, not African culture transplanted to the U.S.A., but African-American culture.

Given this relationship between African-American culture and European-American culture, one may reasonably assume that any serious inquiry into the nature of African-American theatre and the culture from which it emerges must raise questions about the values of European-American culture. These questions are not raised here to evaluate the worth of Eurocentric values to Eurocentric culture. Instead, the purpose is to determine whether or not it would be in the best interest of African Americans for African-American culture to be more Afrocentric and less Eurocentric in its values. In order to address this question effectively, the term "values" must be thoroughly understood. Our dictionary defines the words "value" and "values" as:

> value, --n. 1 the real worth; proper price: . . . 2 high worth; excellence; usefulness; importance: . . . values, Sociology. the established ideals of life; objects, customs, ways of acting, and the like, that the members of a given society regard as desirable: "Man lives by

values; all his enterprises and activities ... make sense only in terms of some structure of purposes which are themselves values in action" (Will Herberg).

Our dictionary's sociological definition fails to emphasize important characteristics that are requisite to a useful understanding of the term values in this context. Values are unconscious and often permanent. These characteristics constitute essential differences between values and attitudes. Attitudes are external manifestations of such internal phenomena as thoughts, opinions, dispositions, moods, and emotions. Attitudes can, therefore, be controlled, to some extent, through the use of will power. So, racist attitudes can, and often are eliminated, or at least reduced, in adult Americans through a combination of education, will power, and enforcement. Values are more basic, more internal, and more enduring than attitudes. Values are learned during childhood and are seldom altered thereafter. So racist values usually do not change in adults, even when the readily recognizable manifestations of these values are eradicated.

Our dictionary provides examples of how some racist values may be sustained and disseminated. The definitions of terms that have been cited earlier are not isolated instances. These terms that have been defined here are useful in establishing a context in which the terms "culture" and "values" may be examined from an African-American point of view. There is still another term for which a dictionary definition seems to be worth citing in order to establish this context. That term is "ethnic:"

> **adj. 1** having to do with the various racial and cultural groups of people and the characteristics, language, and customs of each; ... **2** of or having to do with people of foreign birth or descent: ... **3** having to do with nations not Christian

BLACK THEATRE

The third definition of ethnic assumes that people and nations that are, for example, Islamic or worshippers of Shango, rather than Christian or Jewish, are heathen and pagan and therefore, "ethnic." Dictionaries label definitions that are no longer in current use "archaic" or "obsolete." These definitions of "ethnic" are not labelled archaic or obsolete in the 1979 edition of *The World Book Dictionary*. People who are not Christian or Jewish are regarded as heathen and pagan by contemporary writers and speakers who are important and influential enough to be used as sources for dictionaries. The notion that groups of people who are different must be categorized as inferior or superior to each other rather than merely different provides a foundation for the racist values that permeate the word "ethnic."

Some persons have been inculcated with a set of values that regards all people who do not belong to their particular racial and religious groups as heathen and pagan. Some other persons find it normal and acceptable to be tolerant of some other forms of organized religion, while regarding other religions as strange or weird, and still other religions as totally unacceptable. Almost all of us regard some other set of religious beliefs to be heathen and pagan, even if we are too tolerant to use those words. Once we become adults, altering the negative values that we have about those heathen and pagan practices is possible only under extreme and unusual circumstances. The words that we use to describe religious beliefs and practices that are quite different from our own provide an example of attitudes that are based upon values. We may, indeed, change our attitudes. For example, we may train ourselves not to use certain words that refer to some other group that members of the other group find offensive. But simply learning to avoid so-called "value loaded" words does not necessarily alter the values that caused those words to be used in the first place.

CULTURE AND VALUES

Values are internal and personal. As a result of the manner in which values are acquired, people with similar backgrounds tend to have similar values. By the time we reach adulthood, we have been programmed to relate everything that we perceive in the world around us only in terms of our values.[9] This is true, not only of other people's behavior, but of literally everything that we perceive. For example, an earthquake or a tornado may be regarded as an explainable scientific phenomenon or as an indication that the gods are angry. We may regard a person who eats with chopsticks as normal, or as strange and picturesque, or as primitive and vulgar. How we relate to these various stimuli is directly connected to the values we have acquired.

We acquire our values from the sum total of our experiences during our so-called "formative years." But, certain major sources of information tend to impact significantly upon the formation of values. These information sources include: family, friends (and their families), church and other activities of organized religion, school and other activities of formal education such as books, and media (especially electronic media). The electronic media are relatively new sources of information in the formation of values, but extremely powerful ones. In the U.S.A., the importance of geographical region and family income has been greatly reduced in the values acquisition process. These two factors were of considerable significance in the not-too-distant past. But they have been overwhelmingly replaced by television and recorded music as major factors in the acquisition of values.

Values are acquired individually, non-rationally, and at a very early age. Psychologists generally agree that within the first three or four years of our lives, the basic personality is formed. This personality formation tends to remain intact for the rest of our lives. The first seven years of values acquisition are regarded as an IMPRINTING process. We

31

acquire the ability to walk and to walk NORMALLY. The same can be said for such things as eating and talking. And we also develop extremely complex conceptual structures such as how to behave as an adult.

In the general age range of seven to thirteen, MODELING is the principal mode of values acquisition. Heroes are identified and emulated. Heroes may be chosen from among those who are very close, such as parents, or from among those with whom there is no direct personal contact, such as sports and motion picture stars. Among the seven to thirteen age group, the critical nature of the electronic media in the modeling process is evident in the widespread hero identification with the stars of recorded music and of television. But the hero identification is only a symptom of a much more complex phenomenon. The most significant effects of electronic media upon values acquisition have to do with the content of the material presented. On television, all problems are solved quickly and effortlessly. All pains and anxieties can be immediately eliminated by simply using the right deodorant or toothpaste or taking the right pill. The most complex of international (even intergalactic) entanglements are regularly resolved within the standard one-hour time frame. And the people who solve the problems always survive--usually without even working up a sweat. In the face of these media-generated modeling examples, such values as delayed gratification, self discipline, and the work ethic are difficult to instill through such traditional sources as family, church, and school.

Within the general age range of fourteen to twenty, the dominant urge is toward SOCIALIZATION. We want to be like "everyone else" in every detail. Within this age range, we derive our most significant information for values acquisition from others who are like us in terms of interests, age, and the other major factors that shape our values. People intuitively recognized this phenomenon long before it was described in scientific terms. Segregation with race or religion or sex as its basis has most often focused upon persons between the ages of fourteen and twenty. In this age range, the importance of family decreases and the importance of friends increases in the values acquisition process.

The process of acquiring values continues from birth until approximately age twenty-one. We acquire rational information from several sources, including our families. We also acquire information from these sources about what is pleasant and what is not. From these sources, massive amounts of information about various prejudices are absorbed. During the socialization process, we test a great deal of this information. For example, one might regularly be given a long list of "thou-shalt-not's" as well as some indication of certain horrendous consequences for violating them. But when one of the "thou-shalt-not's" is tested, and if it turns out to be fun, then a shift occurs in the values that are being formed. On the other hand, if the testing process verifies the information, then the information eventually becomes locked into our values.

Social systems are sometimes developed to help insure that the prejudices that the family has inculcated will survive the period in which such values are tested on the "significant others" in the socialization process. For example, if a White family inculcates in its children the value that African-American people are generally poorer because they do not possess the discipline or the intelligence to be more successful, then it is imperative that the children in that White family not be given an opportunity to test the validity of that value. If the White children go to school with African-American children and discover that some African-American children have more discipline and intelligence than many White children do, the values of the White children may shift in a

33

direction that the parents find undesirable. If, on the other hand, a child only comes in contact with others who have very similar values, those values will probably not be altered significantly before adulthood is reached and the values are locked in. At approximately age twenty-one, an individual's values are locked in. Each person's basic "gut level" responses to the stimuli the world provides have been set for life. Only a major emotional upheaval can generate a change in one's established system of values thereafter.

Values operate on a subconscious level and on a continuing basis. Values provide individuals with instant programmed responses to the constant stream of stimuli with which we are all bombarded. These instant programmed responses inform individuals that each given stimulus is right or wrong, good or bad, normal or not normal. And the information that forms a person's values is received almost totally before the age of twenty-one. Any analysis and interpretation of art is impossible except within the context of the values of the person making the analysis and interpretation. More importantly, the reader of any analysis and interpretation of art must understand as much as possible the values of the person who wrote the work. When we examine the way in which White people respond to African-American theatre and other events that are controlled by African-American values, the date upon which the response occurred is not indicative of the values that control the response. The most reasonable and fair evaluation of such a response is probably obtained by examining how African-American people and African-American culture were regarded in the time span and environments that the White responder spent his or her first twenty-one years.

Many White people whose values cause them to exhibit relatively subtle forms of racial prejudice object to having their behavior described as racist. Generally, White people

34

who voice such objections have a view of racist behavior that
includes inflicting deliberate physical harm and vituperative
communication upon another human being because of race.
On the other hand, African Americans and other traditional
targets of racism in the U.S.A. tend to regard other less violent
forms of behavior as racist as well. In order to avoid
protracted debates about what behaviors the word "racist"
includes, we have chosen to use a term we regard as a more
specific nomenclature. We use the term "Afrophobia" or
"Afrophobic" behavior to describe non-belligerent behavior
that appears to grow out of values that result in a general fear
of African people and African culture.

Individuals who suffer from Afrophobia often avoid facing
this fear by ignoring Africa, its culture, and its people. For
example, when planning a trip, we called a major U.S.A.-based
airline to ask if it had flights to Africa. They said they did
not. But, upon reading the airline's brochures, we discovered
they had flights to the country we wished to visit--Egypt. A
well-trained museum director once lamented to an audience
that his museum did not have an African art collection, while
boasting of the museum's collection of ancient Egyptian art.
Somehow Egypt has been removed from the continent of
Africa and put into a place called the middle east. To further
illustrate our point, in 1969 or 1970, NBC did a special
program in prime time about Ethiopia. The program opened
with the statement "The Ethiopians are a dark-skinned
Caucasian people." That statement is the only thing about the
program we still remember, except that the Ethiopians were
characterized as a good and proud people who are descended
from an important ancient civilization--thus, the need to
separate them from their Africanness. Afrophobia distorts
geography, history, and aesthetics, causing its victims to be
blinded by their fear of proximity to things African or to
disassociate from its Africanness something they regard as
good.

BLACK THEATRE

Most of the highly influential historical analysis and interpretation of African-American theatre in America has been written by White people whose values were "locked in" before 1954. Thus, the values that provide the basis for most of the widely held views of African-American theatre are the same values that regarded racial discrimination and segregation as normal, ordinary, and inevitable, not only in churches and schools but in the Army, Navy, and Air Force and nearly every work place in America, even if an individual's values regarded racial discrimination as inappropriate. Racial discrimination in virtually every other aspect of American life prior to 1954 seemed equally normal, ordinary, and inevitable within the value systems of those in control. The decade following the end of World War II witnessed an extremely gradual change in the value programming of Whites in America on the subject of racial discrimination. Progress has undoubtedly been made with regard to reducing racism in American values during the decades following the Supreme Court decision outlawing segregated public schools. Thus far, the progress that has been made has had very little impact upon how African-American theatre in America is perceived and interpreted.

ENDNOTES

1.   Carlton Molette, "Aristotle's Union of Rhetoric and Dramatic Theory," *The Southern Speech Journal*, 34, No.1 (Fall, 1968), 47-51, suggests that the art versus rhetoric dichotomy is a false one, even in as Eurocentric a conceptual framework as Aristotle's.

2.   The technique they use to determine the meaning of words is described in the following quote by the editors: "*The World Book Dictionary* is based on an extensive quotation file containing more than three million quotations collected by

experienced readers over a period of twenty-five years. These are culled from a wide sampling of contemporary magazines, newspapers, scholarly and technical journals, and books. Through an extensive reading program, the dictionary staff of editors and researchers constantly accumulates information on words, meanings, and usages. . . .", 4.

3.   Cheryl M. Fields, "Controversial Book Spurs Scholars' Defense of the Legacy of Margaret Mead," *Chronicle of Higher Education* (May 11, 1983), 28.   The quote is by George E. Marcus, chairman of the anthropology department at Rice University, Houston, Texas.

4.   Cheikh Anta Diop, *Civilization or Barbarism: An Authentic Anthropology*, trans. Yaa-Lengi Meema Ngemi, ed. Harold J. Salemson and Marjolijn de Jager (Brooklyn: Lawrence Hill Books, 1991), 362.

5.   Maulana Karenga, selected and retranslated, *Selections from The Husia,* (Los Angeles: The University of Sankore Press, 1984), 95.

6.   Karenga, 41-42.

7.   Diop, *Civilization or Barbarism*, 129.

8.   Cheikh Anta Diop, *The Cultural Unity of Black Africa* (London: Karnak House, 1989), 148.

9.   Morris Massey, *What You Are Is Where You Were When*, video cassette (Farmington, Michigan: Magnetic Video Corporation, 1976).

Chapter Two

VALUES AND INTERPRETATION

Values significantly impact upon the analysis and interpretation of art. The relationship between the values of the historian and the resultant analysis and interpretation of historical data may be exemplified by examining historical information that is central to an understanding of the history of African-American theatre: "The First African-American Theatre" and "The First Theatre."

African-American theatre has existed in the Americas since the very first performance in the Americas by people who came from Africa. That performance was not exactly as it would have been had it taken place in Africa instead of the Americas. Black theatre in the Americas grows out of African-American culture. The values of that culture are reflected and perpetuated by Black theatre. The terms "Black theatre" and "African-American theatre" are not used here to describe the Black revolutionary theatre movement of the 1960's exclusively. That movement helped to repopularize the term "Black" and had a number of other positive effects upon the cultural awareness of African-Americans as well. The result was a reawakening of African cultural identity. Neither a new culture, nor a new theatre was created. Black theatre and Black culture are older than recorded history. We know that Black theatre began many thousands of years ago.

VALUES AND INTERPRETATION

THE FIRST THEATRE

Now in its sixth edition, *History of the Theatre* by Oscar G. Brockett, is widely regarded as the standard theatre history textbook in the United States. Brockett asserts:

> Although the influence of Egypt on Greece apparently was considerable, one important difference remains between their performance traditions. The Egyptians maintained an advanced civilization for some three thousand years (a period longer than the one that separates us from the beginnings of Greek drama) and never developed theatrically beyond ritualized performances, repeating the same ceremonies year after year for centuries. Theirs was a relatively static society which resisted changes that might have led to an autonomous theatre, whereas the Greeks went on to develop a theatre in which new plays were presented each year. Thus, despite the achievements of the Egyptians, it is Greece that took the decisive step toward an autonomous theatre.[1]

Two fundamental aesthetic differences between Afrocentric theatre and Eurocentric theatre are illuminated by this passage. First, the assumption is made that the rapid change in Greece from religious-based ritual theatre to secular theatre constitutes progress. Afrocentric philosophy, as codified by the ancient Egyptians, contends that there is no differentiation between the religious and the secular because religion permeates every aspect of human existence. In contrast, Eurocentric philosophy contends, not only that such separation is possible, but that the development of institutionalized secular art constitutes progress in the development of civilization.

Second, the assumption is made that competition, a
fundamental characteristic of Greek theatre, fosters
excellence. Competition held no value for the ancient
Egyptians, concerned with abiding by the guiding principles
of Maat--Truth, Justice, and Righteousness. These governing
moral values "stemmed from a collective, sedentary, relatively
easy, peaceful life, once it had been regulated by a few social
laws."[2] The Greek idea of the dramatic contest presupposes
that it is better to perform new scripts every year than it is to
do a better job of performing the same old scripts year after
year after year. The ancient Egyptians, by virtue of their
behavior, would obviously disagree with this contention.
Further, a continuation of the philosophical view of the
ancient Egyptians is seen in the current Afrocentric aesthetic
ideal and will be described in the section of this book that
deals with contemporary African American ritual theatre.
Here, it is sufficient to note that the Eurocentric aesthetic
ideal places a greater value on the presentation of new content
than the continuation of traditional values through ritual. In
African ritual, there is an internal motivation to perform the
ritual well--possibly, to perform the ritual better than it has
ever been performed before--but there is no contest; there is
no need to proclaim winners and losers. On the other hand,
ancient Greek drama evolved into an annual competition in
which winners and losers were declared. The competitive
nature of Greek drama, along with its secularization,
undoubtedly fostered the development of new theatrical
content. However, the unanswerable question remains: To
what extent did the secular competitive nature of Greek
drama reduce its effectiveness in instilling the values of truth,
justice, and righteousness in its audience?

Brockett indicates that there are more than fifty surviving
"pyramid texts" from the period 2800 to 2400 B.C. and that
certain passages may have been traditional by that time and
may have originated 1000 years earlier. These texts generally

portray the values and beliefs that governed the lives of the ancient Egyptians. Brockett also points out that some scholars contend that these texts were scripts to be performed while others "disagree violently over the degree to which these texts should be considered dramatic" contending that they were literary pieces not intended for performance.[3] In addition to the "pyramid texts," Brockett mentions that there are texts related to the coronation of pharaohs; a text called the "Memphite Drama" that was performed on the first day of spring, dating back to 2500 B.C.; and a text that some scholars call the "Abydos Passion Play" that was performed annually from about 2500 until about 550 B.C."[4] The "Memphite Drama" was composed during the first dynasty and rewritten by Shabako about 700 B.C. on a stone, which now resides in the British Museum. The "Memphite Drama" commemorated the unification of upper and lower Egypt by Menes about 5500 B.C. and "is in reality the libretto of a drama or stage-play which was probably acted when certain important festivals were celebrated at Memphis.[5] The "Abydos Passion Play" is based upon the myth of Osiris and Horus. The term "Passion play" is traditionally used to describe a type of Medieval Christian drama that focuses on the death and resurrection of Jesus. The myth of Osiris and Horus is considerably more than 2000 years older than the similar Greek myths that deal with death and resurrection or rebirth. According to the Greek historian Herodotus:

> Almost all the names of the gods came into Greece from Egypt. My inquiries prove that they were all derived from a foreign source, and my opinion is that Egypt furnished the greater number.[6]

Brockett recognizes that some scholars consider these texts the earliest recorded theatrical productions while others "have vigorously objected."[7] Brockett also presents a photograph of a relief sculpture from a tomb at Saqqara [or, Sakkara] that clearly illustrates some individuals performing a dance while others "seem to be providing a clapping accompaniment."[8] Thus, there are paintings that depict ritual dancing; there are texts that describe dramatic action; and there are highly respected scholars who have validated the conclusion that the texts were enacted in the form of dramatic ceremonial rituals.

Most of the widely disseminated information that recognizes the theatre and drama of ancient Egypt implies that the ancient Egyptians were committed to their religious beliefs and practices to the extent that they seem to have been a humorless people. Yet, a scholar of considerable Eurocentric respectability, E. A. Wallis Budge, indicates that ancient Egyptian drama and theatre was not limited to serious plays. Budge states "The lapses of the gods and goddesses, moral or otherwise, did not stir men to anger, but did provoke men to regard them with a sort of kindly and good-humoured ridicule."[9] He uses the hieratic text, "The Contendings of HORUS and SET," translated by Alan Gardiner to illustrate the point. Budge writes:

> This contains what I believe to be the 'book of words' of a play, . . . which may rightly be described as 'a Mythological Drama.' The narrative is slight, but the speeches of all the actors are given at length, and a connected story can be constructed. This play represents the gods assembled as a Court of Justice with RA as chairman, and they have to decide a simple issue, viz. whether the son of OSIRIS, the youthful cripple HORUS, is to succeed to his father's office, or whether it is to be given to his bold, handsome and free-living uncle (or brother) SET. RA is in favour of SET, but many of the gods are not. They lose their tempers, contradict and insult each other, and wrangle together like the members of a local or municipal Miglis in EGYPT at the present day. The delay of the

law is laughed at, and the indecision and vacillation of the gods is made clear. The gross social customs of a bygone age are pilloried in the story of the criminal assault which SET made on HORUS whilst they were occupying the same couch, and in the account of the obscene relations which existed between ISIS and her son HORUS. The ribaldry of NEITH, the whorish behavior of HATHOR, the daughter of RA, the lasciviousness of SET, the quarrel of SET with the gods when he threatened to slay them one by one, the quarrel of HORUS with ISIS when he cut off her head, . . . are all lightly but clearly brought out. The gods adjourn and change the site of their court, but come to no decision, for they ignore the advice of the old gods, and the evidence which they ask for and obtain from them and snub their referees. Finally, forgetting their precarious position, they address disparaging words in their letters to OSIRIS, but his reply is so menacing that they fulfil straightway his command to make HORUS his successor, and give SET a position in the sky where he can act as the god of thunder. This play makes good reading and is a thoroughly 'human document', but it is difficult to think that those who saw it played would find their reverence for the gods increased.[10]

The ancient Egyptians left further evidence that the extant scripts were actually performed by indicating who the performers were. Diop supports the contention that these works were performed in *Civilization or Barbarism*. He observes:

> Up to the first Tanite dynasty, the royal family itself acted in Osiris' drama,. . . . Then later, only the priests would act, before the royal family, in the passion of Osiris, the mystery of his death, and resurrection.[11]

BLACK THEATRE

One approach that theatre scholars use to aid in determining whether or not a work was performed in its historical context is to perform the work. The assumption is that texts that were not intended to be performed usually do not result in a polished performance without modification, while a work that was intended to be performed usually has undergone whatever modification is necessary to enable a polished performance. Further evidence that these texts were performed is provided by Diop, thusly:

> The British school of Egyptology has translated one of these plays written in hieroglyphics; a team of disguised British actors performed it, following the texts faithfully. The film that was made of this unique document was shown by the dramatist and poet G.M. Tsegaye, during the 1973 Pan-African Congress in Addis-Ababa.[12]

In the face of this evidence, the proof that theatre art existed in Egypt by 2500 B.C. and continued for at least 2000 years would seem to be substantial, but many scholars reject this notion. However, what if there were evidence that the ancient Egyptians had constructed a performance space with scenery? And what if this performance space had been constructed of stone in 2778 B.C.? And what if it had been constructed in the same place (Sakkara) as the relief sculpture reproduced in Brockett depicting a performance? And what if this performance space still exists? Would this provide sufficient evidence?

In 1896, Sir Banister Fletcher published the first edition of his seminal work, *A History of Architecture on the Comparative Method*. This work has been considered so significant that, although Sir Banister Fletcher died in 1953, the work continues to be revised and re-printed. Thus, the failure to recognize that Sir Banister Fletcher has described a

VALUES AND INTERPRETATION

performance space in the following quote cannot be attributed to a lack of access to the material. We owned a copy of the book for approximately twenty-five years without making the connection. Only as a result of visiting the Step Pyramid of Zoser in 1988 and having the sense that we were in a space that was intended for theatrical performance did we "discover" the significance of Sir Banister Fletcher's discussion of this milestone in architectural history to the history of theatre. Fletcher states:

> The **Step Pyramid of Zoser, Sakkara** (2778 B.C., beginning of Third Dynasty) is remarkable as being the world's first large-scale monument in stone. King Zoser's architect, Imhotep, was greatly revered both in his own and later times, and in the Twenty-sixth Dynasty was deified.[13]

Fletcher goes on to say the pyramid indicates that there were at least five changes in the plan during the course of its construction. The final dimensions were "411 ft from east to west by 358 ft wide and 200 ft high," with the addition of "two more steps to the height, making six in all."[14] From the perspective of theatre history, the iconoclastic information is contained in the following quote (italics ours).

> Surrounding the pyramid was a vast rectangular enclosure, 1790 ft from north to south and 912 ft wide, with a massive Tura limestone wall, 35 ft high, indented in the manner of the earlier mastaba facades. Around the walls were bastions, fourteen in all, and each had *stone false doors*. The only entrance was in a broader bastion near the southern end of the eastern face. In the fact that there is a small offering chapel (with stelae, offering table and a statue of Zoser) and a well-developed mortuary temple, containing two courts, a maze of corridors and many rooms, the

buildings inside the enclosure show some relation to earlier developments of the mastaba; but these two buildings abut the north face of the pyramid, instead of the east as was to be the common practice, and *all the rest of the structures are quite exceptional and unique to this complex. They are dummy representations of the palace of Zoser and the buildings used in connection with the celebration of his jubilee in his lifetime. Most of them therefore are solid, or almost so, comprised of earth or debris faced with Tura limestone.* ... Just inside the enclosure entrance a narrow corridor runs deviously northwards to the Heb-sed Court, the principal scene of this festival lined with *sham chapels*, each with its small forecourt, those on the western side representing the provinces or 'nomes' of Upper Egypt and those on the eastern, of Lower Egypt. These *virtually solid structures* ... might have symbolized the two kingdoms.[15]

The only reasonable explanation for the existence of these unique "dummy representations" seems to be that they were intended to evoke a sense of place or places for the performance that occurred in this "vast rectangular enclosure." These structures were unusable in the traditional architectural sense because there was no space inside these structures that could be occupied by a person. The ancient Egyptians would not have built these structures unless they served some purpose. Their purpose, in current terminology, must have been that of stage scenery. Therefore, it seems reasonable to assert, based upon this evidence, that the first known designer and builder of what we now call stage scenery was Imhotep in approximately 2778 B.C. in Sakkara, Egypt. Diop lends further credence to this idea of a performance at the Step Pyramid of Zoser:

VALUES AND INTERPRETATION

In Egypt, it is the Pharaoh Zoser who seems to have inaugurated the ceremony of the symbolic death of the king, of his regeneration.[16]

As one seeks answers to questions about the origins of theatre art in Africa, an interesting pattern in Eurocentric scholarship becomes evident. This pattern is one of consistent failure to recognize information that seems to us to be obvious in establishing that theatre art reached a remarkable level of sophistication in the Nile river valley on the continent of Africa 2000 years prior to the "golden age" of Greek drama.

But recent scholarship has re-discovered and disseminated evidence more widely that seems to be forcing a change in dominant views about many aspects of the ancient civilization of the Nile river valley. As this "new" information is disseminated to a broader segment of the population, efforts to classify the inhabitants of this time and place as Caucasian seem to have intensified. Brockett acknowledges that:

> Archeological discoveries in recent years seem to establish that human beings evolved first in the Rift Valley of eastern Africa. Thus, the oldest humans and the first rulers of Egypt may have been black-- information which some recent scholars see as having been de-emphasized because of racial prejudice.[17]

The examples of dark brown skin color as the pigment of choice in the paintings and the facial features and hair texture that is represented in considerable detail in the sculpture produced by these people over a span of more than three thousand years, provide obvious and ample evidence that the people of the ancient Nile valley civilization exhibited the physical characteristics that have been used in the U.S.A. to define people traditionally called "Negro" and, since the mid-1960's, "Black."

47

Negro, *n., pl.* **-groes,** *adj.--n.* **1a** a person belonging to any of the black races of Africa, characterized by brown or black skin, coarse, woolly hair, and a broad, flat nose. The chief peoples of Africa south of the Sahara are Negroes. **b** a member of any other dark-skinned people. **2** a person having some black ancestors (subject to precise definition by law in certain states and countries).

Further, there is convincing evidence that the root of the word "Kemet," used by the people of the ancient Nile valley civilization to refer to themselves, is also the word that represented the color of charcoal in their language.[18] These are the people who built the great pyramids at Giza, the temples at Abu Simbel, the two great temples at Thebes with their connecting avenue of sphinxes, and many other astounding architectural achievements. Among their earliest architectural wonders is the step pyramid at Sakkara and the surrounding structures. Thus, the people of ancient Egypt (1) exhibited physical characteristics identical to those used in the U.S.A. to define people who are called "Negro" or "Black" or "African American;" (2) built the first known structures for the performance of theatre; and (3) wrote the earliest known dramas and the oldest extant drama. In 2778 B.C. the step pyramid at Sakkara was constructed. In 1492 A.D. Columbus "discovered" what he thought was a sea route to India. In the 4270 years between these two events, scholars have documented a southwesternly migration by the inhabitants of the Nile river valley. By the time the capture and transport of Africans to the Americas had become a significant factor in the European economy, the culture of West Africa had been heavily influenced by the culture of the ancient Nile river valley. Hence, there is a direct cultural connection between ancient Egyptians and African Americans.[19]

VALUES AND INTERPRETATION

THE OLDEST EXTANT AFRICAN-AMERICAN SCRIPT

When historians apply Eurocentric values to African-American theatre history, they have generally concluded that African-American theatre did not exist. For this reason, African-American theatre history prior to the Confederate Rebellion has been almost completely ignored. Most African-American theatre history since then is also ignored and for similar reasons. We do not intend to cast blame on those White theatre historians who have ignored or misinterpreted African-American theatre history. These individuals can only be expected to respond to the evidence before them as their values dictate. And so they have.

White historians have managed, whether deliberately or unconsciously, to avoid communication about significant cultural achievement within an African-American cultural context by African-Americans. White historians have, on occasion, convinced us that they were helping by applauding those cultural achievements by African-Americans that either supported preconceived notions about the inferiority of African-American people or mimicked European-American culture. For example, a book was published in 1969 under the title *Negro Playwrights in the American Theatre 1929-1959* by Doris Abramson, a White woman.[20] The only "Negro" playwrights in the American theatre, according to the content of Miss Abramson's book, are those whose plays have been produced under White economic auspices in the city of New York. According to this definition of African-American theatre, the plays of such historically important and artistically competent African-American playwrights as John Ross, Randolph Edmonds, Thomas Pawley, and Ray McIver are excluded simply because their plays had not been performed in New York prior to 1959. The preceding statement is by no means intended to imply that those African-American playwrights whose work has been

49

produced in New York have been treated fairly. Therefore, theatre historians whose values are in harmony with the values of African-American theatre must provide a fair analysis and interpretation of the historical evidence that is available.

The casual student of African-American theatre might easily conclude that the first African-American play was *The Escape: Or a Leap to Freedom* written by William Wells Brown and published in 1858.[21] Even a work of the stature of John Hope Franklin's *From Slavery to Freedom* makes such an assertion.[22] But, according to Miss Abramson, *The Escape* is not really even a play, nor is *Caleb, the Degenerate*, written by Joseph S. Cotter in 1903. She says that both of these plays are "crude" and they are "really tracts, meant for the library or the platform." According to the dictionary, "crude" means uncultured. But according to whose culture? These plays are neither lacking in African-American culture nor do they deserve such a negative evaluation, except when examined from within a context of White values that were locked in prior to the mid-1950's.

The Escape: Or a Leap to Freedom provides an excellent opportunity to gain insight into some aspects of the life of a slave from the point of view of a former slave. William Wells Brown's comic irony exposes a view of both Whites and African Americans in the South during slavery that no White writer of the period managed to create. Walker, a slave trader, says to Dr. Gaines, the "kind" plantation owner:

> The price of niggers is up, and I em gwine to take advantage of the times. Now, doctor, ef you've got any niggers that you wants to sell, I em your man. I am paying the highest price of any body in the market. I pay cash down, and no grumblin'.

VALUES AND INTERPRETATION

DR. GAINES   I don't know that I want to sell any of my people now. Still, I've got to make up a little money next month, to pay in bank; and another thing, the doctors say that we are likely to have a touch of the cholera this summer, and if that's the case, I suppose I had better turn as many of my slaves into cash as I can.

WALKER   Yes, doctor, that is very true. The cholera is death on slaves, and a thousand dollars in your pocket is a great deal better than a nigger in the field, with cholera at his heels ...

The Reverend Mr. Pinchen, while this discussion is going on, proclaims:

... I tell you, Mr. Walker, I've been in the gospel ministry these thirteen years, and I am satisfied that the heart of man is full of sin and desperately wicked. This is a wicked world, Mr. Walker, a wicked world, and we ought all of us to have religion. Religion is a good thing to live by, and we all want it when we die. Yes, sir, when the great trumpet blows, we ought to be ready. And a man in your business of buying and selling slaves needs religion more than any body else, for it makes you treat your people as you should. Now, there is Mr. Haskins,--he is a slave-trader, like yourself.   Well, I converted him.   Before he got religion, he was one of the worst men to his niggers I ever saw; his heart was as hard as stone. But religion has made his heart as soft as a piece of cotton. Before I converted him, he would sell husbands from their wives, and seem to take delight in it; but now he won't sell a man from his wife, if he can get any one to buy both of them together. I tell you, sir, religion has done a wonderful work for him.

Later, as Walker is about to depart with the slaves he has purchased from Dr. Gaines, Rev. Pinchen asks:

> ... What kind of niggers sells best in the Orleans market, Mr.Walker?
>
> WALKER   Why, field hands. Did you think of goin' in the trade?
>
> REV. PINCHEN   Oh, no; only it's a long ways down to Natchez, and I thought I'd just buy five or six niggers, and take 'em down and sell'em to pay my travellin' expenses. I only want to clear my way.[23]

Of course, William Wells Brown's use of language is compatible with the style of production with which he was familiar--a mid-nineteenth-century European-American style of production. Therefore, the language of Williams Wells Brown sounds stilted to European-American ears over one-hundred years later. But so does the language of his White contemporaries. A playwright's style is bound to be influenced by the existing theatre practices of his time and place. There is one aspect of mid-nineteenth century European-American theatre practice that William Wells Brown did not adhere to, however. He did address a subject that was generally avoided by his White counterparts. He dealt with the multiple standards of sexual behavior on Southern plantations with frankness and with insight during a period when frank public communication on the subject of sex was rare, and interracial sex was simply not supposed to be mentioned.

During the previously mentioned scene, Walker, the slave trader, asks Mr. Wildmarsh, a neighbor of Dr. Gaines, if he "... had any niggers to sell." Wildmarsh explains that he does

VALUES AND INTERPRETATION

not, having just sold ". . . the smartest gal I've ever raised. . . ."
Walker then inquires:

Then she was of your own raising, was she?

WILDMARSH Oh, yes; she was raised on my place,
and if I could have kept her three or four years longer,
and taken her to the market myself, I am sure I could
have sold her for three thousand dollars. But you see,
Mr. Walker, my wife got a little jealous, and you know
jealousy sets the women's heads a teetering, and so I
had to sell the gal. She's got straight hair, blue eyes,
prominent features, and is almost white. . . .

WALKER Why, Squire, was she that pretty little gal
that I saw on your knee the day that your wife was
gone, when I was at your place three years ago?

WILDMARSH Yes, the same.

WALKER Well, now Squire, I thought that was your
daughter; she looked mightily like you. She was your
daughter, wasn't she? You need not be ashamed to
own it to me, for I am mum upon such matters.

While attempting to decide which slaves to sell, Dr. Gaines
tells his wife:

My dear, I'll sell any servant from the place to suit
you, except Melinda. I can't think of selling her --I
can't think of it.

MRS. GAINES I tell you that Melinda shall leave this
house, or I'll go. There, now you have it. I've had my
life tormented out of me by the presence of that
yellow wench, and I'll stand it no longer. I know you

53

love her more than you do me, and I'll --I'll --I'll write --write to my father. (Weeps.)

Dr. Gaines later tells his wife that he has sold Melinda, the attractive young mulatto referred to earlier by Walker. Actually, Dr. Gaines spirits Melinda away to a cottage he owns that is some ten miles away from the plantation house where he keeps her under guard. When Dr. Gaines is finally able to visit Melinda, he tells her:

> ... I will set you free, let you live in this cottage, and be your own mistress, and I'll dress you like a lady. Come, now, be reasonable!

> MELINDA   Sir, let me warn you that if you compass my ruin, a woman's bitterest curse will be laid upon your head, with all the crushing, withering weight that my soul can impart to it; a curse that shall cling to you throughout the remainder of your wretched life; a curse that shall haunt you like a spectre in your dreams by night, and attend upon you by day; a curse, too, that shall embody itself in the ghastly form of the woman whose chastity you will have outraged. Command me to bury myself in yonder stream, and I will obey you. Bid me do any thing else, but I beseech you not to commit a double crime,--outrage a woman, and make her false to her husband.[24]

Although Melinda's speech sounds stilted to contemporary ears, William Wells Brown apparently sought to make his statement through this speech in a manner that was permissible in polite public performance in the mid-nineteenth century.

William Wells Brown used elements from several aspects of his cultural heritage--both European and African--and in the process created a work of art that is neither pure European nor pure African, but a mixture of the two. So, when a critic--no matter how responsible, no matter how fair--has been value programmed to understand and appreciate only the White or European aspect of Williams Wells Brown's cultural heritage, while either ignoring or despising his African cultural heritage, that critic is likely to conclude that *The Escape* is a crude play.

So long as White people continue to superimpose Eurocentric values with regard to aesthetic acceptability upon African-American culture on the grounds that White values are universal ones, misunderstandings will, in all likelihood, continue. The reverse of this is not necessarily true, since African Americans are generally value programmed to hold the basic rudiments of White American culture in the highest esteem through a system of rigidly enforced requirements, such as the public schools. African Americans learn about White culture and are taught to value it to a degree that few, if any, Whites learn to value African-American culture. Only after some recognition of the legitimacy of African-American culture and the values of that culture is one able to begin to understand and appreciate the art of African Americans.

THE FIRST AFRICAN-AMERICAN THEATRE

When we deal with African-American theatre history, even from a Eurocentric perspective, we discover that 1929 was not the beginning, nor was 1858. In 1816 or 1817, a man known as Mr. Brown opened a tea garden in what was by then a thriving community of free African-Americans in New York.[25] Although the two men have been identified as the same on occasion, this is not the same Mr. Brown as William Wells Brown. The latter Mr. Brown, that is William Wells, could not have been more than two or three years of age when the former Mr. Brown began what eventually became the first professional African-American theatre company in the city of New York.[26] Mr. Brown gave up his job as a steward on a ship that sailed between New York and Liverpool, England to open the tea garden in New York. Among the early entertainers at the tea garden was a man named James Hewlett, whose entertainment consisted of portraying the roles of several different characters in one performance. By 1821, Mr. Brown had built a theatre seating three or four hundred people.[27] In this theatre, a group called the African Company performed. One member of the company, Ira Aldridge, went on to become one of the most renowned actors of 19th century Europe.[28]

But what of the African Company itself? Playbills of the African Company's performances indicate that they may have performed as regularly and definitely charged as much as the other professional theatres operating in New York at the time.[29] Still, the African Company has been labeled by a few White theatre historians as a group of amateurs who made no significant mark upon the history of theatre short of being "picturesque." On the other hand, most White theatre historians ignore them completely. An African Company playbill dated June 7, year unspecified, but probably from 1822 or 1823, announces an African Company production of *Tom and Jerry, or Life in London*. They probably drew heavily upon the original (1821) Pierce Egan script. However, the African Company added an extra scene entitled, "On the Slave Market." The playbill lists "Mr. Smith" as the "Auctioneer" and "Slaves" are portrayed "By the Company."[30] One may reasonably assume that the purpose of this additional scene was to galvanize existing anti-slavery sentiment among the audience members who were among the few free people of African origin in the United States at the time. Since the scene was added to a popular British melodrama, there is a strong probability that the means of achieving this anti-slavery theme was through the use of comic irony. How could such an event be regarded by responsible historians as of no historical significance or importance? Even from a frame of reference of White racist values, arriving at such a conclusion seems rather difficult.

We consider it important to note that Mr. Brown and his African company were among the first American theatre organizations to produce Pierce Egan's *Tom and Jerry, or Life in London,* a play that "... began a trend toward the melodramas of contemporary life and local color."[31] The play was adapted by other groups and became *Life in Philadelphia or Life in New York.* Thus, one might reasonably conclude that the African Company was among the pioneer theatre groups in the United States in the movement away from the exotic and the supernatural in melodrama and toward the urban folk hero who did not emerge into full popularity until the 1840's.

A later playbill announced that on June 20 and 21, 1823, the African Company would present, for the second time, a play called *King Shotaway.*[32] The play was billed as portraying a slave insurrection on the island of St. Vincent and based upon the actual experiences of Mr. Brown, who was both playwright and manager of the company. The indication on the playbill that Mr. Brown actually took part in such a slave insurrection could very well be a fabrication designed to help sell tickets. Such marketing techniques were as commonplace in the theatre then as they are today. On the other hand, was not a play written and produced by an African American in 1823 about a slave insurrection a significant mark upon the history of the theatre?[33] Again, we may reasonably assume that this production sought to make a statement in opposition to the institution of slavery. Although the available information about the play is limited to the playbill announcing its presentation for a second time, the implications are clear. The title character is regarded as a hero because he was the leader of a slave insurrection. So, the play must have made the thematic assumption that the appropriate way for a slave to behave is to try to escape.

Neither *King Shotaway* nor *On the Slave Market* is extant today as a script. Therefore, they may be completely disregarded as dramatic literature. Even though the scripts may not be analyzed and evaluated as literature, their historical significance as productions is not reduced. On the other hand, a Eurocentric analysis of the issues that Mr. Brown presented in *King Shotaway* and *On the Slave Market* may very well lead to the conclusion that the works could be dismissed on the grounds that the behavior of the characters in these plays was insane. Joseph Baldwin, national president of the Association of Black Psychologists was quoted in an Associated Press article as saying that "Samuel Cartwright, a white psychologist who worked while slavery existed in the United States ... identified two disorders suffered by blacks... 'Drapetomania' was the desire of blacks to run away from slavery, and 'dysathesia aethopica' was a form of rascality where slaves broke hoes or walked over cotton plants or poisoned cows to get out of work." Baldwin went on to explain that although Whites regarded such behavior as crazy, African Americans considered it the logical thing to do.[34]

Undoubtedly, many White people in New York in 1823 would have regarded a public statement by African Americans in favor of slave insurrection as insane or criminal, or both. Even before they presented *King Shotaway*, the African Company had its share of troubles with the New York Police Department. The Company had been harassed repeatedly and on more than one occasion, members of the company were arrested and jailed.[35] What happened to the African Company after their June 20 and 21, 1823, performances of *King Shotaway* cannot be accurately documented at this time.

VALUES AND INTERPRETATION

The hostility of an influential segment of the White community in New York, as reflected in the newspaper coverage of the African Company's encounters with the police, would seem to suggest a possible explanation for its demise.

Herbert Marshall and Mildred Stock have provided an outstanding example of thorough and unbiased scholarship in their book entitled *Ira Aldridge: The Negro Tragedian*. Chapter four of the book is devoted to Mr. Brown's African Company. Marshall and Stock cite a number of contemporary newspaper accounts of the African Company. Their quote from an article in the *National Advocate* of September 21, 1821, cites at least two occasions when the New York police interfered with the operation of the African Grove--the place that housed both Mr. Brown's tea garden and his African Company. On one occasion the police apparently closed the place altogether and on another occasion they arrested the actors portraying Richard III and Catesby following a performance of Shakespeare's *Richard III*. The values expressed in the *National Advocate* newspaper, with regard to whether or not it is acceptable for Shakespeare to be performed by a company of African-American actors, seem rather transparent and in concert with the police. The *National Advocate* refers to the African Company, at one point, as "These imitative inmates of the kitchen and pantries ..." and to the actor who portrayed Richard III as " ... a dapper, woolly-headed waiter...." The *National Advocate* later describes the same actor as " ... a fellow as black as the ace of spades." The role of Richard III was undoubtedly played by James Hewlett, who is described in a different newspaper as " ... of lighter color than ordinary mulattoes." The latter (lighter) description is also corroborated by a drawing of Hewlett that is reproduced in *Ira Aldridge: The Negro Tragedian*.[36]

BLACK THEATRE

Marshall and Stock cite still another newspaper account of police harassment several months later in the *American* of January 10, 1822.[37] A portion of that article is quoted here to give a sense of how the White population felt about the African Company or at least how one newspaper wanted them to feel.

HUNG BE THE HEAVENS WITH BLACK
--SHAKESPEARE

We have heretofore noticed the performances of a black corps dramatique in this city, at their theatre, the corner of Bleecker and Mercer Streets. It appears that the sable managers, not satisfied with a small share of the profit and a great portion of fame, determined to rival the great Park Theatre, belonging to Messrs. Beekman and Astor, and accordingly hired the Hotel next door to the theatre, where they announced their performances. . . . The ebony-colored wags were notified by the police that they must announce their last performance, but they, defying the public authority, went on and acted nightly. It was at length considered necessary to interpose the arm of authority, and on Monday evening a dozen watchmen made part of the audience. . . .

Several . . . ascended the stage and arrested His Majesty. "Where am I going?" says he. "To de tower?"

"No; to the watch house," said the Knight of the Lantern. Henry, Queen Elizabeth, and the two young princes were escorted in their tinselled robes, to the watch house, into which they marched with royal contempt and defiance.

VALUES AND INTERPRETATION

"Come, come," said the watch; "none of your playacting airs --into the black hole with you." The sable corps were thrust in one green room together where, for some time, they were loud and theatrical; ever and anon, one would thrust his head through a circular hole to survey the grim visages of the watchmen. Finally they plead so hard in blank verse, and promised never to act Shakespeare again, that the Police Magistrates released them at a very late hour.

James Hewlett, who played the title roles in both *King Shotaway* and *Richard III*, managed to continue his acting career. In December of 1825, Hewlett appeared at the Spruce Street Theater in New York, apparently in his one-man show in which he played several different characters in one performance and did imitations of the better known White actors of his day. There is some indication that Hewlett performed his one-man show in England in 1825 as well. February 3, 1826, was announced as his last appearance in the United States (at Military Garden) prior to his return to London, where he was allegedly scheduled to appear at the Royal Coburg Theatre--the theatre that eventually became known as the Old Vic. There are no records at the Coburg of Hewlett's appearance there to substantiate the announcement. Hewlett's appearances in England were, in all likelihood, made at a theatre of lesser importance or possibly in a major theatre (maybe even the Royal Coburg) but in a minor role. However, evidence exists that Hewlett performed in New York as late as September 22, 1831.[38] James Hewlett was an actor of note in the New York theatre beginning with his rise to prominence with the African Company and lasting for at least a decade. The only known reference to his apparently sudden departure from the spotlight is in a letter from Ira Aldridge to a mutual friend in which Aldridge refers to Hewlitt as ". . . poor Jim Hewlett."[39]

BLACK THEATRE

Ira Aldridge did go from the African Company in New York to London and eventually to the Royal Coburg Theatre. In October of 1825, Aldridge launched a European career that eventually led to his being recognized as one of the leading actors in the Eurocentric world. In spite of the special significance of Ira Aldridge's success, recognition during his lifetime occurred only in Europe and in strictly Eurocentric terms. In spite of White America's desire to love and imitate things European, recognition of Ira Aldridge's excellence as an actor came to America begrudgingly and a century late. In Eurocentric terms, Aldridge succeeded and Hewlett did not. In Afrocentric terms, both of these outstanding actors were influenced to abandon the venue of artistic expression they had initially chosen. With the demise of the African Company, neither Hewlett nor Aldridge would again have an opportunity to appear professionally in a play written by an African American, for an African-American audience, with an African-American acting company managed by an African American.

The African Company's early nineteenth century exploits do not fully expose the beginnings of African-American theatre. The true beginnings of African-American theatre involve the evolution of pure African art forms as a result of the impact of the slave experience in America. This evolutionary process occurred with relative rapidity because of the oppressive conditions of the slave experience. In many instances, when African Americans openly used their traditional African modes of communication, the result was brutal punishment of various kinds --whipping, mutilation, or even the severing of various extremities. Survival demanded that African-American art forms evolve within certain rigidly enforced specifications. For instance, the language used had to be English; African languages were generally not allowed. In addition, the use of drums was almost always prohibited.

VALUES AND INTERPRETATION

THE MINSTREL TRADITION

The slave experience mandated a survival technique that must be appreciated if one is to understand the development of African-American theatre. That survival technique employs double meaning. Things were almost never what they seemed to be when heard and seen by White folks. The use of double meaning was a common characteristic among the practitioners of the early forms of communication art from which African-American theatre developed--minstrel performers, singers of spirituals, storytellers, and preachers. White historians who have attempted to describe the beginnings of the "Negro Minstrel" have generally made precisely those misinterpretations that African-American minstrel performers intended for them to make. During the early days of the minstrel, the survival tactics of African-American people in this country required that Whites be misled. This deception had to be done because the minstrel invariably included some rather caustic satire on the subject of the ineptness of White folks. A quotation from a play by Loften Mitchell entitled *Star of the Morning* is included in his historical account of African-American theatre in New York entitled *Black Drama* as a means of explaining what minstrel entertainment meant to African-American people before White people co-opted it. The character who speaks is Oliver, an elderly ex-slave and minstrel man. Oliver is talking to the leading character in the play, Bert Williams. He tells Bert Williams that, when he was a slave, minstrels were done on plantations ". . . to poke fun at Old Master." He stresses the importance of getting a house Negro to be the interlocutor. Oliver explains:

> We used to take off on that house Negro 'cause he was the Master up and down.
>
> (Imitating Tams)

Tams would say: "Mistah Stafford, do darkies go to heaven?"

(Moves over, imitates Bones)

Old Bones would say: "Yes suh, Mistah Stafford. Do us darkies go to Heaven?"

(Moves back, imitates the house Negro)

House Negro would say: "Now, why would you darkies be going to heaven? That's for white folks!"

(Imitates Tams)

Tams would say: "We just wanted to know who opens them Pearly Gates for white folks to get inside?"

(All laugh. OLIVER becomes serious now)

That's how it was. Them white folks come from up North and copied what we was doing. They made me a fool, and now I got to go out there and make money laughing at me![40]

In the original African-American version of minstrel routines, the focus of the comic irony is upon the White slaveholder's values. These values allow him to feel that he is superior to African-American people while simultaneously being obviously dependent upon African Americans to perform many of the simplest and most basic tasks that are required for human survival. Further, the buffoonery by White Americans when they portray African-American people's enthusiastic failure to imitate well, along with other stereotypical characteristics such as laziness and stupidity, create laughter for White Americans by demeaning African Americans.

The "Negro Minstrel" that contemporary African-Americans find so demeaning was invented by White people. It was, no doubt, an accurate reflection of what their values caused them actually to see and hear when witnessing an African-American minstrel performance. But this White invention represented a reversal of the values of the African-American minstrel performances held on plantations in the South for the enjoyment of African-American audiences.

There are some elements of the original African-American minstrel form that may serve to clarify its values and functions: first, the physical arrangement of the performers --the "master" in the middle, the "darkies" on the ends; second, the obsession with calling the interlocutor "mister" with such frequency as to become ludicrous and trite--unless we assume that it was a lampoon of how Whites expected to be treated by African Americans; and third, the tradition of using a light skinned African American who could "talk like White folks" as the interlocutor. The original African-American minstrel performances not only entertained African-American people but made life tolerable for African-American slaves in the U.S.A. by ridiculing, through the use of comic irony, the White slave owner--the key figure in the system that caused their oppression. Of course, the ridicule had to be presented in a manner to insure that, while African-American people were certain to understand and appreciate it, White people were certain not to understand. The successful functioning of this type of African-American theatre was a significant factor in the mental health and physical survival of African-American people within the slave experience.

The preceding examples of African-American theatre, from the period prior to the Confederate Rebellion, suggest certain functions of African-American theatre for African-American audiences that are manifestations of the values of both artists and audience. Although the style of the language and other such surface characteristics may have changed through the years, there is no indication that the intended functions of theatre for African-American audiences have changed concurrently. The combined use of double meaning and comic irony as a contributor to survival within an environment of systematic oppression appears to be a recurring function, as does the galvanizing of existing anti-slavery sentiment. If some of the more contemporary meanings of the term "slavery" are recognized, both of these functions continue to be important manifestations of the values of African-American theatre artists and their audiences. These values that are transmitted by African-American culture and the African antecedents to African-American culture comprise the PREMISE of Afrocentric theatre.

ENDNOTES

1.   Oscar G. Brockett, *History of the Theatre*, Sixth Edition (Boston: Allyn and Bacon, 1991), 10-11.

2.   Cheikh Anta Diop, *The African Origin of Civilization: Myth or Reality*, trans. Mercer Cook (Westport: Lawrence Hill and Company, 1974), 230.

3.   Brockett, 9.

4.   Brockett, 9.

5.   E.A. Wallis Budge, *From Fetish to God in Ancient Egypt* (New York: Dover, 1988), 263.

VALUES AND INTERPRETATION

6.   Herodotus, *History*, Book II, trans. George Rawlinson (New York: Tudor, 1928), 99, quoted in Diop, *The African Origin of Civilization*, 234.

7.   Brockett, 10.

8.   Brockett, 7.

9.   Budge, *From Fetish to God in Ancient Egypt*, 23.

10.   Budge, *From Fetish to God in Ancient Egypt*, 23-24.

11.   Diop, *Civilization or Barbarism*, 337.

12.   Diop, *Civilization or Barbarism*, 337.

13.   Sir Banister Fletcher, *A History of Architecture on the Comparative Method* (New York: Charles Scribner's Sons, 1963), 27.

14.   Fletcher, 27.

15.   Fletcher, 30.

16.   Diop, *Civilization or Barbarism*, 320.

17.   Brockett, 8.

18.   Cheikh Anta Diop, "Origin of the Ancient Egyptian," *General History of Africa*, Chapter 1 in Vol 2 (The UNESCO Press, 1981), in *Egypt Revisited*, Vol. 10, *Journal of African Civilizations*, ed. by Ivan Van Sertima (New Brunswick: Transaction Publishers, 1989), 9.

19.   Cheikh Anta Diop, *Precolonial Black Africa* (Westport: Lawrence Hill and Company, 1987), 212-234. Diop documents this migration with linguistic evidence and describes this migration from the perspective of physical artifacts and social patterns.

20.   Doris E. Abramson, *Negro Playwrights in the American Theatre, 1925-1959* (New York: Columbia University Press, 1969), 14.

21.   William Wells Brown, *The Escape; or, A Leap for Freedom* (Boston: 1858; rpt. Philadelphia: Rhistoric Publications, n.d.).

22.   John Hope Franklin, *From Slavery to Freedom* (New York: Vintage Books, 1969), 232.

23.   William Wells Brown, Act I, Scene 1, pp.17-20 and Act I, Scene 2, p.23.

24.   William Wells Brown, Act I, Scene 1, pp.18-21 and Act III, Scene 5, p.33.

25.   Several writers have attributed different first names to Mr. Brown. James Hatch and Omanii Abdullah, *Black Playwrights, 1823-1977: An Annotated Bibliography of Plays* (New York: R. R. Bowker, 1977), 29; call him Henry Brown. Johnathan Dewberry, "The African Grove Theatre and Company," *Black American Literature Forum*, 16, No.4 (Winter, 1982), 128; calls him William Henry Brown. Oscar G. Brockett, *History of the Theatre*, 6th ed. (Needham Heights, MA: Allyn and Bacon, 1991), 422; calls him James Brown. Fannin S. Belcher, Jr., *The Place of the Negro in the Evolution of the American Theatre, 1767-1940*, Diss. Yale 1945 (Ann Arbor: University Microfilms International, 1969), 292; states "There is no infallible evidence that 'James' was his first

name, but it seemed the most probable one in the list of Browns in the volumes of the New York City Directory for 1820 and 1821. The entry reads: 'Brown, James black, 56 Mercer [Street]."

26.   Benjamin Brawley, *The Negro Genius* (New York: Dodd, Mead and Company, 1937), 59. Brawley puts William Wells Brown's birth year in 1815, give or take a year. Brawley states that William Wells Brown escaped from slavery in 1834 when he was about nineteen years old. Even if we allow for a reasonable margin of error in the exact birth date of William Wells Brown, it is clear that he would not have been old enough to start a second career as the owner-manager of a theatre by 1817. Certainly, William Wells Brown was not a free adult living in New York in 1817.

27.   George C. D. Odell, *Annals of the New York Stage* (New York: Columbia University Press, 1928), III, p.35 lists the "first reference with which I am familiar" as *The National Advocate*, August 3, 1821.

28.   See Herbert Marshall and Mildred Stock, *Ira Aldridge: The Negro Tragedian* (New York: Macmillan Company, 1958), 31. They quote the *Anglo-African Magazine* of January, 1860, having asserted on p.11 that it is ". . . the only known piece of printed matter dealing with Aldridge's early life, and the correctness of which is confirmed by his own statement in a letter to the author some months after its publication. It was written by Dr. James McCune Smith, a schoolmate of Aldridge at the African Free School in New York."

29.   "Professionalism" is generally addressed by two standards in the theatre: (1) recognized standards of artistic quality and (2) sufficient financial remuneration to provide the theatre artists with an opportunity to pursue the development of their arts on a "full-time" basis. Participation

by such actors as Ira Aldridge and James Hewlett ought to provide adequate reason to assume that the African Company met the minimum standards of artistic quality of their time and place. Ticket prices ought to address adequately the issue of financial remuneration. Admission prices at New York theatres in 1822 and 1823 as cited by Odell are as follows: The price of admission at the performances of the African Company were--box, 75 cents; pit, 50 cents; gallery, 37-1/2 cents (p.70). "Tickets at Vauxhall Gardens . . . were high 50 cents" (p.79). "With Hilson's arrival, the prices at the City Theatre were raised to 75 cents in the boxes, and 50 cents in the pit; the gallery remained at 25 cents" p.66). "Bad luck in Warren Street is indicated by the fact that admission to the pit was not reduced to 25 cents" (p.68).

30. Odell, 70, and Laurence Hutton, "The Negro on the Stage," *Harpers*, 79 (June, 1889), 133.

31. Brockett, *History*, 335 and 377.

32. Odell, 70.

33. Although Brockett mentions that this is an event of some significance in the 2nd ed. through the current 6th ed. of his *History of the Theatre* (pp.376-377), there is no mention of the African Company in the 1st ed. (1968) of this important work. The paragraphs preceding and following the 2nd ed. mention of the African Company are on p.492 of the 1st ed. Brockett's 1974 edition of *History of the Theatre* apparently represents the first serious recognition of the historical significance of the African Company by Eurocentric sources.

34. "Psyches different between races, psychologists say." *Houston Chronicle*, 22 May 1983, Sec.3. p.4. col.1.

35.   As quoted in Marshall and Stock, pp.33-34 from The National Advocate, Sept.21, 1821; on pp.34-36 from *The American* of January 10, 1822.

36.   As quoted in Marshall and Stock, pp.33-34 from *The National Advocate*; p.38 from the Star of December 22, 1825; also, see Plate 2, between p.40 and 41.

37.   As quoted in Marshall and Stock, 34-36.

38.   Marshall and Stock pp.37-39.

39.   As quoted in Marshall and Stock, p.39 from a letter by Ira Aldridge to Dr. James McCune Smith, who was, according to Marshall and Stock (p.11), ". . . a schoolmate of Aldridge at the African Free School in New York. Dr. Smith studied at the University of Glasgow, receiving his B.A. in 1832, his M.A. in 1833, and his M.D. in 1834, and became an important figure in the medical profession in New York as well as a scientific writer of note."

40.   Loften Mitchell, *Black Drama* (New York: Hawthorn Books, Inc., 1967), 30-31.

Chapter Three

EVALUATION OF ART

Evaluation of art is directly connected to the aesthetic values of the evaluator. Although values, in general, impact upon this evaluative process, narrowing the scope to aesthetic values enables one to focus more effectively upon factors of major significance. The dictionary definitions of "aesthetic" and "aesthetics" provide parameters for focusing upon those values that have the greatest impact upon the evaluation of art.

> **aesthetic**,adj., n. --**adj.1** having to do with the beautiful, as distinguished from the useful, scientific, or moral; based on or determined by beauty rather than by practical or moral considerations: . . . **2** (of persons) having or showing an appreciation of beauty in nature and art. **3** (of things) showing good taste; artistic; pleasing: . . .

> **aesthetics**, n. the study of beauty in art and nature; philosophy of beauty or taste; theory of fine arts. . . .

The classic question that is raised in the study of aesthetics is: What is beauty? The answers to that question have been many and varied in different times and at different places. Standards of what constitutes good and beauty will be as different as cultures and values are different. These aesthetic values determine the qualitative standards by which the art of any culture is judged. One can only regard as beautiful that which one's values allow to be regarded as beautiful. Most people hold a strong personal attachment to their notions about what is beautiful and what is not, what is valuable and what is not, and more specifically, what makes them and their art better or worse than other people and their art. There is usually a good bit of flexibility within a culture that allows for variations in individual taste. Nevertheless, all cultures impose parameters for what may or may not be considered beautiful. Those parameters differ from culture to culture. Therefore, aesthetic concepts that are used to evaluate art will vary according to the cultural context in which the art occurs. In addition, evaluative insights into the artistic creations of any culture are more likely to be valid when preceded by an appreciation, as well as an understanding, of the aesthetic values of the culture in question.

The study of aesthetics raises both general and specific questions about what beauty is and the creation, evaluation, and uses of beauty. We are then faced with several fundamental questions: Who in a given society determines and controls the standards of beauty? Who decides what constitutes good taste? These same questions are applicable to the term "art." How is art created, perceived, evaluated and used? When can it be said, with validity, that a work of art is good? What does a group of people expect of its art?

In every society, some segment of the population determines and controls the standards of that society with regard to what is good and what is beautiful. The segment of the society with this power is able to dictate taste and define art by influencing the values of the society. In the United States, Eurocentric aesthetics dominate because the group that dictates taste and defines art is Eurocentric. The values of those Europhiles who are in control filter concepts of beauty and art as well as other cultural phenomena. Filters allow some classes of things to pass through while preventing or drastically reducing the passage of others. Thus, all cultural traditions, the values upon which they are based, and their works of art are filtered by the elitist Eurocentric criteria of those who control the dissemination of information in the U.S.A. Those who control the dissemination of information operate such an effective filtering mechanism that any need they might have to exhibit force in order to dictate values, tastes, and evaluative decisions about art is obviated.

Beautiful things that are created and evaluated are often called "fine art" by Europeans and Eurocentric Americans. The term "fine art" is used to describe a type of art that is, within this Eurocentric context, alleged to be superior to "un-fine" art, applied art, or craft. In more extreme instances, such artifacts that do not fit into the category of "fine art" are called base or coarse or crude or primitive or uncivilized. The determining factor that seems to relegate the "un-fine" arts to a lesser status is that they are used for non-aesthetic purposes as well as for aesthetic ones. Fine art is, by Eurocentric American definition, useless. Art that deliberately serves some functional purpose in the society is relegated to a lesser status than art that does not. A fine art sculptor, for example, would not want to use his or her talents to produce a table, a chair, a door, or anything that is overtly and intentionally useful to people. In this Europhile American context, a chair that is used to sit in should not be considered fine art no matter how beautiful it may be. On the other hand, a painting of the same chair could be considered fine art because a painting of the chair cannot be used for sitting; its only probable function is for its intrinsic beauty to be seen and contemplated.

Connected to the concept of fine art is the notion of art-for-art's sake. This concept assumes that art, and even the act of creating art, has intrinsic significance, meaning, and value in and of itself. Conversely, there are those who believe that the value of any work of art is, in part, related to its usefulness, that is, art-for-people's use. The term "fine art" is inappropriate to the understanding, appreciation and evaluation of African-American works of art since overt and intentional usefulness in a work of art is not held against it in an Afrocentric context. The African (and Afrocentric American) concept of art is that art is inextricably connected to life. Art is supposed to be useful to society in contrast to the Eurocentric elitist art-for-art's sake tradition. Within a context of Eurocentric fine art, playwrights should try to avoid doing anything on the stage that is intended to be useful to society from an Afrocentric perspective. Afrocentric American playwrights, on the other hand, ought to be concerned with providing something useful to an African-American audience. For example, it is appropriate for an African-American playwright to disseminate intentionally information that helps African-American people control their own lives, for their own betterment, on their own terms. The concept of actively seeking to control one's own life is a political concept. So the work of African-American playwrights is often attacked with such slogans as, "Art and politics don't mix." Such slogans can only have significance in the process of evaluating art if we first accept the notion that fine art must not seek to be of any significant use from an Afrocentric perspective.

One might reasonably ask, "If art is supposed to communicate ideas and feelings, then why does a person need to take courses in college in order to develop the ability to appreciate Eurocentric art?" Most Eurocentric American art museums and theatres are designed to exclude all but certain elite groups of people. Only people who have acquired both the information and the system of values to understand and appreciate their art, and in the case of theatre, the wealth to afford the prices charged for it, are included. Only wealthy and highly educated people are encouraged to go to the theatre; other classes of people are, by inference, encouraged to stay away. Theatre in the Eurocentric tradition in America seems to discourage attendance by the non-elite through such devices as deliberate non-communication resulting in boredom with the theatre event. The non-elite are fully aware that other events such as athletic contests are sometimes boring as well. However, they are taught to believe that with athletic contests, boredom is the exception, whereas with art, boredom is the rule.

The criteria for determining who is admitted to membership in the elite group are NOT based upon intelligence, or sensitivity, or love of language. Instead, the criteria are based upon the acquisition of a rather specific set of prior experiences that result in the acquisition of a rather specific set of values. Persons who are not of the "right" ethnic background and economic class (and, to some extent, even regional environment) often encounter extreme difficulty getting exposure to the "right" set of experiences that will result in the acquisition of the "right" set of values. Those in the elite group tend to think that most other people lack the refinement to appreciate the fine arts. In a real sense, then, the difference seems to be more one of economic class than of race or cultural identity. But that economic disparity is only superficial. White elitists have been remarkably successful in getting Whites who are not elite to adopt elitist attitudes, at least insofar as those attitudes are useful in defining non-elite Whites as superior to non-Whites. Irrespective of social and economic class, White Americans generally regard themselves as better, that is more civilized, than African-American people of a similar socioeconomic status. Even White Americans who like pop, rock and roll, and the more contemporary styles of American music, consider their music to be more refined than blues, rhythm and blues, and other African-American musical idioms.

76

EVALUATION OF ART

Appreciation of the fine arts serves as a symbol of status for an elite group of Eurocentric people who have accumulated money, formal education, and leisure time. Efforts at outreach programs by Europhile arts institutions are designed to cause those who are not part of their elite group to cherish the resources, the acquired information, and the system of values of these Eurocentric Americans who control these Europhile arts institutions. These outreach programs actually seek to attract people who are not a part of the Anglo-Saxon and Teutonic aristocratic traditions. African-American people and other people of color in America are encouraged to participate in outreach programs. Their participation provides a constant but infinitesimally small supply of tokens who are examples of how non-aristocratic Caucasians and people who do not look like Europeans can become acceptable if they learn to behave in a manner that is sufficiently Europhile and aristocratic. Predictably, then, the most efficient and effective way for an African-American artist to become acceptable to this elite group of Europhile Americans is to go to Europe, spend some time there, achieve a modicum of acceptability there, and then return to the U.S.A. able to love Europe and its arts with greater fervor and with more specificity than most White Americans. This description of how some African-American artists have gained respect among Eurocentric patrons of the arts is not intended to demean any African-American artist who has chosen to pursue a career in Europe. Most African-American artists who have chosen to spend time in Europe appear to have done so in an effort to avoid the negative impact of American racism and Afrophobia on their art.

Europeans and European-Americans make the distinction between fine and applied art, at least in part, to reinforce class differences. Class distinctions are made between people who must create or find beauty in things that are useful to them on the one hand, and people who possess enough material wealth so that they are able to purchase things that have no immediate use. Status is achieved through the conspicuous consumption of all manner of goods and services. Ironically, the conspicuous display of large American-made automobiles has become so widespread among persons of relatively low socioeconomic status that the practice has become nearly worthless as a status symbol among members of the upper socioeconomic class. Admittedly, a few automobiles (imported from Europe) cost enough to retain their capacity to serve as status symbols. But an automobile, no matter how expensive, may be used for pragmatic transportation. On the other hand, very few people can find anything truly pragmatic to do with a yacht. So owning a yacht carries a much higher status value than owning an automobile that costs as much as a yacht.

The highest degree of status is achieved through the conspicuous purchase and display of items that, in addition to their great monetary value, are considered beautiful to look at or listen to or both, but are of little or no real use to the owner or to anyone else. Since some people buy books to read, reading might appear to have some pragmatic outcome, even when none is deliberately intended by the reader. Therefore, books displayed for status must overtly avoid the appearance of pragmatism. They must look expensive, elegant, and above all, as though they have been read seldom if ever. Such books are sold, or at least advertised for sale, on the basis of the elegance of their covers (genuine leather with gold lettering, hand sewn, etc.), often with only vague mention that the contents of the books are "classic" or "great."

Eurocentric "highbrow" performance arts provide opportunities to be seen in attendance at "the right" public events and to have one's name included on lists of patrons that are part of the printed programs distributed at performances. Memberships on boards of directors and auxiliary organizations of arts institutions provide still another kind of status symbolism. These are only examples of the many factors that create the Eurocentric concept that leisure time and a "highbrow" education are necessary for the appreciation of fine art. The same Eurocentric concept conversely asserts that persons who do not have the requisite education, leisure time, and the financial resources and social status that usually accompany them, are not able to appreciate the finer things in life, especially fine arts. The purveyors of Eurocentric art accomplish several other things while reinforcing class differences. They secure financial security and status for themselves, financial security and status for their artists, and respect for the art that their artists do. In doing all of this, the purveyors of Eurocentric art must provide those in control with an array of products (the arts) that they are willing to endorse by attendance at events, financial contributions, and service on boards.

The art-for-art's sake philosophy provides a mechanism for ignoring or dismissing ideological content in art. The purveyors of highbrow art may authoritatively repeat the art-for-art's sake story authoritatively whenever it appears to them that some work of art might actually threaten the status quo in some way. So the reinforcement of class and status differences may be incidental to other accomplishments of the art-for-art's sake philosophy such as embracing the perceived value of the status quo. The issue of fine art versus applied art as a means of supporting class and status differences is essentially a Eurocentric issue. For those who would like to pursue this issue in much greater depth, we recommend beginning with Thorstein Veblen's *Theory of the Leisure Class*.[1] This definitive work on this essentially Europhile subject provides a highly detailed analysis, appropriately, from a Eurocentric American point of view. On the other hand, the establishment of such class and status differences by and among persons of European heritage has a definite and important impact upon non-Europeans in a Eurocentric society such as the U.S.A. The negative potential of such an impact is evident in recent restrictions placed upon the National Endowment for the Arts by the U.S. Congress. However, we will not pursue this issue in any greater depth than this mention of its existence.

Still another series of questions that gets raised in the study of aesthetics has to do with the nature of the artist. We may reasonably assume that, in order to have art, there must be an artist. Who is an artist? How does the artist fit into the society? What are the artist's responsibilities to the society? What are the society's responsibilities to the artist? Do we identify and differentiate between creators, interpreters, and imitators of art? If so, how? While discussing people and their behavior, still another aspect of aesthetics deserves consideration. How do people respond to art? Can these responses be measured objectively? Is it likely that people from different times and places will respond in a universal manner to a given work of art, or will their responses differ according to experiential differences, or racial differences, or both?

In the study of African-American aesthetics, we are concerned with all of the previously mentioned questions as they relate to African-American artists, art, and responders to that art. We must ask such questions as: What do African Americans perceive as beautiful? What are the characteristics, criteria, and standards of beauty among African Americans? What do African Americans consider to be good art? In what specific ways do African-American people respond to things beautiful and to art? What kinds of expectations do African Americans have of their artists? What kind of an effect should African-American artists have upon other people? These questions impact upon several specific groups of African Americans including the general population, art theorists, and artists. Also, we must ask: How do the answers to these questions differ among such specific groups of African Americans? And, do African Americans have significantly different answers to these questions from the answers of European-Americans? These questions can also be asked with reference to specific art forms, such as theatre. Such questions must be addressed if an understanding of the aesthetics of African-American theatre is to emerge.

Each one of these questions raises a concurrent question: How does one know that a particular answer is valid, correct, true? In order to address such questions, we must be concerned with epistemology as well as with aesthetics. What, then, is the epistemological basis for an analysis of African-American aesthetics going to be? How do we determine that any given concept or theory or idea about African-American aesthetics is valid, correct, or true? How do we derive knowledge about the subject of aesthetics? How do we know that we know something about African-American aesthetics? In very general terms, there are two approaches to this issue that have been widely used. We call one a contemplative approach and the other a perceptual approach. The contemplative approach tends to turn inward to one's own inspiration or insight, or both, as a means of arriving at transcendental knowledge--that is, knowledge that transcends data. The perceptual approach takes data that can be perceived by the senses and measured, and attempts to organize and analyze that data by measuring it in some way. Although many people apparently assume that one of these approaches is superior to the other, we contend that both are necessary and that neither approach is very useful without the other.

Examples abound of valid knowledge gained through the contemplative approach--inspiration, creative vision, insight, and the like. Of course, there are also many examples of valid knowledge gained through the perceptual approach--the organization and analysis of data that has been perceived and measured in some way. Both methods are valid ways to gain knowledge. In European-American academic settings, knowledge gained through the conceptual approach tends to be rather lightly regarded. Further, these two approaches to knowledge have been viewed by some within the European-American academic community as mutually exclusive opposing positions. They are not. In fact, the depth of understanding that a good artist must possess demands the use of both faculties in a holistic manner. Our intention is to study the nature of African-American art from a descriptive rather than a prescriptive approach. Of course, we must be concerned, at various levels, with what ought to be. However, we believe that preliminary to a concern with what ought to be, we must discover, to some reasonable degree, what is, as well as what the group generally agrees ought to be.

Some African-American scholars express a great deal of concern that many African-American concepts of aesthetics are so totally a product of White oppression that we ought not to glorify them. Some scholars have taken the position that we should consciously reject traditional African-American art that is clearly connected to oppression. As African Americans, our choices of what we consider to be beautiful have been limited by conditions of oppression. For example, Black folks have developed foods, such as chitterlings, that White folks considered unfit to eat. Eventually, some Black folks came to regard chitterlings as a delicacy. But the enslaved African-Americans who ate chitterlings on southern plantations prior to the Confederate Rebellion were only able to obtain chitterlings and several other delicacies because the White plantation owners did not consider them fit for White people to eat. African Americans proclaimed chitterlings a delicacy without alternative foods to use as a basis for comparison that included escargot, broiled beef-steak, lobster tails, and other Eurocentric delicacies. Should soul food cooking, blues and spirituals be discarded because they were originally created, in part, as responses to oppression? All cultures develop an idea of beauty out of the materials that are available to them. For instance, the architects and sculptors of ancient Egypt worked with stone because, among other things, timber in sufficient quantity and size was not readily available to them. Greek architects and sculptors of the Fifth century B.C., building upon the legacy of the ancient Egyptians, made similar choices for similar reasons more than two thousand years later.

Conditions of neither oppression nor geography have invalidated African-American aesthetic concepts. Martin Luther King, Jr. often said that unwarranted suffering is redemptive. Without theorizing about either the ethical or the theological desirability of unwarranted suffering, we contend that oppression may have forced certain depths and subtleties of artistic perception that would not have existed among African Americans in such large measure otherwise. For example, the subtle meaning in the lyrics of the spirituals is directly attributable to the impact of oppression. Systematic oppression of an entire group may actually increase the tendency of the members of the group to be creative. Oppressed people are usually perceptive enough about their condition to be dissatisfied with the status quo. In order for any behavior to be creative, it must somehow destroy some aspect, no matter how minute, of the status quo by adding to or replacing something that had existed before. In order to be creative, then, one must change some aspect of the status quo.

Oppression has also been responsible for some incongruities in African-American standards of beauty. Some social scientists who focus their attention on African-American studies have postulated that oppression manifests itself through the characteristics of rage, impotence, and fantasy. But, while these characteristics do have their negative manifestations, they may also provide the ingredients for creativity.

Moreover, we would assert that one of the useful functions of African-American art is to counteract or overcome, these characteristic manifestations of oppression. In other words, African Americans use art (the acts of producing and reacting to beauty) to keep from being destroyed by rage, impotence, and fantasy.

In seeking to answer the question, "What is beauty?" one may presuppose, as Plato did, that beauty is eternal and universal. That is, a study of beauty involves a search for those elements of beauty (assuming that there are some) that transcend time and place. The traditional European-American method of analyzing beauty presupposes, as Plato presupposed, that there are some specific characteristics of beauty that are eternal, ideal, and prototypical. On the other hand, we may presuppose that beauty exists within a cultural framework. Within this framework, beauty could be regarded as a universal concept without necessarily assuming that there are some specific characteristics of beauty that are universal. In other words, all cultures probably regard something as beautiful. However, a specific object or a specific characteristic that is thought to be beautiful within one cultural framework might be considered ugly in some other. For example, music is often alleged to be more "universal" than art forms that depend upon language as a means of expression. Yet, we have rarely found an American of either African or European descent who did not find the sound of Chinese classical opera to be distasteful.

Those who believe that beauty is culturally relative usually consider it to be temporally relative as well. In other words, that which constitutes beauty changes over a period of time even within a cultural group. If one believes that what constitutes beauty is eternal and universal, one will probably prefer to seek knowledge about universal aesthetics and universal theatre, rather than pursue knowledge about

84

aesthetics or the nature of theatre within a cultural or temporal framework. On the other hand, if one is willing to concede that characteristics of ideal beauty may vary according to time, place, and culture, then there may be some basis for believing that the study of African-American theatre aesthetics is a legitimate intellectual pursuit.

Although we assume that the study of African-American aesthetics should be as far removed from Eurocentric morality as possible, we cannot reasonably expect a totally amoral reaction with respect to any given work of art. Each individual's value system contains both aesthetic and moral values. These important aspects of an individual's value system do not always reconcile easily. Many important creative developments in the history of African-American music have been ignored because the music was often played as background entertainment in places that provided prostitution or gambling or both as the main attraction. Because the music was heard in places that housed activities that have been proclaimed by Eurocentric "moral leaders" to be immoral, the music was frequently called immoral.

When attempting to discern what constitutes grace or beauty of movement among members of a particular cultural group, analytical observation of the way that members of the group behave in informal situations may provide an important source of information. However, if the persons being observed are thought to be imitating the behavior of pimps or prostitutes or anyone who is regarded as immoral, then analyzing that concept of grace without making moral judgments about it becomes very difficult. We do not mean to imply that such moral judgments ought not to be made. Such moral considerations are virtually impossible to avoid. They should simply be recognized for what they are--moral judgments, not aesthetic ones. Persons often make moral judgments with regard to certain kinds of movements. They judge them to be "dirty" or "suggestive" or "lewd" and, therefore, ugly. The difficulty arises when one assumes that an activity which appears to be "suggestive" (a moral judgment) must also be ugly (an aesthetic judgment). This difficulty becomes more complex when examined from a cross-cultural perspective. What a specific movement is "suggestive " of to persons of one culture may be quite different from what it suggests to persons of some other culture.

An example of this complexity is illustrated in the film, *Ethnic Dance: Roundtrip to Trinidad* featuring Geoffrey Holder.[2] He does a dance called "The Yavalu" in the film. Dhambala, the god in the dance, inhabits the body of the dancer, whose movements resemble those of a snake. As the dance begins, the movements are in the upper region of the torso and spread to the arms, head, pelvis and feet, and finally encompass the entire body. When Geoffrey Holder saw the dance performed in a nightclub in New York, he heard people around him whispering about how sexy the dance was. Geoffrey Holder relates that "there is no sex in this dance." He explains that the torso is the life center and everything rotates from that point. The possession of the dancer by the god Dhambala demands that the dancer release this energy. Holder suggests that the Eurocentric New York audience was unable to appreciate the dance aesthetically because their moral indignation over the pelvic movements interfered.

Some people have discredited African-American social dance on aesthetic grounds when their actual objections are to the movement of the torso that occurs within the dance in question. Their objections invariably grow out of moral judgments about the lack of social respectability of those movements. Eurocentric moral objections to Afrocentric movement usually focus upon the pelvis. The Afrocentric aesthetic ideal differs from the Eurocentric aesthetic ideal with reference to movement of the entire spinal column up to and including the neck. Afrocentric ideals of graceful movement value flexibility of the spinal column. On the other hand, Eurocentric ideals of graceful movement, which are in concert with Eurocentric moral standards, demand that the entire spinal column remain straight from the pelvis to the head. Eurocentric ideals of grace are further characterized by pointed toes and rounded arms. Moreover, the hand follows the arm. But, most important of all, the torso MUST remain rigid.

A behavioral style occurs among some African-American males that is frequently labeled with the expression "pimping." In this instance, the term simply describes a style of walking and talking, and to some extent a style of dressing, that some African-American men affect in order to look good. Analysis of this style of behavior outside of the context of Eurocentric morality reveals the employment of a number of important Afrocentric aesthetic principles. A casualness and looseness must be affected that is, in actuality, thoroughly studied and practiced. These movements do not come naturally. But they must appear to come naturally. And more importantly, they must appear to come easily.

Probably the most noticeable aesthetic characteristic involved in pimping is asymmetry. The principle of asymmetry must manifest itself both visually and rhythmically. Rhythmically, the standard European-American assumption about walking is one of symmetry. The assumption is that, when one is walking, one should spend the same amount of time on the left foot as one spends on the right foot. This achieves a rhythmic symmetry. Visually, the Eurocentric standard assumption is that when one is walking, the body should achieve symmetrical balance. One side of the body ought to be, as nearly as possible, a mirror image of the other side. These aesthetic assumptions are obvious, for example, in the music of John Philip Sousa. On the other hand, the African-American behavior style that we are focusing upon prefers both visual and rhythmic asymmetry. Visually, the body must achieve an asymmetrical balance by leaning the torso to one side and then positioning the arms and legs in such a way that the body is balanced, but in such a manner that one side is not simply a mirror image of the other side.

This visual asymmetry contributes remarkably to the success of the other important quality that must be achieved--rhythmic asymmetry. The amount of time spent on one foot must differ by a fraction of a second from the duration on the other foot. The foot that receives the longer duration is on the side toward which the torso is leaning. The high value that is placed upon the aesthetic goal of asymmetrical balance is far more widespread than previously mentioned examples might tend to suggest. African-American dance, music, theatre, and the visual arts, in both religious and secular settings, are all significantly influenced by the same cultural factors that have created the behavioral style known as "pimping."

A culture may affirm a very high value with reference to something that is scarce in that culture, although mere scarcity does not always increase value. In the economic theory of capitalism, this theory is called "the law of supply and demand." European-Americans place a very high aesthetic value on people with blonde hair and blue eyes. One of several factors that causes this high value is their scarcity. On the other hand, if people with blonde hair and blue eyes were totally absent from the European-American experience, they probably would not place such a high value upon these traits. Does our rage/impotence/fantasy lead us to the belief that blonde hair has some sort of magical power? Do brown-skinned blondes have more fun too?

EVALUATION OF ART

These seemingly frivolous questions lead to other questions: What factors exist within the institutional process of transmitting culture in the U.S.A. that promote and enhance the values expressed in the slogan "Is it true blondes have more fun?" Moreover, what are the ramifications of indoctrinating African-American children with such values? Is it beneficial for the processes of human development of African-American children to include such an abundance of information that places a much higher aesthetic value upon blonde hair that is straight than upon black hair that is curly? If African-American children are taught a set of aesthetic values that lead them to consider themselves ugly, or at least less beautiful than minimum standards of acceptability, what must they think about the beauty of a work of art that portrays African-American people? What kinds of value assumptions will they tend to make about both African-American art and African-American artists? And, much more importantly, how will they evaluate their own worth as human beings?

Developing and articulating Afrocentric ideas about what culture is, what aesthetics does, and how aesthetics can function within a culture to control the behavior of individuals and groups is important. Only after such ideas are polished through interaction can we expect to pursue a valid analysis of the past or present artistic production activity of African-American culture. Inherent in this effort to describe an Afrocentric aesthetic is the assumption that Afrocentric art is, by nature, different from Eurocentric art. Some African Americans would say, "A work of art ought to stand or fall on its own merit, in terms of whether or not it is accepted or rejected by the people--the African-American people, that is." Under ideal conditions such an idea might have some validity. However, African people in America, particularly in the United States of America, do not exist under ideal conditions.

BLACK THEATRE

One of the most unfortunate circumstances of African-American people's existence in the United States has been the attempt, whether conscious or unconscious, to destroy African cultural heritage and to discredit its subsequent evolution into an African-American culture. This attempt has not been totally without results, especially among more highly educated African Americans. Therefore, a concerted effort to educate some African Americans in the traditions of their own culture is necessary. One does not exaggerate when asserting that there are some African Americans who are more thoroughly educated in the traditions of Europhile American culture than they are in their own. Likewise they have been miseducated into believing that the dominant culture is also an innately superior one.

An artist cannot possibly create a work of art that is not influenced by his or her own culture. Nevertheless, there are instances of African-American novelists, playwrights, painters, and actors who have made public pronouncements about the virtual nonexistence of African-American art. They proclaim "I am an artist who just happens to have a darker complexion," or "a birth certificate that says 'Negro,'" or something similarly irrelevant to the end product, the work of art. Clearly, these individuals do not want their work to be regarded as African art because they consider such an identification to be demeaning to them. Only with supreme difficulty can we imagine a British playwright, or an Italian sculptor, or a German composer proclaiming, "I am not a British/Italian/German artist! I am simply an artist!" Why, then do some African-American artists find it necessary to renounce their cultural identity in their quest for a reasonable level of acceptability as an artist and as a person? Hopefully, the miseducation process, to which all African Americans have been exposed, can be reversed.

EVALUATION OF ART

This miseducation process has been, to a large extent, carried on in the public school systems of the United States. One of the main purposes of these school systems is to instill into the value systems of all young Americans that the European sources of American culture are superior to the non-White cultures of the world. Young people are required to understand and appreciate examples of European and Europhile American literature, visual art, music, dance, drama, and philosophy that are reputed to be masterpieces. Further, standardized examinations that reflect this understanding and appreciation are required of nearly all young Americans, often as an absolute prerequisite for employment. How often are students required to partake of similar experiences from the other cultures that have influenced the culture of the United States? More importantly, one must recognize that this miseducation process has been carried on for so long, so well, and with such success that its techniques have now taken on the appearance, to those who have been subjected to the process, of being endowed with such admirable characteristics as logic, truth, objectivity, and universality.

One of the principal techniques that has been used in this miseducation process is the use of European-American criteria to judge the art that is created from within the framework of African-American culture, as well as other non-White cultures. Suppose we decided to pass judgment upon what makes a good orange by using apples as a standard for judgment. We would undoubtedly reach the conclusion that all of the oranges that we had observed were of an inferior color (too yellow on the outside, not white enough on the inside), too acid a taste, too juicy a texture; and we could go on and on with our list of inferiorities. This analogy is not as farfetched as some might like to believe. Just as we must know what an orange is supposed to look like and taste like in order to determine whether or not any specific orange is a good orange or a bad

91

one, a specific production of a work of art for an African-American audience cannot possibly be judged with validity unless African-American aesthetic standards are known and appreciated by the individual doing the judging.

Our approach to an analysis of Afrocentric aesthetics includes the study of at least four aspects of aesthetics: (1) works of art, the finished product, methods and materials of achieving the finished work; (2) the persons who create art; (3) the intended audience and its responses to art as well as its behavior generally; and (4) other people's theory and analysis of art and people's responses to art. In observing these four aspects of aesthetics as they function in African-American culture, we will not assume that everything in our environment is beautiful simply because it is there. However, we will describe some fairly widespread goals that groups of African Americans strive for--to talk, gesture, and dress in certain ways. In addition, we will examine certain abstract concepts that are thought to be of greater value than others. These goals and concepts manifest themselves in the more traditional art forms that groups of African Americans are willing to patronize. A subtle and complex system of determining that a given thing is more or less beautiful than other things of the same kind is present in African-American culture. This system is flexible enough to allow for considerable individual variation. If an artist is to practice some form of art with some degree of effectiveness for an African-American audience, he or she must relate to these concepts about beauty that exist among African Americans.

ENDNOTES

1.   Thorstein Veblen, *The Theory of the Leisure Class* (1899; rpt. New York: New American Library 1953).

EVALUATION OF ART

2.   *Ethnic Dance: Roundtrip to Trinidad*, conceived and written by Martha Hyer and featuring Geoffrey Holder and Carmen deLavallade. Produced for the National Educational Television and Radio Center by the Lowell Institute Cooperative Broadcasting Council, WGBH, Boston, 1960. Black and white film, 29 minutes.

Chapter Four

OBJECTIVITY AND UNIVERSALITY

The study of any aspect of African-American theatre will necessitate some understanding of the aesthetic foundations upon which African-American theatre is built. Any process that attempts to evaluate African-American theatre must begin by determining some parameters within which the process functions. Probably the most frequent cause for controversy about the relative merits of individual products of African-American artists in the United States of America is a widespread misunderstanding with respect to the goals of African-American art generally and African-American theatre specifically. The prevailing practices with regard to the criticism of products of African-American art seem to suggest that the success or failure of the work of art in question may be evaluated without first taking the trouble to discover what constitutes success within the context of African-American art from the points of view of the African-American creative artist and the African-American receiver of the artistic messages. This kind of evaluative process would warrant little, if any, serious attention were it not for its widespread and frequent occurrence among persons who are generally regarded as critics, and the apparent assumption that their work is legitimate and ought to be taken seriously.

People generally and Eurocentric evaluators of works of art, specifically, must deal with whatever they perceive from within the context of their own concepts of reality, truth, and beauty--their own values. This valuation is coupled with a

94

rather obvious tendency among Eurocentric evaluators to assume that their own concepts about reality, truth, and beauty are the only ones that are correct; therefore, anyone whose concepts about reality, truth, and beauty are different from these evaluators, must be wrong. If these different concepts are not wrong, they are at least inferior to the evaluators' concepts. Consequently, when persons who do not possess a thorough understanding and appreciation of Afrocentric values make an analysis of African-American theatre, they will more than likely make some incorrect judgments. We will cite two examples to support this contention.

First, if one assumes that all of the best American plays get produced on Broadway, then historians must conclude that African-Americans have done very little of value or significance in theatre except as performers and have achieved nothing worth mentioning as playwrights. This conclusion is frequently reached by serious theatre historians and drama critics. On the other hand, one might safely assume that the only people in this country with enough money or the influence to raise enough money to produce a Broadway play are almost all White; and rare is the White producer who is willing to gamble a small fortune, as well as his or her reputation as a producer, on the artistic and the ticket-selling potential of an African-American playwright. Further, to provide such an opportunity to an African-American playwright is a *de facto* denial of that production opportunity to a White playwright. In the light of the preceding assertions, we find the production of even one African-American play on Broadway a remarkable occurrence. We must conclude that a Broadway production or the length of a Broadway run has no validity when used as a standard for determining the quality, or lack of it, of an African-American play.

Numerous examples document White producers of plays and motion pictures perpetuating negative stereotypical images of African-American people as a highly successful device for selling tickets to White audiences. D. W. Griffith's film, *The Birth of a Nation* is generally regarded by White experts as a success, not only financially but artistically as well. From an African-American point of view, *The Birth of a Nation* cannot be regarded as anything but a disaster. The stereotypes portrayed on Broadway have generally been more sophisticated than those portrayed in *The Birth of a Nation*. In many respects, the more sophisticated stereotypes from *Porgy* and *The Emperor Jones* to *Ain't Misbehavin'* and *Dreamgirls* are more effective in their negative impact upon how African Americans are perceived, because they appear on the surface to portray African-American people and their behavior in a sympathetic manner. On the other hand, since the Broadway opening of *Simply Heavenly* in the late 1950's, a few plays by African-American playwrights have appeared on "The Great White Way" that have been supported at the box office in large measure by African Americans. These plays illustrate that just as Broadway production and box office success does not necessarily mean that a play is good for African Americans, Broadway production and box office success does not necessarily mean that a play is bad for African Americans. Neither critical acclaim by the White establishment nor financial success at the box office can be depended upon to serve as a reliable indicator of African-American artistic achievement--not even as a reverse indicator.

Our second example of an incorrect analysis of African-American art, resulting from a lack of familiarity with the values that the art reflects, has to do with the evaluation of certain African sculpture and sculptors. White art experts concluded that carved human figures from some parts of Africa were out of proportion. The White art experts noticed, for instance, that many of the figures were sculpted with heads much larger in proportion to the bodies than those of actual human figures. Until very recently, almost all of the White art experts who wrote about this subject concluded that these allegedly disproportionate figures were indicative of the primitive state of the African-American artist who carved the figures. The Eurocentric art experts reasoned that the Afrocentric artists in question were not culturally and intellectually advanced enough to get the proportions right. Of course, these art experts were assuming that the universal goal of all sculptors is to accurately reproduce external surface characteristics and details. They seldom, if ever, thought to ask an African sculptor what he was trying to achieve. The African sculptors in question considered the accurate reproduction of the surface details of a human figure unseemly. The sculptors were accomplishing precisely what they intended to accomplish, and what their people valued and considered proper and right and beautiful.

These are examples of incorrect judgments being made about African-American art because the evaluator failed to first ascertain the values of the artist. The Eurocentric values of racial and cultural superiority that lead to such errors in judgment have caused a number of African-American analysts of African-American art to suggest that few, if any, White critics have any business attempting to make judgments about African-American art. On the other hand, those Eurocentric critics articulate their racist values through such statements as: "Black folks are unable to maintain objectivity in an analysis of works of art that grow out of the values of their own culture. They get emotionally involved. They do not analyze; they support, defend and apologize." These same Eurocentric critics seem convinced that they are able to analyze their own values and their own culture dispassionately, and without indulging in apologetic rhetoric. In other words, they claim they can be objective. Examples to

97

the contrary are so abundant that to cite one or two might serve to imply that there are not thousands of other equally valid examples. Further, to refute such allegations may serve to legitimize them.

Ironically, while African-American artists are often negatively evaluated for the art they produce, a White copy of the African-American original may be judged praiseworthy by those who initially made the negative evaluation of the African-American original. Many aspects of African-American culture are being assimilated into Eurocentric culture in a manner that filters out those Afrocentric elements that most significantly conflict with Eurocentric values. The origin of popular music in the United States is a prime example of this adaptation of African-American culture to Eurocentric values. A significant percentage of the popular recorded music hits among European-American young people is, in effect, European-American performers imitating African-American musical performances. In other cases they actually copy a previously released record by an African-American artist that has become popular among African Americans--copying every syllable, every intonation, but usually failing to even copy well by African-American aesthetic standards. Occasionally, the imitation has been so accurate that even some African-American people have had difficulty in determining that the singer was White. Elvis Presley's early hit *Hound Dog* is a notable example. Another similar example is Bill Haley and the Comets. They were, by African-American standards, a mediocre imitation of what African Americans had been doing better for years.

The popular appeal of Bill Haley, Tom Jones, Englebert Humperdink, Janis Joplin, and countless others is directly connected to their ability to mimic the work of African-American artists. The feature film *Blues Brothers* uses the comic irony of this phenomenon very effectively. But, even when an African-American artist is credited by Whites with some innovation, the validity of such credit must be questioned. For instance, Chubby Checker recorded the song, *The Twist*, several years after The Midnighters did. The song, *The Twist*, and the dance that inspired it, were popularized among African Americans by the Midnighters several years before Chubby Checker popularized them among Whites. Credit for artistic innovation, therefore, was not totally determined by race since The Midnighters are African American and Chubby Checker is also African American.

The judgment to credit Chubby Checker with an innovation that was actually made by The Midnighters was undoubtedly regarded as an aesthetic judgment by those who made it. Actually, the judgment grows more out of a moral reaction to the pelvic movement of the dance--movement regarded as suggestive in European-American culture. The Midnighters had, by White standards, too much front-to-back undulating movement of the spinal column, especially in the pelvic region, in their twist. In contrast, Chubby Checker practically eliminated pelvic movement in his version of the dance. It is important to recognize that Chubby Checker kept his spinal column in a nearly straight line and accomplished his dance movement by rotating his torso from side to side. Further, movement of the arms while held away from the torso was an important element in his version of the twist, whereas movement of the arms was of little consequence in the Midnighters' version. The dance movements that Chubby Checker did while singing were actually "Whiter" than Elvis Presley's. In other words, Chubby Checker's movements were more in keeping with European-American moral values than were those of Elvis Presley and considerably more Eurocentric than the Midnighters.

Another reason for crediting Chubby Checker with inventing the twist rather than the Midnighters is discernable. Most of

99

the fans of the Midnighters were African Americans, whereas a large portion of Chubby Checker's fans were White. Therefore, the logic that allows the conclusion that Chubby Checker invented the twist is similar to the logic that allows the conclusion that Columbus discovered America. The people who were fans of the Midnighters and the people who greeted Columbus on his arrival in this hemisphere are defined into non-personhood by those who control Eurocentric standards.

Ray Charles, Chuck Berry, Muddy Waters and many other African-American performers developed musical concepts and popularized them with African-American audiences, while others received greater financial rewards and greater status for imitating them among the European-American public. Some of those so credited have been African American. However, whether the recipient of the credit is Black or White, the authority bestowing the credit must always be White. More importantly, the standards that determine who gets public recognition and acclaim must be Eurocentric standards. The bestowing of such credit has generally been accepted by Eurocentric Americans as recognition by experts of universal artistic quality. They have assumed that their authorities are objectively analyzing the inherent nature of the thing being analyzed. But an individual's reaction to whatever is being analyzed must exist within the context of the totality of his or her previous experiences.

Afrocentric art that is not extolled by Eurocentric art experts cannot be deemed unworthy of praise, nor can the work be deemed worthy of praise. The bestowing of public recognition and acclamation in America today is largely a matter of the leveraging of power or influence or money. For artists, acclamation is largely a function of such White-controlled, non-aesthetic concerns as the acquisition of bookings into facilities that provide optimum public exposure and the acquisition of media coverage. Recognition and acclamation for artistic achievement is not directly related to artistic quality, not even in Eurocentric terms. This assertion is not to suggest that poorer quality always triumphs among Eurocentric people. Rather, we suggest that, when accorded optimum exposure and effective marketing, an artist of poorer quality is not significantly less likely to triumph than one of higher quality who has less effective marketing and exposure.

The relationship of Afrocentric art to Eurocentric public recognition and acclamation has even less to do with Afrocentric standards of quality. Power, influence, and money are used to market art and artists in the United States in much the same manner that other products are marketed. Those who can bestow public recognition, acclaim, and the status that accompany them usually expect either to turn a profit or increase their own status among those they wish to impress. Afrocentric art seldom serves either purpose for Eurocentric entrepreneurs. On those rare occasions when Eurocentric entrepreneurs perceive some advantage in marketing Afrocentric art, they generally operate on the assumption that they can increase profitability or their own status, or both, by altering the art so that it will, in their estimation, be more palatable for Eurocentric audiences. They usually insist that what they are actually doing is making the art have a more universal appeal.

Several years ago, we happened to see a thirty-minute television news documentary about the marriage England's Anne and Mark Phillips. One of this country's best known and most highly paid television news commentators had been sent to England to cover the story. On several occasions during the program, she referred to England as "... the most enduring monarchy of them all." We are not seeking to champion monarchy as a political system, but what about Ethiopia? Apparently Ethiopia is not in the universe--at least, not in the Eurocentric universe. However, when the documentary was made, the world's most enduring monarchy was Ethiopia; the Ethiopian monarchy dated back, in a continuous line, to a time when England was inhabited by primitive barbarians who had not even evolved a concept of nationalism. We recognize we are using the terms "primitive" and "nationalism" in a way that contradicts one of those most cherished beliefs of European-American culture. When Europhile Americans speak of African people, nationalism is called tribalism. On the other hand, a centuries-old tribal conflict persists in Ireland between the Celtic tribes and the Anglo-Saxon tribes. Further, the tribal conflicts in the general vicinity of Germany have precipitated two world wars. Most recently, tribal conflicts have caused the destruction of the Union of Soviet Socialist Republics. But the term "tribe" is studiously avoided whenever the reference is to these, or any other White people. This simple device is used to reinforce the notion that all of the ancient civilizations of Africa may be defined as primitive tribal societies in order to imply that they are of no great significance.

If one approaches any humanistic issue from an African-American point of view, one must critically examine the most cherished beliefs of Europhile Americans. A real dilemma is created for African Americans by the constant repetition, in the form of a nearly overwhelming environmental mantra, of such statements as "Columbus discovered America," "Africans are primitive," and "England is the most enduring monarchy of them all." These statements are so totally without substance as to make virtually impossible the presentation of a mature, sensible, reasonable argument against them. One of Europe's most influential 20th century leaders, Adolph Hitler, almost parlayed that rhetorical technique into an empire. He was remarkably adept at a rhetorical technique known as the big lie. One cannot reason with the big lie.

OBJECTIVITY AND UNIVERSALITY

Another cherished idea in European-American culture is "bigger is better." There is among European-Americans a cultural affinity for bigness. Again, so many examples exist that to mention a few may reduce, by inference, the impact of the idea. But we will mention a few examples, nevertheless. One example has recently become slightly less cherished. "Big automobiles are better than small ones" is an idea that is no longer beyond question. And the automobile example is one that has been enthusiastically accepted by many African-American people as well.

Another example of "bigger is better" is Stone Mountain--the biggest rock you ever saw. More accurately, it is the world's largest exposed piece of solid granite. Also, Stone Mountain has, carved upon it, the largest piece of sculpture in the world. We have never heard of any serious claim that it is the best sculpture or even a pretty good sculpture--just big. The Mount Rushmore fans may want to question this claim. Well, the folks in Georgia explain that they have the biggest single sculpture. Mount Rushmore has several different ones, and each of the individual ones is smaller than the one on Stone Mountain. But, the point is that both at Stone Mountain and at Mount Rushmore, the attribute of size seems to eliminate any concern for aesthetic qualities that would otherwise be the determining factors in an evaluative judgment.

Freedom is certainly among the most cherished ideas in European-American culture. Western democratic institutions are allegedly traceable back to the Greeks, who also embraced the institution of slavery and did not regard women as citizens. Only a very small percentage of the people who lived in what is now the country of Greece in the Fifth century B.C. enjoyed a democratic form of government. The allegedly democratic government that, by implication, is regarded by many as the national government of Greece was actually the municipal government of Athens. Whatever the origins of the

Eurocentric idea of freedom may be the idea that the best freedom is the present-day United States' brand of freedom is an idea that one must not question. An African playwright named Chiek N'dao pointed out to us that freedom in the American frame of reference includes the individual's freedom not to help his brother. In some cultures, a person does not have the right--the freedom--to stand by and watch his brother or sister drown, or get robbed, or go hungry.

Very closely connected to this concept of freedom is the concept of individualism. In the United States, this concept is often called rugged individualism. Basically, this idea of individualism promotes the point of view that the individual is more important than the community. This ideal is quite apparent in the aesthetic position that promotes individuality of characterization in European and American works of art. The ideal is also apparent in the ethical position that makes heroes of criminals such as Achilles, Robin Hood, Billy the Kid, Jesse James, Al Capone and a number of more recent criminals who have used political power instead of guns. This ethical position is even supported by the Eurocentric scientific community. Darwin, Freud, and their contemporary counterparts tell us that hatred and avarice are natural human instincts and that only the fittest will survive. Others have interpreted these concepts to justify "scientifically" the enclosure and hoarding of natural resources for the use of the powerful and to the exclusion of others; the withholding of basic supplies from the sick, wounded, and starving; and the violent overthrow of those who are either unwilling to commit acts of violence or not powerful enough to hold on to what is rightfully theirs. If your brother is homeless or hungry, that is the way life is--only the fittest survive.

Ironically, the same ethical position that permits one to withhold from his brother the essentials to sustain life, permits one to provide simultaneously unsolicited advice.

OBJECTIVITY AND UNIVERSALITY

African-American people call this practice "meddling in other people's business." And, of course, all of these practices are mirrored in and promoted by the art that European-American culture produces. Further, the standards of taste of popular culture in the U.S.A. are determined, to a great degree, by the adolescents of the society. What could possibly cause people of such a culture to assume that they have the competence, the right, yes, even the responsibility, to pass judgment on the creative products of other people's cultures?

Within an African-American aesthetic context, a strong distinction is made between creators and imitators of art. The ability to make such distinctions requires, among other things, a historical frame of reference that is seldom found in adolescents. Adolescents have been known to assume that something new and innovative has been discovered without looking back in time to determine whether or not that which appears to be an innovation from their limited historical frame of reference is a cliche from someone else's frame of reference. The time frame needed to make such a determination is often only three or four years. The absence of such a time frame among adolescents seems to be an understandable adolescent characteristic. On the other hand, this characteristic ought not to be blatantly present among the principal evaluators of the arts and the artists of a society.

The practice of distinguishing between creators and imitators of art should not be confused with several other distinctions that must be made between different kinds of artists. For example, there are creative artists and there are interpretative artists. Both kinds of artists are necessary to the creation of certain performing art forms. Even among creative artists, a distinction may be made between those artists who adhere to a classical form such as the ballet, the sonnet, the symphony, or the blues, on the one hand, and those who are innovative and seek to move beyond traditional forms or ways of

105

arranging a work of art on the other. In addition to these various kinds of artists, there are those who simply copy or imitate the arts of others. In an effort to illuminate this concept, we will quote from a newspaper commentary that was written in response to the massive outpouring of grief by European Americans that occurred following the death of Elvis Presley in August of 1977.[1]

Rip-off King

Forty million Americans remain largely unaffected by the death of white America's favorite singer, Elvis Presley. Most Black Americans cannot fathom the hysteria and mania that surrounded Presley's live stage appearances. The publicity and the mass demonstration of public sentiment about his demise exceeds that which has occurred following the deaths of recent American Presidents. How is it that a boy born and bred in Mississippi and who later called Memphis his home, was catapulted into such prominence? Was it his voice? Or was it his guitar virtuosity? The answer is obviously negative to both questions. Perhaps, the one valid answer to the question of his success would be Thomas Andrew Parker, Elvis' manager. "Colonel" Parker, as he is usually called, deftly guided Elvis' climb to fame and fortune. Parker cleverly orchestrated the recording aspects of Elvis' career so that, in later years, public appearances were held to a minimum. Through Parker's maneuvering, Elvis was proclaimed by a rabid public as "The King of Rock and Roll."

An example of Parker's business acumen can be seen in the story surrounding Elvis' recording of "Hound Dog." The lyrics for "Hound Dog" were written by two white adolescents, Jerry Liber and Mich Stoller. Johnny Otis,

> a white R and B musician, and Otis Rene, a black song writer who wrote the music for "Sleepy Time Down South," collaborated on the tune. The song was recorded by Willie Mae "Big Mama" Thornton on the Peacock label in Los Angeles. Don Robey, a black Houstonian, owned Peacock Records. . . . Black folks were humming "Hound Dog" all over the U.S.A. long before Elvis made his recording. . . . The song is not a masterpiece, but [it] was a success among black record buyers [primarily] because of the monumental voice of "Big Mama" Thornton.

The column goes on to explain that by the time he recorded Hound Dog, Elvis owned the publisher's rights, even though the song had been previously published. The publisher of a song controls permission to record the song and also garners a major share of the royalties collected for recordings and public performances, as well as for sheet music sales. Although Don Robey is alleged to have negotiated a much better financial arrangement than African Americans usually received in those days, Elvis acquired a much greater share of the revenues from record sales than one would reasonably expect a singer to get for a song that had been previously recorded and with fairly successful results. Of greater concern is the recognition that Elvis' record was a blatant, though mediocre, imitation of "Big Mama" Thornton's earlier recording of Hound Dog.

Since Elvis Presley's death, a story that suggests more widespread imitativeness on his part has emerged. A man named Otis Blackwell has come forth to proclaim that he wrote such Elvis Presley hits as *Don't Be Cruel* and *Fever*. Further, he claims that, although he never met Elvis face to face, he prepared demonstration tapes of every song of his that Elvis recorded. Elvis apparently learned to mimic those tapes very well. We are not aware of any other plausible explanation for Elvis' suddenly acquired ability to achieve both a vocal production quality and an articulation pattern that were considered to be exclusively Negro characteristics in the mid-1950's especially in the South. After hearing Otis Blackwell sing, it is readily apparent that either Elvis imitated Otis, or Otis imitates Elvis with great precision.

In fairness, we must point out that the widespread dislike for Elvis Presley among African-American people is not completely due to the mediocrity and imitativeness of his music. The previously mentioned newspaper column points out that:

> There is a well known quote attributed to Elvis Presley that many black folks believe is the truth. He may have said it, and he may not have said it. The point is, many Black people believe that he said it. And, it is indicative of how most black folks feel about the dear departed one. Elvis is believed to have said that, "The only things a 'boot' can do for me is to buy my records and shine my shoes."

In retrospect, the concluding line to that column should have been: Most African-American people are proud to proclaim that they have never done either.

These anecdotes about the imitativeness of Elvis Presley's music are not intended to suggest that he was a success because he was an imitator rather than a creator. He was more successful than the African Americans who created the musical style that he imitated because he was White and marketed effectively, and they were not. Can some small part of the success of Elvis Presley be attributed to a widely felt need to reduce the likelihood that some African-American male singer might emerge as a popular sex idol among young White females? This question is not intended to imply that the White public acceptance of Elvis was forced in any way. However, public acceptance follows public exposure. The issue, then, has to do with the decisions that get made about who receives massive public exposure and who does not. The general public only gets to choose from among those artists who receive such public exposure.

The preceding discussion of White imitators of the African-American creators of a certain style of music does not rule out the possibility that some of these imitators have themselves been African American. In 1981, William Cockerham of the *Hartford Courant* wrote a newspaper article about a man named Joe Boatner who bills himself in his nightclub act as the only surviving member of the original Ink Spots. Although the original members of the Ink Spots have all been dead for several years, Boatner says he joined the original group when Hoppy Jones died in 1943. Cockerham's research led him to conclude that, except for the first seven or eight years, the Ink Spots were one of the biggest "frauds" in American entertainment history. Boatner claims that there were as many as fourteen groups, billed as the Ink Spots, performing all over the world. Cockerham quotes Boatner as saying:

> "The public didn't know. All they saw were four black faces and four white suits. The only member of the group whose name they did recognize was Bill Kenny's, the distinctively high tenor with the 'good diction,' and if anyone ever asked about him, they'd say he was sick, that he had a sore throat or something."[2]

The important thing to recognize here is that the Ink Spots were, as Boatner puts it, according to Cockerham:

". . . a black group, but a white act. Ninety-nine
percent of the clubs we played were white. Black
people didn't come to the clubs to hear us sing. Black
people were into rhythm and blues back then."[3]

Cockerham portrays Boatner as an intelligent, sensitive man--a
man who ". . . worked his way through Atlanta University and
later the Cleveland School of Music." Why would such a man
wait until long after the Ink Spots were a "hot item" in the
record and nightclub businesses to expose the fact that there
were as many as fourteen groups claiming to be the Ink Spots?
Was it that African Americans had no scruples about
perpetrating such a fraud because those who were "taken"
were virtually all White? Boatner suggests that the singers
who were billed as the Ink Spots simply wanted an
opportunity to work at their chosen profession. Cockerham
further quotes Boatner:

> "You have to understand the segregation patterns back
> in those days. No one did business with a black person.
> You did business with the White agents. They
> controlled you and your money, and this went on right
> up until the late 1960's."

. . . .

Boatner said that theatrical agents also perpetuated the
myth of how the Ink Spots came up with their name.
The agents said the name came by accident during a
record contract session; when one member of the group
took out his fountain pen to sign the contract, it leaked
and formed ink spots all over the legal form, and the
group's name was born.

"The name didn't come by any accident. The name
meant a lot. The white public was clamoring for a

black singing group and they needed a name that would let everyone know they were black. Originally, they wanted to call us the Sambos. If we were called the Four Niggers, it would have been the biggest act in the country," Boatner said.[4]

An African-American group that performed almost totally for White audiences was certainly in no position to change the way White folks do business with other White folks.

When the *Houston Chronicle* carried William Cockerham's story, the newspaper printed three photographs from their files of three different groups that played Houston in 1953, 1963, and 1975, all claiming to be the Ink Spots. With fourteen groups touring all over the world, the assumption would be that, spread out over a thirty-year period like that, no one would notice the difference. But Boatner claims that, on one occasion, the Ink Spots were being advertised at two different Manhattan clubs on the same street. This phenomenon would seem to indicate that some people paid to see a group called the Ink Spots knowing that the group they paid to see was not the only group bearing that name. Although the promoters of the Ink Spots may have pioneered the practice of "multiple billing," evidence exists that suggests that they are not the only promoters ever to engage in such a practice. But, to the best of our knowledge, those few African-American groups that have engaged in such a practice have performed almost totally for White audiences, under the control of White management.

The previous quotes from Boatner are indicative of a prevalent attitude among a much larger segment of the population than White managers of African-American artists. This prevalent attitude may be characterized by the assertion that a small group of White men (few, if any women, or members of non-European racial groups), most of whom have college degrees, are best qualified to determine what is beautiful and true and good. This attitude seems to be the basis for a great deal of the behavior that is identified as cultural imperialism by some of the people who are not a part of this elite group of educated White males who seek to set universal standards of taste and judgment.

We have interpolated the following definition of cultural imperialism from our dictionary's various definitions of the two words: Cultural imperialism is the act or fact or policy of dominating another people's structure or system of what constitutes good in feelings, thoughts, tastes, manners, customs, arts, conveniences, socially inherited artifacts, and the development of the mind or body by education or training, especially when such domination occurs without actually taking physical or governmental control.

Within the Europhile American missionary concept or point of view, the practice of evangelism requires a set of assumptions that are almost identical to the assumptions that are requisite to the practice of cultural imperialism. There are those who would say that evangelism is simply a specific form of cultural imperialism. The only real difference between evangelism and cultural imperialism seems to be that most White Anglo-Saxon Christians regard evangelism as an unequivocally good and worthwhile activity. Some would assert that failure to participate actively in evangelical activity constitutes failure to do good, and is, therefore, bad. On the other hand, cultural imperialism is often regarded by enthusiastic advocates of evangelism as a negative activity. The negativism grows out of the term imperialism--a term that is more often used to describe someone else's covert activity aimed at the takeover of political, military, and economic control of people who, initially, have fewer resources. People in the U.S.A. have a tendency to want to cheer for the underdog. Nevertheless, an evangelist begins with the assumption that his or her way is a better way for everyone and it is his or her duty to convert one and all to that way. Whether or not the person being converted would rather continue in his or her traditional ways is simply not recognized as a valid concern.

Imperialism is a term that is used to describe someone else's behavior. When White Americans have wanted to acquire political, military, and economic control, they have generally used a rhetorical device to describe what they were doing that implies a far more positive mode of behavior than the word "imperialism " does. The term "manifest destiny" is such a device. Arthur Schlesinger, Jr. attributes the phrase "manifest destiny" to John L. O'Sullivan who was a proponent of the westward expansionist movement of the 1840's. O'Sullivan is credited with writing the credo in the *Democratic Review* in 1839 that was the justification cited by the territorial expansionists. According to Schlesinger, O'Sullivan said, "The 'mission' of America . . . was to spread the four freedoms through the world--'freedom of conscience, freedom of person, freedom of trade and business pursuits, universality of freedom and equality.'" Schlesinger refers to this view as "the new imperialism." The phrase, "manifest destiny," was used by O'Sullivan in an article supporting the United States' right to claim Oregon . . . "by the right of our manifest destiny to overspread and to possess the whole of the continent which Providence has given us for the . . . great experiment of liberty."[5] "Manifest Destiny" was a popular rallying cry of those who believed in American democracy as Walt Whitman believed. "It is for the interest of mankind, . . . that its power and territory should be extended--the farther the better."[6]

Manifest destiny was "the new imperialism" of the 1840's. Once established, the tradition of manifest destiny lasted well into the 20th century. Its values are still with us today and can be seen in the rhetoric that seeks to justify continued U.S. ownership of the Panama Canal. A century and a quarter after manifest destiny became the philosophical justification for territorial imperialism, overt political and economic control over every increasing territory was no longer a desirable goal. Cultural imperialism has replaced territorial imperialism. Cultural imperialism has as the basis for its philosophical justification the myths of OBJECTIVITY and UNIVERSALITY.

Since the previously mentioned elite group of European-Americans created and disseminated the mythology of objectivity and universality, the possession of these highly valued attributes in relatively large amounts by the members of that group should not come as a surprise. The result is that a small group, made up almost exclusively of White males, has created and disseminated a mythological structure that describes their most prevalent behavioral characteristics as the criteria for persons with influence or control to make important decisions. Persons who do not belong to this elite group are told that their opinions and suggestions are not valid. Such persons are never told that their opinions and suggestions are rejected because they are offered by persons who do not belong to the elite group. Instead, they are told that their opinions and suggestions are not objective, not universal, or both.

The number one definition of objective, both as a noun and as an adjective, describes a goal or an aim. This use of the word occurs outside the mythological structure to which we have alluded. Objective also means:

n. . . . 2 something real and observable.

-adj. . . . 2 existing outside the mind as an actual object and not merely in the mind as an idea; real. Buildings

114

and actions are objective; ideas are subjective. **3 about outward things, not about the thoughts and feelings of the speaker, writer, or painter; giving facts as they are without a bias toward either side; impersonal: an objective analysis of a poem or painting. An "objective test" is often true or false or multiple choice. A scientist must be objective in his experiments. The policeman gave an objective report of the accident. . . .**

The myth of objectivity is embodied in the concept that all that is real is observable by members of an elite group of White males. Therefore, they assert that phenomena which are not observable by them are not real. Further, most of the European Americans who do not belong to this elite group of White males believe the myth. From our point of view, then, objectivity is a condition that is most common among persons of Eurocentric culture and ethnic background. The condition is particularly widespread among the males of the group. The near absence of spirituality, imagination and creativity are the most notable characteristics of this condition. Members of this group hold the ability to be objective in such high esteem that from early childhood, they systemically teach each succeeding generation to practice their techniques for stifling those behaviors that grow out of spirituality, imagination, and creativity. Eurocentric males are taught that behaviors that grow out of spirituality, imagination and creativity are emotional behaviors and ought to be eliminated, or at least muffled or hidden. Further, these important Eurocentric cultural traits are extensions of Greek culture. Not Athens, but the city-state of Sparta is generally regarded to have been the original exemplar of these traits. Skill in the practice of objectivity is an important prerequisite step in developing the ability to use the process that allows this group to impose its will upon others. And mastery of this process of imposing one's will upon others is the foundation for oppression, cultural imperialism, manifest destiny, and evangelism.

BLACK THEATRE

The myth of objectivity has an interdependent relationship with the myth of universality. As we have stated, members of this group of White males claim that what is not observable by them is not real. That fallacy is the myth of objectivity. Now, the myth of objectivity alone would allow the rest of us to recognize that their failure to perceive something that the rest of us perceive is their problem. Hence, the need for the accompanying myth of universality, which enables this elite group to convince most of the rest of us that what they observe is observed by all who know how to observe well. They are even magnanimous enough to offer to teach the rest of us to observe things the way they do so that we will no longer be "culturally deprived." Many of us even learn to observe the way they do in order to be regarded by them as objective. When they claim to have recognized some universal trait, we must claim to have observed it too. The reason that we often believe that we must make such a claim has to do with how the term "universal" is defined.

> -adj. 1a of all; belonging to all; concerning all; shared by all: **Food is a universal need.** . . . b coming from all; shared in by all: **a universal protest.** c understood or used by all: **the universal language of love.** . . .

Most of us who do not belong to this elite group of people but who live in a Eurocentric environment are reluctant to admit to being the only person on the face of the earth who does not, for example, comprehend "the universal language of love."

A great many of the very important and most highly valued characteristics of European-American theatre are objectively considered by many to be universal characteristics. "Universal," then, is a very weighty term to be so lightly bestowed. Some theatre and drama critics and instructors regularly attribute the quality of universality to a given play, or to a character in a play. They insist that the human

116

qualities they perceive are universal while they virtually ignore the cultural traditions of three-fourths of the world's population. And, of course, they will tell you that they are being objective in their analysis.

Ideas that are thought to be of central social significance in non-Western societies of the world--filial piety, for instance-- may be considered quaint, picturesque, primitive, and naive by persons who are steeped in the traditions of Europhile American ethical behavior. And, of course, other non-Western ideas and values are regarded as equally inferior. One set of values grows out of the assumption of reincarnation; another set of values grows out of the assumption that real property is in the public domain; and still another set of values grows out of the assumption that polygamy is the basis of family structure. These values affect people's observations of reality. No real evidence suggests that any one large group of people has values that are more or less objective and universal than any other large group of people.

Seldom do European Americans consider that, although other people do not look and act like European Americans, those differences alone do not necessarily constitute evidence of other people's inferiority. In addition, the modes of communication--usually referred to by European Americans as style--vary enough from one culture to another to make the whole business of universality in a given work of art of no significance on those rather pragmatic grounds alone. Further, the specific characteristics of the human condition that are most frequently talked about by European Americans as having a universal quality operate in a rather paradoxical fashion as they relate to standards of excellence in the art of the theatre.

Jealousy, for instance, is frequently mentioned as a universal characteristic that is illuminated by Shakespeare's Othello.

Let us assume that jealously, in very general terms, is a universal element of the human condition. But, jealousy that grows out of a monogamous married situation in which the husband believes that the chastity of his wife has been violated, as it specifically relates to *Othello*, is not a universal element of the human condition--since chastity is not a universally valued condition among adult women in all societies. Obviously, monogamy is not a universally valued behavior pattern either. Further, the entire concept of romantic love, which provides the basis for the marriage of Othello and Desdemona, was a concept that was only a few hundred years old when Shakespeare wrote the play. In addition, the so-called universality of the jealousy exemplified by *Othello* does not function independently of the overall quality of the work. Witness all the soap operas that thrive upon precisely that same kind of jealously, yet are condemned by those same Anglophile Eurocentric critics who praise *Othello*. So, undoubtedly something about the play causes it to be of great value among Anglophile Eurocentric critics other than its portrayal of jealously that grows out of a husband's suspicion of extramarital sex on the part of his wife. Although the play is excellent, within the framework of Anglophile Eurocentric art, to claim that *Othello* is universal is an exaggeration.

On some other occasions when the term "universality" is used in praise of a work of art, the term is used to mean, in effect, longevity. A work of art is praised because it is valued now and it has been around for a very long time. However, longevity in a work of art is at least as dependent upon the vicissitudes of war and climatic conditions as it is upon the quality of the work. Those highly valued Eurocentric works of art that "have stood the test of time" are generally not regarded as being of high quality except by those Eurocentric people who have the "refined taste" to appreciate antiques and also the power or influence to demand that others be taught

118

that these works are of sufficiently high quality to be regarded as masterpieces. From a Eurocentric perspective, the *Mona Lisa*, *Hamlet* and *Oedipus Rex* are masterpieces. The issue is whether or not they are masterpieces from Afrocentric and Asiocentric perspectives, thereby providing some basis for the claim that they are universal masterpieces. Further, we question the implication that the lack of awareness by Eurocentric scholars of artifacts of similar quality from some ancient civilization in Africa is evidence of that African society's inferiority to the one that produced *Oedipus Rex*. More importantly, we recognize that many masterpieces of ancient African cultures exist and that many Eurocentric scholars have chosen to ignore these masterpieces.

What often remains from antiquity is not determined by aesthetic quality but by complex sets of circumstances. Those who created the artifacts and the larger group for whom they were created had very little impact upon which things were actually preserved as representative of their culture. The artifacts that remain from a given culture may not have been the best of that culture. This assertion is especially true in instances when the descendants of a culture discover that their ancestral shrines are being broken into pieces for shipment to such places as the British Museum. One may reasonably assume that the best and most sacred works of art might have been hidden or even destroyed in order to keep them from being stolen by the British. The British are singled out here because some of the most significant art treasures, not only of the African continent, but of Greece, Mexico, and other nations were "removed" by the British and now reside in the major museums of England. Whether or not one regards these art treasures as stolen is essentially a question of the cultural identity of the person making the decision. From the perspective of our cultural identity, these art treasures were stolen.

BLACK THEATRE

Many people at many different times and places have simply decided that they have more important things to do than to preserve artifacts and written records of everything they do for posterity. So, to conclude that those societies have produced no artistic masterpieces simply because their best works of art have not been carefully preserved so that they are extant several centuries later is invalid. Some societies have an oral tradition rather than a written one. No evidence supports the Eurocentric assumption that oral records are less accurate in societies with an oral tradition than written records are in societies with a written tradition. Oral records are not inherently unable to maintain a society's drama accurately over a period of hundreds of years. More importantly, a work of performance art that has special religious significance would undoubtedly be kept secret from any aliens who might be likely to desecrate the work in some way. Therefore, most English-speaking scholars are probably not aware of the greatest artistic achievements of some other societies.

The Memphite stele--the stone upon which the Memphite drama is inscribed--provides an important example of the possible consequences of a work of great significance falling into alien hands. The Memphite stele, inscribed in around 700 B. C., was originally upright "but was thrown down from its pedestal and was probably walked on by many generations of men or it may have formed part of a wall." Although the Memphite stele has been in the British Museum since 1805, it was nearly destroyed during the centuries prior to its "rescue" by the British. Whereas the British undoubtedly regard their theft of this artifact as a rescue, the Egyptians probably do not. If there were still practitioners of the religious doctrines of the ancient Egyptians among us today, they might prefer the destruction of their religious icon to the desecration it now endures.

120

OBJECTIVITY AND UNIVERSALITY

European-American society places such an unusually high value upon the maintenance of written records that U.S. tax money is used every ten years to make an accurate count and a published statistical record of, among other things, the indoor toilets in the United States. Some other societies would, no doubt, consider that another project, for instance the elimination of hunger, would make better use of a nation's money and manpower than counting its indoor toilets. Since Eurocentric values hold written records in such high esteem, one should not be surprised that the absence of such records are presumed to be evidence of the absence of civilization.

The quality of a work of art is subject to a number of variables that have little, if anything, to do with the mythological standards of objectivity and universality, even when the work of art in question is European-American. But the mythological attributes of objectivity and universality have become virtually self-perpetuating. And, ironically enough, the elite group that is actually responsible for the perpetuation of these mythological attributes seldom, if ever, finds it necessary for any of its members to appear to force their acceptance upon the rest of us. The rest of us voluntarily perpetuate the myths. Hence, to deny the myths is tantamount to an open denial of one's humanity.

One does not have to be particularly astute to notice that those who control government possess similar characteristics to those who control the economic resources and to those who control the dissemination of ideas. In addition to being White and male, these individuals appear to be quite similar in dress, speech, and other easily observable behavior patterns. They enjoy similar recreational activities, for example. They are certain that they are civilized and that they are objective. Therefore, when they proclaim that some object or activity has some universal quality, they do so without any anxiety that their proclamation will be challenged by those of us who do not belong to their group. We do not want to be singled out as less sophisticated, less refined, and less knowledgeable than all other human beings. So, to contradict an affirmation of universality is to risk much more than the particular controversy that results. For example, if some universal response ought to occur as a result of viewing the *Mona Lisa*, then to admit that one does not perceive such a response after viewing the painting is to say that one has failed to achieve a level of human refinement that virtually all other human beings have achieved. Even those of us who are not very objective are reluctant to admit that we are devoid of some such universal perception. To admit to the absence of several such perceptions will probably cause one to be accused of being less than civilized--possibly even less than human.

ENDNOTES

1.   Barbara and Carlton Molette, "The Ripoff King," *The Informer and Texas Freeman* (Houston), 15 October, 1977, 6.

2.   William Cockerham, "One of the Biggest Frauds in History?" *Houston Chronicle*, August 23, 1981, Zest, 8 and 39.

3.   Ibid.

4.   Ibid.

5.   Arthur M. Schlesinger, Jr., *The Age of Jackson* (Boston: Little, Brown and Company, 1945), 427.

6.   Schlesinger, 450.

PART TWO

PRESENTATION

n. 1 the act of giving; delivering: ... **2** the gift that is presented: ...**3** the act of bringing forward; offering to be considered: ... **4** an offering to be seen; exhibition; showing: **the presentation of a play or a motion picture.**

African-American culture provides the basis for a definition of African-American presentation. African-American culture grows, in part, out of the oral traditions of Africa. These traditions, as described by Wole Soyinka, are "... sophisticated in idiom. Our forms of the theatre are quite different from literary drama. We use spontaneous dialogue, folk music, simple stories, and relevant dances to express what we mean."[1]

African-American culture is also influenced by the literary traditions of Europe. African-American theatre is a total event that may include narrative storytelling, storytelling in dialogue form, persuasive speeches, sermons, song, dance, or instrumental music in any number of conceivable combinations. African-American theatre can be either an event that evolves orally or a specific set of words fixed for all time upon a page.

African-American theatre emerged from a societal context in which Africans were brought to America, some slave, some free, all oppressed. Out of this societal context, African-

123

BLACK THEATRE

American slaves held their White captors up to public ridicule, among themselves, in what has since been co-opted into the Negro minstrel. From this societal context came African-American preaching, storytelling, dancing, singing, and the standards by which such presentations are evaluated. These presentations function, not only as art, but as implements for the transmission of history, mythology, and ethical standards. African-American presentation of art has traditionally functioned as a prime conduit for the communication of Afrocentric values. The roots of contemporary African-American theatre are embedded within this societal context.

This inquiry into the nature of African-American theatre as presentation will seek to encompass the variety of forms by which the presentation of art has been used to communicate Afrocentric values. In addition, this inquiry will seek to focus upon what African-American performing artists seek to accomplish through presentation and what African-American audiences, both actual and potential, value and consider to be proper, right, and beautiful in the presentations they witness.

During the 1960's and 1970's, the dominant strategy for achieving a more overt acceptance of Afrocentric aesthetic values by African Americans seemed to necessitate a thrust that has appeared to some observers to be a negative one. But such a step was undoubtedly necessary in order to achieve a positive thrust as the next step in the process. This seemingly negative thrust was to educate African Americans to reject the idea that White artistic standards are universally appropriate. As this rejection of prior miseducation is accomplished, African-American people may be properly educated in the appreciation of Afrocentric aesthetic standards. Many Whites have condemned this rejection by African Americans of the imposition of Eurocentric artistic standards upon Afrocentric people as "racism in reverse."

PRESENTATION

A comparison between attempts at African-American liberation and the imposition of Eurocentric values as universal ones is not valid for several reasons. A pivotal reason is that African Americans are not attempting to enslave Whites but to free African-American people from the mental enslavement of Whites. As Carter G. Woodson pointed out over a half-century ago, physical oppression is not necessary--except to make examples of a few of us who get "uppity" from time to time--in a society that provides such effective and abundant miseducation. The contemporary Black theatre movement has never been especially concerned about having a significant influence upon the kind of theatre Whites do for other Whites--and certainly the Black theatre movement has not sought to impose Afrocentric aesthetic values upon White people.

White objective universalists have indicated, by virtue of their condemnation of a theatre of, by, and for African Americans, that they still "know what's best" for African Americans. Underlying such an assumption is a broader assumption that the White objective universalists understand what African-American artists are doing and why. With the aid and comfort of these assumptions, White objective universalists paternally inform African-American artists what they should perceive as beautiful and what they should not. This process is not altogether a function of racism, since an elite group of White Americans also tells other White Americans what they should and should not perceive as beautiful.

White objective universalist critics do not consider some Eurocentric art (quilts, embroidery, wood carving and so forth, that is done by White people and exhibited at fairs) to be fine art just as they do not regard most African-American art as fine art. Both kinds of work are defined into an inferior status by persons with sufficient influence to accomplish such judgments. The concepts of beauty of White

125

objective universalists have succeeded, in some instances in the past, in altering African-American theatre to Eurocentric theatre, performed in natural blackface, on the pretext that the only culture of worth is the White man's culture. Eurocentric Americans who subscribe to the tenets of objectivity and universality continue to promote the notion that production standards are production standards. When African-American people say, "Our productions ought to be judged by different standards," White objective universalists misconstrue the statement to be a plea to be judged by lower standards. African-American theatre must be judged according to its own standards of beauty and excellence. Although such standards are often quite different from those of European-American theatre, they are not lower standards. Presentations of art that is about, by, and intended for African-American people must not be subjected to Eurocentric criteria.

An Afrocentric evaluation of theatre is made difficult by the imposition of Eurocentric concepts delineated by Eurocentric terminology. This difficulty is not confined to Afrocentric artists in the U.S.A. Ghanaian dramatist Efua Sutherland adroitly verbalizes the misunderstandings that are created by imposing Eurocentric terms upon African dramatic expressions. Ms. Sutherland described this phenomenon as ". . . a clash of concepts" in a lecture presented at Spelman College in 1969. She argued that this clash of concepts results from ". . . an insistence on using foreign terminology to describe African dramatic expressions. . . . Each African language has precise and indigenous terms for its dramatic concepts and conventions, for every variety of performance. . . . Outside of a small sprinkling of people, the words drama, theatre, stage, audience, etc., are foreign words and incomprehensible in Africa."[2] English language terms, then, need to be used with care in order to position the concepts within the parameters of Afrocentric values to the greatest possible extent.

PRESENTATION

Africans who speak English frequently reposition words in the English language in order to get concepts to fit within the parameters of Afrocentric values. Efua Sutherland provides an example of this practice by explaining how the word "concert" came to be used by Ghanaians to mean any presentation in a European physical arrangement. The term "concert" evolved as Ghanaians experienced European performances. The staged programs of songs by school children were called concerts by the European colonizers. The performers were on a platform in front of an audience that sat in chairs arranged in rows. Ghanaians, in time, associated the term "concert" with all performances given on a stage before which people sat in rows and listened. If Ghanaians perform on a stage before an audience seated in rows of chairs, they too are giving a concert. The content of the material presented has no bearing on what is called a concert. The Eurocentric manner in which the environment of the presentation is arranged determines its classification as a concert. The term "concert" was appropriated by the Ghanaians and conceptualized in a way that has meaning for them.

We find ourselves confronted with a clash of concepts. Our observations and evaluations are written in English language words. But we use these words in ways that enable us to get the concepts symbolized by these words to fit within the parameters of our Afrocentric values.

ENDNOTES

1. Lewis Nkosi, *Home and Exile* (London: Longmans, Green and Company, Ltd., 1965), 108.

2. Efua Sutherland, "The Drama-Theatre Argument: A Clash of Concepts," *Encore* (1970), 3-8.

Chapter Five

AFROCENTRIC RITUALS

Rituals are sets of practices that evolve over a period of time into formalized behaviors. These formalized behaviors are used to indoctrinate members of societies by validating the system of values of the group. The rituals evolve out of the group's consensus. Further, the group must regard the ritual as having some functional effect. The rituals that are most often described by scholars and journalists are solemn ceremonies. However, some rituals are not solemn ceremonies. Whether they are solemn ceremonies or not, rituals will have all three of the following characteristics: (1) Behavior becomes formalized through an evolutionary process; (2) Group consensus regards the behavior as having some specific and important functional effect; and (3) The ritual validates the group's system of values. Afrocentric rituals provide a way to describe the traditions and ideals that cause Black theatre to be different from White theatre. If one understands the traditions and ideals of Afrocentric rituals and understands that these traditions and ideals are as important to Black theatre as Dionysian rituals are to Greek theatre, one is less likely to discredit Black theatre for failing to accomplish things that it never intended to accomplish.

Rituals evolve out of the behavior of a group of people with a common set of values. Rituals, in the traditional sense, cannot emerge full blown overnight and be thrust upon a group of people. In recent years, the word "ritual" has been used to describe another kind of behavior: a performance in and for a cultural community that attempts to alter the values of that community. These so-called rituals were developed and performed by several Black revolutionary theatre groups during the 1960's. Although they were solemn ceremonies, these so-called rituals had not been formalized through an evolutionary process, nor did a broadly based Black community regard them as having a specific functional effect.

The rituals created by Black revolutionary theatre groups seem to have deliberately sought to change the values of African Americans rather than to validate or strengthen existing ones. Therefore, the rituals do not function as rituals in the way the word is traditionally used. The apparent intention of the Black revolutionary theatre groups that created rituals was to cause these events to become eventually so ingrained in the African-American consciousness that they would thereby become rituals. For the most part, this goal has not been realized. We note, however, that at least one such set of practices established in the U.S.A. in the 1960's, the celebration of Kwanzaa, seems to be growing in acceptance among African Americans to the point that it may soon be regarded as a ritual in the traditional sense of the word.[1] Also, Asante and other Afrocentric humanists have established rites of passage for young African American males.

Performances that are called rituals by Black revolutionary theatre groups are attempts to recapture a lost sense of values. These values embody the spirit and the spirituality of our African predecessors. These performances do not successfully duplicate the actual ritual events of our predecessors because that is not their goal. These performances are not attempts to achieve some kind of archaeological revival of the rituals of the past. Instead, the goal is to adapt traditional Black ritual concepts to contemporary African-American culture in order to achieve the spiritual responses that traditional African rituals are able to achieve in their own environments.

BLACK THEATRE

Accuracy in reproducing the surface details of the rituals of our African predecessors is not a major goal of the rituals of Black revolutionary theatre. Consequently, unfavorable criticism based upon a lack of authenticity is invalid as a standard of judgment for these presentations. The valid standards for determining the success of Black revolutionary theatre rituals are more likely to be found in the responses of those for whom the rituals are performed than by comparing the rituals to an external model.

Information about what African Americans value in their performing art can be obtained by examining rituals that are highly regarded by African Americans. Since church services contain ritual elements that are held in high regard by African Americans, a determination of the most highly valued ritual elements in such church services will provide important information about Afrocentric aesthetic values. Our descriptions of these elements of African-American religious rituals are based upon our accumulated observations of Afrocentric church services. But we must hasten to point out that we do not regard all church services that are carried on by African Americans as African-American church services. Some are very nearly European-American church services carried on by individuals who just happen to be Black.

At least two essential differences exist between Afrocentric and Eurocentric culture with regard to the subject of religion. First, traditional Afrocentric religion is for the community whereas Eurocentric religion is for the individual. Second, Eurocentric religion is conceptually separate from ordinary everyday life whereas traditional Afrocentric religion is everyday life. Afrocentric culture regards religion as a total way of life for all of the people in the society--a continual day-to-day and minute-to-minute activity that encompasses everyone. Nevertheless, Eurocentric scholars have accused ancient Egyptians as having "religious obsessions" in the conduct of their daily lives.[2]

Dr. John S. Mbiti is an African theologian who is an expert at generalizing about traditional African religions in a manner that is meaningful to non-Africans. Although Dr. Mbiti's work is not directly concerned with the retention of African culture by African Americans, his statements on the subject of traditional African religions provide an excellent basis for assessing these retentions. Dr. Mbiti has said that "Because traditional [African] religions permeate all the departments of life, there is no formal distinction between the sacred and the secular, between the religious and non-religious, between the spiritual and the material areas of life."[3] The entirety of Dr. Mbiti's statement suggests that the secular does not exist, in a traditional African sense. Since all of life is religious, there can be nothing that is not religious. Persons who are born in a traditional African environment do not make individual choices to accept or reject the religion of their community. Religion is the entirety of everything, so such people are inevitably religious; choice with respect to religion is nonexistent. Traditional African religion encompasses the total existence of a community and is for the community to which the individual belongs rather than for the individual. Therefore, the ordinary and mundane artifacts and activities of everyone of the community have as much religious significance as any special artifacts, activities, or individuals.

Eurocentric religion is special. It is not ordinary. Eurocentric culture tends to regard the practice of religion, the church, and the clergy as a special thing, a special place, a special group of people. These exist outside of and exclusive of the normal day-to-day activities of the world. People who are regarded as worldly only come in contact with the religious when they attend the special place called church on a special day and time. The sacred is fundamentally different and distinct from the secular in Eurocentric thought. Diop attributes the separatism of the secular and sacred to the materialism of the Greeks who "were never to pass beyond material, visible man, the conqueror of hostile Nature." He contends the "rugged life on the Eurasian plains apparently intensified the materialistic instincts of the people living there, . . . it forged moral values diametrically opposite to Egyptian moral values. . . ."[4] Ironically, this fundamental difference permits some African Americans to conceptualize the religious and the secular as having separate and different kinds of ritual and theatre, although the Afrocentric view does not.

Eurocentric culture makes a fundamental distinction between ritual and theatre, whereas the Afrocentric view does not recognize such a distinction. From an Afrocentric view rituals can be considered a performing art. By definition rituals must have some functional effect. To that extent, the Eurocentric notion of art for art's sake and the definition of fine art do not apply to rituals. The aesthetic worth of fine art must be based upon criteria that do not include usefulness. Therefore, persons who believe in art for art's sake cannot reasonably be expected to accept the notion that what causes a work of theatre art to be regarded as valuable can be the same as that which causes a ritual to be considered valuable.

The pervasive influence of Eurocentric concepts upon African Americans might lead one to assume that there are some significant, basic, and essential differences between religious rituals and secular ones in African-American culture. Such an assumption could serve to confuse the issue, if applied too rigidly. For Black people who regard religion as an all encompassing phenomenon, the separation that occurs between the religious and the secular is largely a matter of style and convenience in the arrangement of the presentation. Our analysis of the ritual theatre characteristics of traditional

AFROCENTRIC RITUALS

Afrocentric American church services is, therefore, applicable to secular presentation as well.

One of the most striking expressions of this absence of significant difference between the religious and the secular in traditional African-American art was voiced in the early 1970's by Dr. Wendell P. Whalum, then Chairman of the Department of Music at Morehouse College. When lecturing on the subject of the evolution of Black music in America, he has said that there are two, two-syllable words, "Jesus" and "Baby," that may be used to alter a song from a religious one to a secular one. Many songs are interchangeable from gospel to blues with that principal change in the wording, although numerous subtle changes also take place in such a transformation. But the key concern here is to recognize that such changes do occur. Further, this absence of dichotomy between the religious and the secular is only one of several fundamental differences between an Afrocentric point of view and a Eurocentric point of view relative to the relationship between ritual and theatre.

The aesthetic priorities of Afrocentric ritual theatre do not conform to the generally accepted Eurocentric format for the analysis of drama. Eurocentric aesthetics has traditionally used an approach to the analysis of drama that involves its division into six components. These components, as outlined by Aristotle in order of importance, are plot, character, theme, dialogue, music (mood and rhythm), and spectacle. Plot, character, and theme are the most important of these components in the Eurocentric tradition. Plot, character, and theme combined constitute the structure. Dialogue, music (mood and rhythm), and spectacle comprise the texture. "The texture is what is directly experienced by the spectator, what comes to him through his senses, what the ear hears (the dialogue), what the eye sees (the spectacle), and what is felt as mood through the entire visual and aural experience."[5]

BLACK THEATRE

Eurocentric aesthetic standards place a higher value on structure than texture. This dictum was true when Aristotle wrote *The Poetics* and it is true today. Eurocentric playwrights have not sought to supplant this archetype, although some have attempted to challenge it--absurdist drama, for instance. Absurdist drama challenges the conventional Eurocentric dramatic structure and texture archetype in order to expand the limitations that the archetype imposes. Absurdist drama does not, however, attempt to replace the conventional Eurocentric archetype with a different one. Absurdism and several other more recent ventures that have deviated from the middle of the stream of Eurocentric theatre tradition grow out of Eurocentric values. No matter how severely these movements seem to veer away from the middle of the stream, they remain a part of the stream.

The various avant-garde movements in the post-modern Eurocentric theatre do constitute a rebellion against conventional Eurocentric drama. But each avant-garde movement seems to focus upon a particular aspect of conventional Eurocentric thought and challenges that aspect to test the limitations it imposes. For example, absurdist playwrights challenge conventional Eurocentric notions about objectivity by claiming that the universe is irrational. They further assert that reality cannot be reduced to a model of linear logic, as is the case with traditional Eurocentric plays. Nevertheless, absurdist playwrights seem to recreate a perception of surface reality that is very similar to their Eurocentric predecessors. Traditional theatres of Asia and Africa are fundamentally different from Eurocentric theatre. Further the traditional theatres of Asia and Africa have ways of perceiving and expressing reality that are fundamentally different from the manner in which Eurocentric drama reproduces and expresses surface reality. Ibsen and Ionesco are remarkably similar when they are contrasted with the classical operatic forms of Peking or Yoruba culture.

Afrocentric theatre is not a rebellion against conventional Eurocentric drama. Afrocentric drama places significantly more emphasis upon dialogue, music, and spectacle, than upon plot, character, and theme. Moreover, African-American theatre does not violate European-American aesthetic standards. African-American aesthetic priorities are different; as a result, African-American theatre is different from European-American theatre. An aesthetic that grows out of an oral traditional and that regards rhythm as the central factor in presentation must necessarily place a higher value upon texture and a lower value upon structure in its aesthetic priorities.

Structure in Eurocentric drama is often analyzed from the script rather than from the presentation. A certain amount of dissonance may result from the variation in this Eurocentric process of script analysis as opposed to the analysis of presentation. For instance, the term "dialogue" is used to mean both the vocal utterings of the performers and the words that are written in the script. The term "dialogue" is often used in script analysis to describe the cognitive meaning conveyed by the written word. As a result, we must emphasize that when analyzing theatrical presentations from a Eurocentric perspective, dialogue is, as Kernodle puts it, "what the ear hears." In analyzing "what the ear hears," we cannot separate the meaning of the words in a purely literary sense from the vocal qualities of the delivery, the mood, the rhythm, and the visual perceptions that impact upon the person who receives these as a single message.

Dialogue used in an Afrocentric context describes the presentation rather than any literature that may provide the basis for the presentation. An Afrocentric view of dialogue is very similar to the Eurocentric conceptual framework of dialogue that focuses upon "what the ear hears." However, the relative value of the cognitive meaning conveyed by the presentation of dialogue differs. The difference is subtle, but there is a difference.

An old African-American story is often told about the good church-going sister who was asked by a friend, who had been unable to attend the church services earlier that day, "Did Reverend Jones preach a good sermon this morning?" "Oh, yes," the sister answered. "Well, what was the sermon about?" her friend asked. The sister replied, "I don't know what it was about, but it sure was a good sermon." That story may provide some insight into the relative value of the texture as opposed to the structure of African-American religious ritual theatre.

Further insight into the relative values of structure and texture may be gained by examining the African tradition from which African-American theatre continues. Lewis Nkosi explains that because ". . . there is very little pretense toward naturalistic representation . . . an actor can often pause to introduce extraneous matter or explanations to the action or comment on the appearance of members of the audience, drawing extra laughs, without minimising the dramatic impact of the action. The result of all this is to make it very difficult for an African to think of drama merely as literature because the force and integrity of the drama is realisable only in its performance."[6]

In African-American religious ritual theatre, the texture must be examined from an Afrocentric point of view of presentation. The important factor with regard to dialogue is the manner in which words are presented, rather than which words are chosen. Structure must also be examined from an Afrocentric point of view of presentation. For example, a sermon on the 23rd Psalm will probably contain no new thematic ideas or cognitive information through plot or character for anyone in the congregation.[7] But the theme, the plot, and the character are of relatively little importance to the value of the sermon. What is more important is how well the presentation is made. This aesthetic hierarchy is operative, not only in religious presentations, but in other Afrocentric presentations as well. The traditional Afrocentric church presentation simply provides an example that is well known and accepted by a broad array of African Americans. Within the context of evaluating how well the presentation is made, the presenter need not enact a story that has a beginning, a middle, and a conclusion in the way that Eurocentric realistic drama does. Eurocentric realistic drama is based on a play structure that uses language to convey character exposition, character conflict of some sort resulting in a climax followed by a resolution. In Eurocentric realistic drama, the structure hinges on the story--an arrangement of cognitive information conveyed primarily through the use of language.

In Afrocentric ritual theatre, the structure is based upon a dramatic premise. This premise can be as simple and as straight forward as, for instance, the reading of the first verse of the 23rd Psalm. First, the premise is established. Then, the premise builds in emotional intensity as a result of the arrangement of actions within the presentation. Conflict through plot complication is acceptable, but not necessary, since there are other devices available to increase the emotional intensity. The emotional intensity eventually reaches a point of climax, causing an emotional release among members of the congregation or the audience. However, this point of climax and emotional release may occur at different points in time for different members of the congregation. This disparity is possible because the climax is not irrevocably connected to the transfer of cognitive information through the literal use of words or actions. Based on a reading of the translations of some of the hieratic ancient Egyptian ritual texts, we found striking similarities to African-American ritual theatre presentations. Many of the Egyptian rituals are based not on stories but on dramatic premises, as are Afrocentric sermons. Both use such devices as chants, hymns, repetitions, call-responses, and musical instruments to affect emotional intensity.

In Afrocentric rituals, the peak of emotional intensity is followed by a gradual reduction in emotional intensity, but it is not a Eurocentric denouement, since its purpose is not to resolve conflict or tie together all the loose ends of the story. This rise and fall in emotional intensity is very carefully organized throughout the entire order of service and is not a function of the sermon alone. For instance, the congregation may tarry for whatever length of time is necessary to arrive at a proper level of emotional involvement before the sermon begins. Tarrying is not simply a means of delaying the sermon until the late arrivals have been seated. It is an important initial step in the process of achieving a dramatic ritual climax. In each church the preacher or a highly respected elder will have the designated responsibility of determining when this proper level of involvement has arrived and taking some pre-determined action that both prompts the beginning of the sermon and notifies the congregation that the sermon is about to begin. A similar function is accomplished in the presentation of secular poems and stories by having those who congregate to witness the presentation repeatedly encourage the presenter to perform until that initial tarrying step has been achieved. The presenter must know when this occurs and offer to begin the requested presentation at that time.

The ordering of actions that elicit empathetic responses is more important in Afrocentric theatre than in Eurocentric theatre where the emphasis is upon language that provides an ordered sequence of cognitive information--a story. We are not saying that there is no story content in Afrocentric ritual drama--only that story content is less valuable, less important, less necessary to the success of the event than the ordering of the actions to achieve the proper emotional responses. Afrocentric ritual theatre does not rely upon a story to create a conflict leading to a climax that causes an emotional release on the part of the audience as Eurocentric theatre does. Story complications are unnecessary; therefore, no need exists for a denouement or resolution of the story complications. Thus, a play script structured around a story line that begins and concludes, as in a conventional Eurocentric drama, is not necessary and sometimes not even desirable in Afrocentric ritual theatre.

The element of rhythm is a dominant force in Afrocentric ritual theatre. The Afrocentric religious ritual is almost totally dependent upon tempo and rhythm as the means of ordering the presentation into a beginning, a middle, and an end. The tempo builds in rate and intensity, and the volume usually builds to a climax and then recedes. In the process, the rhythmic ideal to be aimed for is asymmetry. On the other hand, the Eurocentric aesthetic tends toward more symmetry and regularity of color, of pattern, and of rhythm than the Afrocentric tradition does. Further, the asymmetry of rhythm in Afrocentric drama is present in the dialogue as well as in the music. Frequently, rhythm is an overriding factor with regard to the choice of dialogue. Syllables may be added or deleted from words. Words or phrases may be repeated several times in order to create a more intense rhythmic response from the audience participants.

For example, a preacher may make a simple straightforward statement like, "The Lord is my shepherd." Now let us assume that he gets vocal acclamation from his congregation of low to medium intensity--a few "Amens," a few "My Lord's." He may then repeat the statement, "The Lord is my shepherd," five or six times while using the intensity of his rhythm and vocal inflections to cause the congregation's vocal affirmation to grow in volume and intensity. What matters is the way he says it, not what he says. And if he says, "The Lord is my shepherd" six or seven times, he will say it a different way each time, with each new and different way aimed at soliciting a more unanimous and more emotionally intense vocal affirmation from the congregation. A syllable, or even a whole word, may be omitted from a phrase if it interferes with the rhythm pattern. This rhythm pattern is the origin of many of the idioms of "Negro dialect." When Black poets alter the pronunciation of words in order to make them conform to a desired rhythmic pattern, they are accused of not speaking "good English." When White poets alter the pronunciation of words, the process is called "poetic license."

Rhythm dominates the communicative modes of speech, music, and movement. African-American preachers will generally regard the rhythmic elements of music, movement, and speech as valid and useful tools for heightening the emotional intensity of religious ritual theatre. All three of these elements are used together to establish an empathy with the congregation that is virtually irresistible in the creation of a response among people of African-American cultural heritage. The movement, music, and speech patterns of the preacher grow in intensity, causing the response of the congregation to grow in intensity.

Most African-American preachers and their congregations would never call their body movements during a sermon "dance." Usually dance in the Eurocentric tradition is secular and is not considered an appropriate religious activity. Some protestant religions label dance "sinful" and "evil." Body movements that are communicative and aesthetically pleasing can be considered dance. Certainly, in Afrocentric ritual drama movement is an essential feature and what the participants in the Afrocentric ritual drama do is communicative and aesthetically pleasing to those for whom it is performed. One of the most salient features of the dance movements of participants in Afrocentric ritual drama is that movement of the torso is more important than movement of the extremities. The ideal of grace in European dance movement generally places a very high aesthetic value upon certain specific kinds of movement of arms and legs, while assuming that the torso ought to remain quite rigid. The best example would be classical ballet, in which any sort of undulating movement of the torso is considered aesthetically displeasing and is absolutely forbidden by the rules.

On the other hand, the African-American and African ideal of grace in dance movement places a very high value upon certain kinds of movement of the torso, reasoning that the torso is the center and source of human life and that rigidly specified movements of the arms and legs are much less important. In addition, the arms and legs are permitted a much greater degree of freedom of movement and flexibility for spontaneous expression within the context of the African and African-American aesthetic. One of the things that this freedom, then, permits is the use of the extremities to provide rhythmic emphasis via movement and sound by the clapping of hands and patting of feet.

African-American rituals must fit within the parameters of certain Afrocentric values. African-American theatre rituals are no exception. African-American rituals must achieve at least three important functions: a sense of community, some useful purpose, and spiritual involvement. The first of these functions is to celebrate the affirmation of a sense of community, a feeling of togetherness. One thematic element that Afrocentric rituals seem to share is the consensus that we, who are gathered here to participate in this event, are and belong together. This sense of community is often emphasized through physical contact, such as the joining of hands. Spiritual togetherness is affirmed and heightened by this ritual type of physical togetherness. The affirmation of togetherness through the use of verbal responses is even more frequent.

Afrocentric theatre that is scripted generally retains the emphasis upon community that is found in more traditional Afrocentric rituals. On the other hand, the masterpieces of the Eurocentric cultural tradition, from *Oedipus Rex* to *Hamlet* to *The Glass Menagerie* to *Who's Afraid of Virginia Woolf*, emphasize the individual and his individuality, his differentness from the other members of his community. Afrocentric ritual theatre has as its fundamental goal bringing together a group of people in celebration of being together as a communal act. Although the stated purpose of traditional Afrocentric rituals is usually to observe some specific event such as birth, puberty, marriage, or death, at the foundation of such specific purposes is the more basic goal of affirming a sense of community. For example, the principal non-theological need that is satisfied by going to church is the fellowship. Fellowship--which is a way to affirm a sense of community--is an important force in validating the system of values of the group.

The tendency for rituals to establish a sense of community is not peculiar to Afrocentric rituals. However, Afrocentric rituals generally have stronger tendencies of this kind than Eurocentric rituals. The strength of this tendency grows, in part, out of an Afrocentric philosophical concept which suggests that things absorb essence and meaning from other things that are in close proximity. So, when things that are in harmony are also in close proximity, the whole may be greater (or stronger) than the sum of its parts. This concept also affects language. For example, African-American language takes English and bends it in the direction of Afrocentric concepts. By so doing, words take on meanings that vary drastically. Thus, to an Afrocentric American, the English word "bad" may mean bad, or it may mean good, depending upon what connects with it to form a whole. The essence of things can flow into other things. This concept is in direct contradiction to Platonic philosophy. Furthermore, this Afrocentric use of language is, from a Eurocentric perspective, not objective.

A second major function of Afrocentric ritual drama is to affect some specific useful purpose. Traditional rituals are expected to have some future effect outside the framework of the ritual event itself. For example, a funeral ritual is supposed to have a certain specific useful future effect upon the soul of the deceased brother or sister. According to contemporary European-American standards, acceptance of the existence of cause and effect relationships that cannot be scientifically explained is a primitive and superstitious belief. Eurocentric aestheticians have therefore defined such notions out of their theoretical framework of theatre. Within this Eurocentric framework of theatre, the goal must not be to cause a future effect. Incidental aftereffects, such as changes in opinion that result from insights rather than deliberately persuasive arguments, may exist within this Eurocentric framework. Afrocentric poets and playwrights whose goal is to affect a useful purpose by teaching, persuasion, or motivation often generate negative responses from Eurocentric critics. These critics dismiss overt efforts to accomplish useful Afrocentric goals as non-theatre. This Eurocentric critical mentality classifies such Afrocentric efforts as propaganda or rhetoric rather than as theatre art or dramatic poetry.

Within this framework, Eurocentric critics of Afrocentric theatre contend that rhetoric and theatre art cannot co-exist. European-American theatre art does not seem to provide a basis for such a contention. The pre-19th century Eurocentric notion that the purpose of drama is to teach and to please has not been driven out of the Eurocentric mind by contemporary Eurocentric values that are more materialistic and scientific. Further, most of the textbooks that describe contemporary American theatre recognize that propaganda or rhetoric can be an integral part of Eurocentric legitimate theatre art. Nevertheless, African-American theatre, when it is not ignored altogether, has usually been dismissed as being propaganda and therefore not theatre.[8]

An apparent dilemma prevails here. Do Eurocentric values regard theatre art and rhetoric as two separate phenomena that should never be mixed, or not? The resolution to this apparent dilemma is that the persuasive message that is being taught must be consistent with Eurocentric values. Europhile American critics really do not object to theatre art that teaches--that combines drama with rhetoric. What they object to is the teaching of Afrocentric values. Europhile American critics often consider the presentation of controversial ideas to be proper--for unpopular positions to be taken--as long as the ideas fit within the value systems of the Eurocentric Americans who comprise the leadership or controlling class.

Apparently, the European Americans who are in control permit certain specific forms of dissidence. This obvious fact--that dissidence is tolerated in the U.S.A.--is often misconstrued. Advocacy of a Eurocentric notion that is as antithetical to American capitalists as Marxism is tolerated if the advocate carefully adheres to the theoretical while totally avoiding the pragmatic. But Marxism is as Eurocentric in its view of history and economics as capitalism is. Although a radical Eurocentric idea may be advocated, one may not assume Afrocentric notions will also be tolerated, even when the notions are not substantially antithetical to those Whites who are in control. Many White people with no real vested interest in the establishment in control have been convinced that they do have such a vested interest simply because they are White. Frequent attacks by those Whites in control on Afrocentric positions, even those not harmful to the establishment, further convince those Whites who have no control that simply being White gives one a vested interest in the controlling establishment.

A third major function of Afrocentric ritual theatre is to create a total spiritual involvement, sometimes referred to as emotional involvement. The African-American aesthetic does not operate on the characteristically European-American assumption that all human behavior is either rationally motivated, resulting in fine behavior or emotionally motivated, resulting in coarse behavior. Further, Afrocentric values do not generally operate upon the assumption that human behavior can be classified in such an arbitrary manner. The African-American aesthetic places a very high value upon what European-Americans call emotionally motivated behavior. Another term that can be used to describe this behavior more accurately is spiritually motivated behavior. "Soul" is a highly valued concept among African Americans. Soulful behavior may be called other things by some African Americans, but its value remains. Soulful behavior is emotionally or spiritually motivated rather than rationally or objectively motivated in the Eurocentric sense.

The characteristics of Afrocentric religious rituals that we have described also occur in varying degrees in African-American theatre that is scripted. *The Amen Corner* by James Baldwin is built upon the rhythms of the African-American church. The action of the play flows to the rhythms of the language and the music of the play. The dominant force in the play is the rhythm. The audience must be swept up in this rhythm and thereby compelled to participate. One of the major goals in the presentation of *The Amen Corner* must be to affect the audience in a similar manner to that of Black church rituals. One important similarity is the empathetic response that the presentation seeks to elicit from the audience through the use of rhythm. Second, the empathetic responses of those who are gathered together (the audience) reinforce their sense of togetherness. Both of these responses are important outcomes of the traditional Black church ritual.

The *Amen Corner* is also similar to Black church ritual with respect to its content. *The Amen Corner* is about love--about the enduring strength that love gives--about the love among four people who comprise a particular Black family. In addition to the immediate family, an extended family love surrounds the congregation on the stage (the actors) and the congregation in the auditorium (the audience). There is a love that transcends all the petty bickering, the jealousies, and the family fights. And this love is made to come alive in the theatre through the use of the same presentation techniques that the Black church uses.

Ironically, *The Amen Corner* is weakest as a play when it is strongest as literature. There are several two-character scenes between the members of the Alexander family that illustrate Baldwin's strength as a novelist. From the perspective of Afrocentric theatre, these scenes reveal too much about the characters through the use of words. All that is told needs to be told; but some of it ought to be told through means other than words. That is what actors are supposed to do. The need to rely almost completely upon words mandates that the tempo be slowed and that the rhythm become less pronounced. On these occasions, the action slows down and the word becomes more important than the deed. This ebb in the action is especially pronounced with the scenes that involve the father, because he is confined to a sickbed. Thus, visual interest through movement becomes very difficult to achieve. In addition, ideas are repeated. The use of repetition can work very well when the goal is to create a rhythmic involvement from the audience through the use of empathy. But in these word-dominated, two-character scenes, Baldwin's repetition does not function well with respect to the creation of such a response.

Although some aspects of *The Amen Corner* exemplify Afrocentric aesthetic priorities, other parts of the play exemplify Eurocentric priorities that regard the word as the principal element of drama. This emphasis upon the word is apparent in the practice of publishing and reading scripts rather than producing and attending plays. Such an emphasis upon the word results in a playwright's being thought of as a "writer" rather than a "wright." As a result, scripts are more highly valued for their literary worth than for their impact in presentation. Critics and audience members who are trained in the Eurocentric tradition of literary analysis seem to have considerable difficulty in accepting the notion that a dramatic presentation cannot be recaptured on the printed page. An unfortunate concept that has grown out of this literary tradition is that improvisational theatre, or music, or dance is regarded as inherently inferior to that dance, theatre and music in which each word or note or movement is written down and then memorized prior to its presentation.

Spontaneity is a valued aesthetic concept in Afrocentric ritual theatre. At least two prerequisites are necessary for the spontaneous creation of good art. These prerequisites are sufficient practice to have mastered the art form and total spiritual involvement in the performance event. Conversely, European-American theatre values the ability to pretend to create an illusion of spontaneity, as opposed to actual spontaneity. The jazz idiom in music provides ample evidence of the artistic validity of spontaneity that grows out of both a mastery of the art form and a spiritual involvement in the event.

147

BLACK THEATRE

In this context, one needs to recognize that Black folks are not "natural" singers or dancers. Those Black people who excel in some performance idiom are able to excel because they first practiced often, well, and with sufficient discipline to master the necessary performance techniques. Also, they have developed the capacity for spiritual involvement in the art that they perform. The ability to create actual spontaneity results from a dedicated and disciplined mastery of one's art. Actual spontaneity is highly valued; it exhibits a high level of artistic accomplishment. In addition, the spontaneity of the responses of both the performing artists and the audience enhance the sense of community that is necessary in Afrocentric ritual.

ENDNOTES

1.   Kwanzaa is celebrated by some African Americans and is sometimes regarded as an alternative to Christmas. The holiday is a week long from December 26 to January 1. The ceremonial aspects honor the family, children, community and nation. Presents are given to the children as a token of the fruits of the labor of the parents and as a reward for being contributing members of the family.

2.   Henri Frankfort, *Ancient Egyptian Religion* (New York: Harper & Row, 1948), p.viii.

3.   Mbiti, p.2.

4.   Diop, *African Origin of Civilization*, p.230.

5.   George and Portia Kernodle, *Invitation to the Theatre* (New York: Harcourt Brace Jovanovich, Inc., 1971), p.209.

6.   Nkosi, p.111.

7.   Although there is no substitute for experiencing actual Afrocentric church services, several excellent examples of Afrocentric sermons are available as audio recordings. Rev. C. L. Franklin, *The Twenty-Third Psalm*, Chess, 9309, n.d. provides such an example.

8.   Opinions that were expressed in widely read and respected periodicals in the early 1970's illustrate the manner by which African-American theatre is demeaned by calling it propaganda.   The sampling of such articles includes a spectrum of Eurocentric writers, including a Pulitzer-Prize winning playwright who happens to be African American.

Eric Bentley, "Must I Side With Blacks or Whites?" *New York Times*, Arts and Leisure, 23 January 1972, pp.1 and 12.

Charles Gordone, "Yes, I am a Black Playwright, But...," *New York Times*, Arts and Leisure. 25 January 1970, pp.1 and 11.

Walter Kerr, "We are left with Only the Nightmares," *New York Times*, Arts and Leisure. 6 December 1970, pp.5 and 7.

Hilton Kramer, "Black Art and Expedient Politics," *New York Times*, Arts and Leisure. 7 June 1970, p.19.

Chapter Six

RELATIONSHIPS IN SPACE AND TIME

In traditional Afrocentric ritual, the dramatic event is not obligated to create an illusion of time and place other than its own. The traditional performance techniques of African-American preachers and narrative storytellers provide evidence to support this assertion. The widespread acceptance of these performance techniques by African Americans suggests that the creation of an illusion of some realistically formulated time and place other than the actual time and place of the theatrical event is not an especially highly valued quality among African Americans. On the other hand, the European-American theatre tradition aims at creating an illusion of reality of time, place, and character other than the actual one. This European-American aim, coupled with a clear and firm architectural separation of the actors from the audience and comfortable seats that are attached to the floor in parallel rows, encourages passive observation of the dramatic event. Except for occasional applause, due to approval after the fact or politeness or just because some other people are applauding, this passivity is rarely interrupted.

The Afrocentric ideal of theatrical presentation that maintains a sense of real and present time and place frees the audience members to participate spontaneously in the theatrical event. This spontaneous participation is a response to the spiritual involvement which the presentation evokes in each audience member. Under optimum conditions there is no such thing as an audience in the Afrocentric theatre only various kinds of participation in the presentation. The most immediate concern in Afrocentric theatre is to stimulate an overt emotional response. This emotionally motivated, spontaneous participation should not be confused with such Eurocentric responses as applause, which is supposed to be rational judgment behavior after the fact. Nor should it be confused with traditional Eurocentric liturgical unison responses which are planned, usually with written instructions as to when to speak, what to say, when to stand, sit, and kneel. In the ideal African-American theatre, all persons are expected to participate in the presentation. This participation does not mean, however, that everyone who is present is necessarily expected to participate in the same manner or to the same extent. We continue to use the terms actor and audience because we are using the English language--a language that is based on a Western European view of the world. However, we are using these terms in an Afrocentric context.

The Afrocentric ideal of evoking unanimous participation by the audience is most optimally achieved among significant numbers of African Americans at this time, by African-American gospel and rhythm and blues musicians, and African-American preachers. Although the preacher or the musician attempts to motivate everyone present to participate fully, each member is expected to "testify" according to the degree of his own personal involvement and commitment. Afrocentric playwrights, designers, performers, and theatre critics must not and do not expect their audiences to sit still and listen passively to the theatrical event. These expectations influence the performance of African-American theatre in many ways. The techniques that an actor uses to concentrate on the performance will be altered, depending upon whether or not the actor needs to listen to verbal responses from the audience and make verbal responses in reply. The manner in which a playwright constructs dialogue will be changed if the playwright knows that the audience will make certain kinds of verbal or even action-oriented responses to the dialogue and actions of the performers. The total physical design--including the Eurocentric categories of architecture, scenery, lighting, costume, and makeup--must be based upon the aesthetic ideal of unity of the presentation space and the audience space. No architectural separation can exist between presentation space and audience space since those spaces are considered to be all one space.

The Afrocentric aesthetic ideal of unity of space is quite different from the Eurocentric ideal of aesthetic distance that permeates the physical design concepts of the European-American theatre. In addition to the physical separation of actor from audience that is an outgrowth of the Eurocentric concept of aesthetic distance, Eurocentric theatre uses this physical distance and the placement of architectural barriers to manipulate empathy. Eurocentric theatre does seek to produce responses between actor and audience. However, the empathy that results is supposed to be detached and non-participatory. The Eurocentric audience is supposed to behave in a manner that exhibits detachment, restraint, and control so that the highly valued Eurocentric attribute of objectivity will be maintained throughout the presentation. Since an abundance of empathy tends to reduce objectivity, Eurocentric realists seek to create a form of empathy that is emotionally detached. This emotional detachment is created, in large part, by using architectural devices that separate the actors from the audience.

Bertolt Brecht did not regard these architectural devices as sufficient to provide optimum audience objectivity. Brecht sought to create a form of theatre that was not only epic in scope but much more objective than conventional Eurocentric realistic theatre. Brecht sought to accomplish this increase in objectivity by making conscious decisions as a playwright to interrupt the empathy being created by the realistic mimetic presentation of the story. Whether or not Brecht succeeded in accomplishing this objectivity as a playwright is both debatable and beyond the scope of this work. On the other hand, Brecht's endorsement of the relatively high value of objectivity in contrast to the much lower value of empathy is an effective articulation of an important contemporary Eurocentric point of view.

Eurocentric thought regards cognitive knowing and feeling as not only different but, in a sense, opposing things. On the other hand, Afrocentric thought regards knowing and feeling as inseparable aspects of the whole process by which human beings receive stimuli from outside themselves and learn from them. Cognitive knowledge is highly valued in both Eurocentric and Afrocentric cultures. Since feeling is more highly valued in Afrocentric culture than in Eurocentric culture, then such emotional stimuli as that of the conventional Afrocentric church service would be regarded as anti-intellectual from a Eurocentric perspective. Those who dominate Eurocentric culture belittle those European Americans who indicate that they value feelings more highly than Eurocentric criteria regard as desirable.

Some Eurocentric theatre companies seek to increase audience participation and involvement. However, the ones that we have observed or read about all seem to encourage participation, not by creating empathy, but by confrontation with the audience. Thus, when the physical separation between audience and actor is eliminated, the psychic or emotional separation remains. These Eurocentric actors generally get audience participation by forcing members of the audience to defend themselves against the verbal, visual, and sometimes even the physical onslaughts of the actors. We do not mean to suggest that these confrontations are always belligerent. Such confrontations may occur in a relatively friendly manner. But, physical proximity and verbal communication do not eliminate the "we/they" relationship separating the actors from the audience in Eurocentric theatre. Many firmly established Eurocentric assumptions about the physical characteristics of theatre contradict Afrocentric ideals with respect to relationships between performers and audience. The achievement of a relationship between performer and audience that is consistent with Afrocentric values is difficult to achieve when the actors are framed by a proscenium arch; the performance space is separated from and raised above the audience space; and the audience sits in parallel rows of seats that are attached to the floor.

Many Eurocentric theatre critics and historians have theorized about the invention of the proscenium arch. Some have said it has crippled the theatre; others have said it has been the best thing that ever happened to the art of the theatre. Most who have criticized the proscenium arch have offered alternative ways of dealing with a fixed architectural entity known as "the theatre." Although the proscenium arch is probably the most difficult of the available arrangements for African-American theatre, the contemporary Eurocentric alternatives--theatre-in-the-round, thrust, and open staging-- do not completely satisfy the space requirements for actor-audience relationships that are appropriate for African-American theatre. These Eurocentric spatial relationships do not provide environments that are in concert with the values of African-American theatre since each of these Eurocentric alternatives contains a fixed architectural element that separates the actor's space from the audience's space. Often a substantial neutral zone increases the distance between actors and audience. The Afrocentric ideal of unity of space permits no such fixed architectural separation.

RELATIONSHIPS IN SPACE AND TIME

An Afrocentric audience spontaneously participates in and comments upon the dramatic action if and when moved to do so. In order to enhance this participatory involvement, the architectural space ought to be free of barriers between performers and audience. An Afrocentric presentation space ought to provide the actors easy accessibility to and from the audience space and the physical space that is regularly occupied by the performers ought to be accessible to the audience. While the audience may not often be requested to enter the performance space and participate in the performance physically as well as verbally, the architecture of the facility should allow for such an eventuality. In addition to occasional need for actual proximity and accessibility, the audience's perception of proximity and accessibility to the presentation space also seems to increase the potential for overt empathetic responses to the presentation. Afrocentric values hold such overt responses in high esteem. On the other hand, Eurocentric values seem to regard these responses as unwelcome intrusions into the action of the presentation and possibly even as uncivilized responses, since behavior that is overly emotional is viewed as insufficiently objective.

The most widely accepted African-American rituals take place in spaces that were designed and built to house similar European-American rituals. Many of the most popular African-American religious rituals take place in buildings that were designed to serve European-Americans as churches, theatres, or motion picture houses. The seats for the audience are usually attached to the floor, in parallel rows, facing in one direction. Often a space greater than six feet wide separates the performance space from the audience space. Further, the space normally contains an architectural barrier, such as a bannister rail or a change in floor level of several feet which prohibits the spatial unity of performers and audience. Eurocentric architects include these elements because the architectural form of the European-American

155

church or theatre has evolved as it has in order to successfully accommodate Eurocentric church or theatre functions. Therefore, when African-American rituals take place in these physical facilities, the ritual performances must overcome these architectural elements that work against the success of Afrocentric rituals.

The space between the front row of audience seats and the raised performance area must be occupied and used in a manner that destroys the Eurocentric goal that caused such a chasm to be regarded as necessary. Eurocentric notions about actor-audience relationships require such a void in order to physically establish aesthetic distance. In some African-American congregations, this space is occupied by the most active respondents to the presentation. These respondents are thereby able to accompany their spontaneous verbal responses with body movements that are not constrained by the people occupying the fixed rows of seats. Although this use of Eurocentric spatial relationships renders the space aesthetically acceptable for African-American presentations, an ideal Afrocentric solution to the use of space for presentation has not evolved.

A theatre for African-American dramatic events should provide an architectural surrounding that is free from fixed spaces or barriers that physically or spiritually separate the audience from the actors. A significant step in this direction via architectural planning was the New Lafayette theatre in Harlem.[1] An example of an extremely effective production from the point of view of appropriateness of environmental conditions, but without a structure that was planned for such a purpose, was the "Celebration of Blackness" commemorating the opening of the Institute of the Black World in Atlanta, Georgia, January 17, 1970.

RELATIONSHIPS IN SPACE AND TIME

The celebration was held in a large "multi-purpose room" in the student union building at Morris Brown College. Black artists from throughout Africa and the Americas were there to perform. Chairs were placed around the perimeter of the room. Some people sat in the chairs, others sat on the floor in front of the chairs, and others stood behind the chairs. But the chairs could be moved and were moved at various times throughout the celebration. Contrary to European-American tradition, the chairs were not bolted to the floor in parallel rows. Food and soft drinks were available on a covered balcony adjacent to the ballroom. People moved in and out of the room and around in the room throughout the celebration. An atmosphere of relaxation, fellowship, and community encouraged moving about, talking to those who were performing while they performed, and talking to others who were witnessing the performance.

In the middle of the room, a vaguely defined area was reserved, more or less, for the various presentations. The presentations did not all take place in that area and the size and shape of the performance area did not remain the same throughout the celebration. Some events, such as the Katherine Dunham Dance Company's performance, required a large, unobstructed area in which to perform. So an area of adequate size for such a presentation was quickly cleared. At the other extreme in space requirements was a performance by Ms. Val Gray Ward. She began her presentation in the midst of a crowd of observers and throughout her performance, she moved among the members of the audience. This celebration is not an isolated, exceptional example. In this kind of an African-American celebration, the orthodox goal for the performer is to achieve a physical and spiritual unity with the people who are there and to be among the people. Rather than remain on the other side of an architectural barrier, the performer unites with the audience.

157

One other significant characteristic of the "Celebration of Blackness" that is representative of orthodox Afrocentric values was the lack of a rigid time schedule. The "Celebration of Blackness" adhered to a traditional African concept of time. A starting time was announced, but the event started when it was time for the event to start--a time that turned out to be somewhat later than the announced starting time. The event concluded when there was a communal sense that the concluding time had arrived. That time occurred when the activity had completely run its course. Hence, the Celebration of Blackness" continued for several hours past the scheduled stopping time. Events begin and end because of a communal sense that it is time for them to begin and end. This concept of time is frequently seen in jazz and gospel music. A given song is played until a communal sense determines that it is time for the song to end.

How African Americans conceptualize time can be understood more deeply if one understands something of the traditional African view of time. Dr. John S. Mbiti explains, "Time has to be experienced in order to make sense or to become real." As a result, things that have not taken place or have no likelihood of taking place soon, he categorizes in English as "no-time." Most of what is called "the future" in English does not exist--cannot be conceptualized. "What is certain to occur, or what falls within the rhythm of natural phenomena, is the category of inevitable or *potential time.*"[2] The reckoning of either actual (experiential) time or potential time is traditionally done on the basis of phenomena rather than on a numerical basis. Therefore, the assignment of numbers to designate a date, or an hour of the day, several months, or years, in the future has no real meaning in traditional African thought.[3]

Afrocentric time is not a linear continuum from the past into the future, but an experiential surround that contains us. We exist in time. Events must begin and conclude in time rather than on time. Mbiti describes the Swahili word "Zamani" as ". . . the ocean of time in which everything becomes absorbed into a reality that is neither after nor before."[4]

The Eurocentric interpretation of time presumes that the Afrocentric phenomenon is primitive while the Eurocentric phenomenon is more advanced, objective, and universal. Both in contemporary urban Africa and among African Americans, the impact of Eurocentric time is pervasive and inevitable. The resulting conflict between these concepts of time penetrates every conscious aspect of African-American life and creates an extremely distressing instance of double consciousness. Further, this African concept of time is often alleged to be primitive on the grounds that such a concept does not permit precise calculation of scientifically predictable future events. Yet there are numerous examples of extremely precise calculations in such disciplines as astronomy and architecture in Africa dating back for four to five thousand years.

Contemporary Afrocentric values differ from contemporary Eurocentric values with regard to time. The Eurocentric value system places a high level of importance upon punctuality. Obviously, if one is a factory owner or holds some similarly high position in the military-industrial complex, punctuality is crucial to the continuation of profits and power. Punctuality, then, takes on the aura of responsibility, respectability, morality, patriotism, and other idealistic qualities. Punctuality is certainly a valid concept for the Eurocentric cultural framework for which it was invented. A mass production economy cannot survive if punctuality is not an important and highly valued behavioral attribute. Eurocentric values suggest that, among the lower echelon workers in a mass production economy, it is better for the entire production line to be on schedule than it is for an individual to aim for personal satisfaction by doing a job well. In an environment that is economically based upon mass production, everyone's life revolves around the time clock at the factory. Subservience to the clock is regarded by those in economic power as necessary for closely coordinated teamwork which is vital in maintaining a high quantity of production. To be late is to let down the team and delay production. Eurocentric culture regards the manager who produces a marketable product as much more important than the personal scheduling idiosyncracies of the persons who comprise that manager's production team.

African culture, African-American culture, and several other cultures (for instance, Native American culture) regard time in a way that is antithetical to the necessities of a mass production economy. These cultures value the excellence of the individual craftsman and the beauty, individuality, and usefulness of his product, rather than the ability to produce large quantities of goods within a short period of time. Such attitudes allow individuals or groups to commence or end activities according to the desires of those involved rather than to acquiesce to the dictates of a mechanical device that uses numbers to measure time. Efforts by persons involved in the production and analysis of performance art to reconcile traditional Afrocentric concepts of time in a Eurocentric environment raise some issues that are difficult to resolve. Should African-American performances begin promptly at the announced time or not? Should African-American performing artists expect their audiences to arrive on time or not? Should African-American audiences expect performances to start punctually at the announced time or not? Should African-American theatres do what African-American churches do-- while members of the audience assemble, provide some sort of interim activity that prepares them to witness that which follows? Frustration and disappointment among audiences and presenters grow out of a lack of uniformity and consistency in resolving conflict between these different concepts of time.

The prevailing concept of time in any given society seems to be influenced by factors that are many and varied. Also variation with regard to concepts of time exists among the individual members of any particular society. For example, our generalizations about Eurocentric concepts of time should not be construed to mean that all Eurocentric people are always prompt. Nor do we intend to suggest that all Eurocentric people strive to maintain a predetermined schedule. However, those who dominate Eurocentric culture insist upon promptness and punish those who are not prompt. Some of these punishments are formal, such as monetary fines for union theatrical workers who are late. Some of the punishments are informal, such as the creation of feelings of guilt about tardiness. Several factors appear to be partially responsible for variations in degree of commitment to the Eurocentric concept of time and related behavioral ideals such as punctuality. These factors include economic class, degree of industrialization and urbanization, racial identity, and climate.

Those Eurocentric people who control industrial production and profit from it stand to gain a great deal more from punctuality than their workers do. Even those workers who are punctual generally appear to be significantly less enthusiastic in their support of the behavioral ideal of punctuality than those who reap the profits of industrial production. Rural agrarian Eurocentric societies are generally less committed to the use of numerical means of recognizing time, such as calendars and clocks, than urban industrial Eurocentric societies.

In the Mediterranean region, the genetic distinctions between Caucasians, Asians, and Africans have been rather amorphous for centuries. People of the Mediterranean coast of Europe seem to be far less committed to the Eurocentric behavioral ideals of time than the people of other parts of Europe. This notion suggests that variations in racial identity among Europeans may have a direct relationship to commitment to such Eurocentric behavioral ideals as punctuality. For example, one may clearly discern a difference between Germans and southern Italians with respect to punctuality. Explanations of this difference have generally focused upon the obvious fact that Germany has a colder climate than the relatively warm climate of southern Italy. Nevertheless, the racial differences between southern Italians and Germans are at least as discernible as the differences in climate. Those parts of Europe that are close to Africa geographically, and where the European racial characteristics are not as "pure," also happen to have a climate that is generally warmer than other parts of Europe. Therefore, race or ethnicity may possibly have as much or more to do with differences in values and concepts of time than climate does.

Some other Eurocentric assumptions are also difficult to reconcile with Afrocentric concepts of performance. These assumptions deal with what an actor is supposed to do and how he is supposed to do it. Eurocentric culture assumes the theatre is supposed to involve mimesis. In Eurocentric realistic terms, mimesis means the acting out of something with the aesthetic goal of creating the impression of reality. The actor aims at acting his role in such a way that the audience will accept him as the real character he is portraying in the play. The Eurocentric audience, then, willingly suspends disbelief in order to accept the actor as the character portrayed. The actor pretends to be another specific human being other than who he is, where he is, and when he is. In doing so, he is supposed to concentrate so deeply and so completely upon the portrayal of this other character that he at least partially shuts out the reality of the audience's presence from his consciousness. African-American actors who have learned to use this modern, realistic technique in European-American acting classes find it quite disconcerting when their concentration is broken by the Afrocentrically proper, overt involvement of an African-American audience.

The African-American actor-audience relationship requires a different approach to the training of actors--an approach that is based upon the aesthetic assumptions of African-American ritual theatre. This approach does not imply a TOTAL rejection of the idea of realistic mimesis. African-American actors must be able to perform as themselves and to portray other characters as well. An actor who is prepared to function effectively in Afrocentric theatre needs to be able to perform in ways that move beyond the linear goal of recreating a character in a real life situation. Afrocentric theatre requires performance skills that allow the actor to perform as himself and to portray one or more characters within a single performance event. The African-American actor must accomplish this feat without resorting to the tactic of blocking the audience out of his conscious awareness. After all, the actor must be able to perceive and respond to the audience behavior that occurs in response to the performance.

Afrocentric presentations allow for interaction between performer and audience during the performance. This interaction may include evaluative comments throughout the presentation. Therefore, setting aside a time immediately following the body of the presentation to permit direct interaction of an evaluative nature between actor and audience is unnecessary. In Eurocentric theatre, a time is set aside for such an occasion. This Eurocentric theatre convention is known as the "curtain call."

Curtain calls provide another example of the phenomenon of double consciousness. Curtain calls contradict some fundamental Afrocentric assumptions about what theatre presentations are for and the relationships that ought to exist among performers and between performers and audience. One fundamental Eurocentric assumption that contradicts Afrocentric values is that the curtain call is a marketing strategy to sell the stars of the production as well as the production. The basis for these assumptions about marketing strategy is the Eurocentric principle that theatre, or any other work of art, is a commodity. Curtain calls are designed to elicit applause and thereby generate positive opinions about productions and stars. Curtain calls help sell the commodity called theatre. Therefore, the primary purpose of curtain calls is not to provide an opportunity for the audience to show its appreciation to the performers.

As a part of our search for a more Afrocentric approach to the presentation of theatre, we (Barbara and Carlton Molette) discontinued the practice of doing curtain calls in our productions in 1969. After a few years, we returned to the practice of doing curtain calls. African-American audiences "demanded" curtain calls. African-American theatregoers insist upon curtain calls because they constitute an important convention of THE theatre--the Eurocentric theatre. Influenced by Carter Woodson's ideas about miseducation and DuBois' concept of double consciousness, we postulate that, if Eurocentric leaders regularly and emphatically claim that something is one of the "finer things in life," then some African Americans will insist upon having their fair share of it. The question of whether or not a particular "finer thing" is of any value or benefit to any African-American person or to African-American people in general, seldom, if ever, arises in this context.

In African-American ritual theatre, behavior--but not necessarily the words--must occur in a specific and expected manner and arrangement. If the appropriate manner and arrangement of performance is not accomplished, then the aftereffect that the ritual is to cause may not take place. Further, this specifically mannered and arranged behavior must elicit a certain kind of overt interaction between the audience and the performer. This response indicates that the level of spiritual involvement needed to cause the desired aftereffect has probably been reached. Both of these are of much greater importance than the creation of an illusion of surface reality through the use of realistic mimetic techniques. African-American ritual drama does not aim to achieve an ideal of pure representation which is the realistic/naturalistic ideal of Eurocentric theatre. Realistic mimesis is not at the opposite end of a continuum from specifically mannered and arranged behavior. These are two different characteristics with differing orders of priority in African-American ritual theatre on the one hand, and Eurocentric realistic theatre on the other.

Human societies have rituals of many types. African-American people are not unique in that respect. However, the major cultural groups of the world have developed characteristic modes of expressive communication that are recognizable as different from those of the other major cultural groups. African, Asian, and European art forms have characteristic styles that permit us to differentiate one from the other. Our concern is with the African-American mode of expression. In this context, our more specific concern is the impact of African-American ritual upon actor-audience relationships in space and time in the contemporary African-American theatre.

Within the realm of traditional Afrocentric actor-audience relationships, the most important thing about rituals is that everyone present is expected to participate. Ideally, presenters and congregation constantly interact. As a result, Afrocentric values that affect actor-audience relationships in space and time are different from Eurocentric values. Since most African Americans have been miseducated to believe that European-American values are UNIVERSAL, African Americans face a dilemma. Eurocentric concepts of space and time create conceptual conflicts when superimposed upon contemporary African-American theatre. African-American theatre ought to manifest Afrocentric values with regard to the use of space and time to create theatre. The sources of this African-American theatre are traditional rituals that manifest such Afrocentric values. But the phenomenon of double consciousness has not allowed for the evolution of a consensus among African Americans with regard to what kinds of actor-audience relationships in space and time ought to exist in contemporary African-American theatre.

ENDNOTES

1.   Ned A. Bowman, "A Roundup of Recent Theatre Buildings." *Theatre Design and Technology*, No.5 (December, 1968), p.20. The architect for the New Lafayette Theatre Project, Hardy Holtzman Pfeiffer Associates, is quoted as saying, "The New Lafayette will require an environment of exploration and participation. In order to unite artist and audience into the theatrical event as one total community, an architectural cohesion between the event of the production and the life of the audience must be found. This cannot be accomplished within traditional terms--they are too well known, too constricting, too redolent of things past." The theatre facility is located at 200 West 135th Street, New York, New York.

2.   Mbiti, 17-18.

3.   Mbiti, 19.

4.   Mbiti, 23.

Chapter Seven

HEROIC VALUES

Heroes and the standards of heroism that a culture projects are important techniques for informing a society of behavioral ideals and expectations. One of the most important functions of heroism is identity bonding by the members of a culture that produce a particular hero. People must be able to connect their own identities to that of the hero in a manner that is consistent with the values of their culture. The linking or transfer of one's identity to another is closely associated with the concept of empathy. But the concept of identity bonding is much broader in scope than the emotional connections associated with the Eurocentric concept of empathy. The bonding of identities is simultaneously emotional and cognitive. It can operate on a personal level, a nationalistic level, or on a number of other sub-nationalistic levels.

Normally, a hero of great depth and truth from within the value system of one culture has some characteristics that will cause some identity bonding among people of other cultures. All cultures have some members who are more cosmopolitan than other members. Therefore, the more cosmopolitan members of a culture will be better able to identify with the heroes of another culture, whereas the less cosmopolitan members of that culture may not. Many of the relatively cosmopolitan members of some groups assume that their ability to identify in some way with a hero of a different culture is evidence of the universality of the hero. The Eurocentric myth of universality is difficult to avoid.

HEROIC VALUES

Whites have conceived, on occasion, a White hero in blackface--Othello, for instance. Such heroes are permissible if the audience understands that these are White heroes. On some other occasions, Whites have created characters with black skins who have actually been models of how some White people would like to have African-American people behave-- Uncle Tom, for instance. If African-American people can be convinced that such characters as Uncle Tom are their heroes, the tendency for them to behave in ways that are in the best interest of Whites will be increased. On the other hand, the tendency for African Americans to act in their own best interest will be decreased. Moreover, the projected behavioral ideals of the modern, intelligent, "Black," African-American heroes on television and in the motion pictures are seldom more than modernizations of the original Uncle Tom. At the decisive moment, the character willingly sacrifices himself for the good of his White folks. In Eurocentric terms, he thereby becomes a hero. The lesson is projected that "the most heroic possible behavior for an African-American is to sacrifice one's own best interests in order to maintain the well being of some White person." Or, conversely, that "African-American people can achieve significant success in America only as a result of the magnanimous help of one or more White people." Identification with a hero is a necessary prerequisite for empathy. And when one empathizes with a hero, the values and behaviors of the hero are reinforced as worthwhile goals. People seek to emulate the behavior and incorporate the values of their heroes.

Heroes in the Eurocentric tradition must have the genetic potential to be heroic. This concept was developed for the purpose of retaining political control within an aristocracy. Further, this concept is based upon the presupposition that heroic qualities, such as honor and dignity, can be genetically transferred. This concept is the source of all the "highborn" and "lowborn" assumptions that are so abundant in European

169

mythology. When confronted with an example of an apparently "lowborn" individual who has performed heroically, the true Europhile will assume that the hero is genetically an aristocrat whose credentials are incorrect. The notion that one who is not born an aristocrat could be capable of true heroism is inconceivable within this Eurocentric aristocratic frame of reference. Even now, when these aristocratic assumptions are allegedly in disrepute in the United States, the debate over the presence of heroism in such works as *Death of a Salesman* continues. *Death of a Salesman* is generally regarded as one of the finer examples of modern European-American drama. Yet, many European-American experts insist upon emphatically proclaiming the play is not a tragedy. When an explanation is offered as to why *Death of a Salesman* is not a tragedy, the crux of the explanation is often based upon these presuppositions about the genetic transferral of heroism. Ultimately, the play is assumed not be a tragedy because Willy Loman is, as his name implies, a LOW MAN.

A hero must be an important person. In other words, a hero must have magnitude. Other people who belong to the group for which the character is heroic must believe that they have a vested interest in the hero's actions and in the consequences of the actions. The group members must also have empathy with the hero. Within a Eurocentric framework, tragic heroes must have the capacity to suffer greatly and the act of suffering must have some significance that transcends the personal discomfort of the character doing the suffering. In an Afrocentric framework, the hero's actions and the outcome of his actions must transcend his individual needs. The hero must be a prototypical manifestation of the hopes, aspirations, and values of the group. An Afrocentric hero in the U.S.A. must behave in a manner that is independent and external to the expectations of the White establishment. The assumption that a hero must be important in the sense that he or she must have magnitude is a legitimate one. However, Europhiles generalize that such magnitude is genetically transferred from father (White, of course) to son.

The generalization that only aristocratic White males are plausible as heroes perpetuates notions of racial and gender superiority. In the Europhile tradition, women, even the daughters of aristocrats, practically never achieve heroism. Of course, there are the exceptions--Antigone and Joan of Arc, for instance. They are definitely exceptions. Thus, they do not disprove the rule. In like manner, the existence of Othello does not disprove the rule. One must understand that the values that perpetuate notions about African-American inferiority exist within a larger context. The same Europhile mythic structure that reinforces racist values also reinforces values that impact negatively upon females and even those White males who have no claim to aristocratic lineage.

The concept of magnitude in a hero can exist outside the context of a White male dominated political aristocracy. Further, a non-racist, non-sexist concept of magnitude is necessary in order to identify and understand African-American characters who are heroic. In some non-Europhile cultures, heroes achieve their magnitude through means other than aristocratic breeding. Among the ways most compatible with traditional European assumptions is the exhibition of excellence in military or athletic skills. But African culture does not require the trait of aggressiveness as a criterion for achieving the status of hero. Instead, the criterion might involve the use of a nonaggressive athletic skill, accompanied by the exhibition of bravery, courage, and wit, to resolve a crisis. Wit can be exhibited in a number of ways. The use of strategy, in lieu of brute force, against an adversary in a serious context and the comic use of the rhetoric of diplomacy are two of the most frequently observed forms of wit that are used to achieve victory over one's adversary.

BLACK THEATRE

The African-American hero who prevails through the use of wit is the major type of African-American hero who manifests a comic point of view. However, additional character traits are obligatory in order to achieve heroism. If a character who prevails through the use of verbal diplomacy is to be truly heroic within the framework of traditional African-American culture, he must do so with comic irony. To talk one's way out of danger with wit and comic irony is looked upon as a manifestation of heroic behavior. In part, Uncle Tom is considered a degrading character within the framework of African-American culture because there is no sense of comic irony in his verbal diplomacy. He takes himself too seriously. But Uncle Tom's behavior would not be nearly so degrading if he did not possess so much inner sincerity in his willingness to subjugate his own best interests in order to better serve the needs, even the whims, of "his White folks."

Verbal diplomacy that is regarded in African-American culture as heroic can be exemplified by a mythological hero called the Signifying Monkey, who is the main character in a poem of the same title. There are many versions of *The Signifying Monkey*.[1] The poem is intended to be performed orally, rather than written down and read silently. In a very real sense *The Signifying Monkey* is designed to be a theatrical performance. *The Signifying Monkey* is not a play in the Eurocentric literary sense; nevertheless, it is a dramatic experience. The traditional method of performing such Afro-American poems as *The Signifying Monkey* involves a definite ritual form. The first step in this ritual form is to cajole the reluctant storyteller into performing. This first step is essential. The principal performer must not begin to perform *The Signifying Monkey* until he or she has provoked a virtually unanimous and relatively demonstrative communal request to do so. Prior to the storyteller's making a final commitment to actually perform the work, overt participation by the audience must be assured. The storyteller must be cajoled into

172

performing--not as a result of a sense of false modesty on the part of the storyteller, but simply because that is what is supposed to happen in the ritual.

The necessity of overt participation by the audience is as important in African-American secular ritual as it is in religious ritual. This need for preliminary cajoling is a similar phenomenon to tarrying in African-American religious ritual, and is only the initial phase of audience participation. The audience is also expected to comment on the quality of the storyteller's performance throughout the presentation. Characteristics of African-American religious ritual presentations, such as asymmetry of rhythm and movement and the use of repetition and empathetic response to emphasize the importance of rhythm, are generally present to a comparable degree in secular ritual presentations as well.

The story of *The Signifying Monkey* is a simple one, as is the entire structure (plot, character, and theme) very simple. The complex subtleties of the work grow out of the texture--the ritual theatre performance techniques and the verbal appeal of the words used to elaborate upon the story as directly experienced by the audience. The scene opens with the Signifying Monkey high in a tree with nothing to do. For no particular external reason, he decides to "start some shit." About this time the "King of the Jungle" happens to pass by. The Monkey calls out to the Lion and relates to him a fallacious, malicious story about how the Elephant has recently degraded the Lion.

The individual storyteller has a certain amount of freedom to *ad lib* in this segment of the presentation in order to exhibit his own virtuosity as a player of "the dozens." He must stay within the rhyme scheme of the poem; but, he is free to add to or subtract from the list of negative things that the Monkey claims the Elephant has said about the Lion. However, the performer must necessarily make some mention, within the context of the poem, of the Lion's alleged cowardice and his inability to fight. Of course, the storyteller ought to have some pointedly negative things to say about the Lion's mother and grandmother, and about the uncertainty of the identity of the Lion's father. The performer, in similar fashion to the traditional rules for this type of spiritual performance, lengthens or shortens this portion of the performance as a direct outgrowth of the amount and intensity of the audience's participation. In each of the other segments of the story, a similar freedom exists to expand or abridge the details of the story.

The story continues with the Lion going off in a rage after the Elephant. When the Lion meets the Elephant face to face, the Lion confidently tells the Elephant how badly he (the Lion) is going to beat him (the Elephant). The Lion then attacks the Elephant. The Elephant wins the fight easily, beating the Lion unmercifully, for some time and with considerable flamboyance as well. The Lion, beaten and humiliated, drags his battered and bloody carcass back through the jungle, where he is once again greeted by the Signifying Monkey from high atop a tree where he can safely "signify." The Monkey makes fun of the Lion by describing in great detail the extent of the Lion's injuries. The Monkey explains how badly the Lion has been beaten by the Elephant. The Monkey also asserts that the Lion is not really the "King of Beasts" after all. Finally, the Monkey proclaims that, given the Lion's present condition, he (the Monkey) is just liable to come down out of the tree and whip the Lion some more, just on "general principle." The Monkey enumerates the various ways he will go about giving the Lion another whipping. The Monkey is so enamored with his own performance that he begins to laugh uncontrollably at the defeated and demoralized Lion. The Monkey slips from his perch in the tree and falls unceremoniously to the ground. Like a flash, the Lion has his paw placed menacingly upon the neck of our hero.

Here begins the Monkey's apology. The Monkey explains that he did not really mean any harm by the things he said. It was all in fun. Everyone knows that the Lion is the "King of the Jungle." The Monkey proclaims that he has the utmost respect and esteem for the Lion. But the Lion is not impressed with this apology. Then the Monkey tries a new tactic. The Monkey musters an attitude of enthusiastic belligerence and yells:

> Get your foot off my neck,
> let my head out the sand,
> and I'll kick your ass
> like a natural man.
> You damned well better be
> holding me down,
> cause if you turn me loose,
> I'll stomp your ass
> six feet under the ground.

And the Monkey continues to yell threats until the Lion eventually gets so angry that:

> The Lion jumped back,
> he was ready to fight,
> but the Signifying Monkey
> was already out of sight.

The Monkey quickly scrambles up into the tree, returns to his perch and continues to signify. This time the Monkey concentrates on the theme of the Lion's stupidity.

Certain key attributes make the Signifying Monkey a heroic character. First, he has heroic magnitude. He is important

175

because he is an allegorical representative of those who are small, weak, and oppressed. Second, he has developed innovative techniques for survival. Because he is small, weak, and oppressed, his survival depends upon his cleverness and innovativeness as well as his persistence and tenacity. Third, his method of survival includes the unabashed exhibition of considerable verbal skill. Further, the Monkey manages to use his verbal skill to parry the hostile aggressiveness of the Lion in a manner that appears to be almost effortless. He exhibits wit that is clearly superior to both the physical strength and hostility of the Lion. In order to be a hero, a character of this type must exhibit all three of these characteristics to some degree.

Shine, in *The Titanic*, is another example of such a hero.[2] According to African-American mythology, Shine is the only African American aboard a ship that is as legendary for its exclusion of Black passengers as it is for its total failure as an example of the superiority of White technology. The TITANIC was a British Steamer of the White Star Line. On the night of April 14-15, 1912, it struck an iceberg and sank approximately 1600 miles northeast of its destination, New York City. Although the ship was widely publicized as being unsinkable, it sank on its maiden voyage across the Atlantic. Only 705 persons survived, in part because there were not enough lifeboats aboard the ship. Most of the survivors were women and children. Three different investigations of the incident fix the number who died at 1490, 1503, and 1517.

Our concern here is not so much the objective facts surrounding the sinking of the TITANIC, but the perceptions of African Americans with respect to the incident. The comic irony that African Americans perceive in this Eurocentric pathos emerges from the policy of racial discrimination in booking passage aboard the TITANIC and the widespread claims that White folks' technology had created an unsinkable ship. Subsequently, when the news of the sinking of the TITANIC spread across the U.S.A., Black folks knew that none of the hundreds of people presumed dead were Black. Black folks further knew that White folks' technology is sometimes not as miraculous as it is reputed to be. As Leadbelly often sang in reference to the good ship TITANIC:

> Jack Johnson tried to get on board,
> The cap'n said we ain't haulin' no coal
> Fare thee well, Titanic, fare thee well.

Shine, the mythological one and only Black person aboard the TITANIC, was deep in the bowels of the ship, shoveling coal. Black Americans knew that a job shoveling coal was the only possible way for a Black person to have gotten on board the unsinkable TITANIC on its maiden voyage. So Shine represents something much greater than a shoveler of coal-- even greater than a trans-Atlantic swimmer. Shine was, from a Eurocentric point of view, the lowest man aboard the ship. Nevertheless, Shine survived in a situation where large numbers of Whites did not. But mere survival would not have been enough to make him a hero. If he had simply made his mythological swim to safety, he would deserve to be commended, but he would not be a hero. He is a hero only because he was able to add the exhibition of verbal skill to his other attributes. These include the physical prowess to swim 1600 miles across the North Atlantic, and the mental discipline to not be diverted from acting in his own best interest, even when the temptations included promise of great wealth and offers of sex by and with the White captain's blonde and voluptuous daughter.

Rhetorical skill is an attribute of great value in African-American culture. At the very least, rhetorical ability is a survival mechanism, particularly as a means of avoiding hostile and aggressive behavior. In addition to its pragmatic value, the ability to use the language imaginatively and effectively may also function to create an art form when synthesized with other elements requisite to the generation of a work of art. The ability to perform certain word games is characteristic of heroes in Afrocentric ritual drama. "The dozens," a juvenile African-American word game, is probably the best known, most frequently played, and most easily identified. The game consists of a series of verbal challenges, usually alternating between two persons. The apparent object of the game is to subdue the opponent by extemporaneously denouncing, in rhyme, the opponent's parents.

Frequently, the structure of "the dozens" is no more than the repeated assertion "I have had sexual intercourse with your mother and so have a wide variety of others under some rather bizarre circumstances." But the important consideration is not the structure. Rather, it is the texture-- how successfully such assertions are directly experienced by the audience. One of the most highly valued abilities in playing "the dozens" is the ability to create visual images with words. When White people display this verbal ability in other contexts it is usually called poetry.

Eurocentric people who analyze poetry generally regard the phenomenon of "the dozens" as unworthy of their attention and ignore it unless they choose to proclaim that it is trash instead. A great deal of the content of "the dozens" is sexually "suggestive" and the language is usually filled with four letter words. Both of these characteristics run contrary to the moral standards of many people. As a result, public presentations of "the dozens" often elicit strong negative responses on moral grounds. These negative responses seem to emanate from both Eurocentric and Afrocentric points of view. In spite of the morally objectionable characteristics that appear on the surface, there are other characteristics of "the dozens" that are worthy of scrutiny by scholars. The artistic competencies that are exhibited by the performers when playing "the dozens" can be examined apart from and uninfluenced by one's judgements about the moral quality of some of the words that are used, and some of the acts that are described.

One must understand that the performers must use the most inflammatory statements possible if the game is to achieve its ultimate social function: to instill in the participants the ability to maintain a calm and aware demeanor in the face of insult and abuse. A decisive win in this game is achieved, in part, by causing one's opponent to get angry enough to exhibit distress and loss of self control. African Americans in the U.S.A. have had to develop the ability to maintain self control when confronted with insult and abuse in order to survive. Playing "the dozens" has made an important educational contribution by teaching many young African Americans to exhibit self-control and calm awareness when confronted with insult and abuse. In this context, one might find a plausible connection between the current increase in young African-American men in prison and a decrease in lessons learned from playing the dozens.

Other word games are less controversial than *The Signifying Monkey*, *The Titanic*, or "the dozens." Overpraise is such a word game. One can overpraise either himself or his opponent. Mohammed Ali provides a well-known example of overpraise of one's self. Of course, one becomes a hero only if the self overpraise turns out to be a reasonably accurate statement about one's actual performance. The reverse type of overpraise is not as familiar a ritual to most segments of American society. The goal of reverse arrogance is to disarm one's adversary by telling him that he is the greatest. Overpraise of one's opponent may appear to the causal observer as "uncle tomming," but it is not. Rather, the underlying theme of overpraise, as expressed through comic irony, is "Not only am I confident that you are not much of an adversary, but I also have so much disdain for your intelligence that I think you are stupid enough to believe me when I tell you that I think you are better than I am."

Sometimes an Afrocentric hero finds it necessary to behave in a self-effacing manner under extremely difficult circumstances for the purpose of achieving his own goals. He does not demean himself for the aid, comfort, or conciliation of his oppressor. He is playing a verbal game in order to survive. And since he outwits the oppressor with a sense of comic irony, he also survives with dignity. The word that seems to be most appropriate for the quality that must be exhibited by such African-American comic heroes is panache. That word is also applicable to African heroes as well. Chief Kwame Ansa's written response to the ranking Portuguese emissary, who attempted to establish a permanent presence in the Gold Coast in 1482, demonstrates a sense of comic irony, wit and the use of overpraise of the enemy. A portion of the message is quoted below.

> I am not insensible to the high honour which your great master the Chief of Portugal has this day conferred upon me. His friendship I have always endeavoured to merit by the strictness of my dealings with the Portuguese, and by my constant exertions to procure an immediate lading for the vessels. But never until this day did I observe such a difference in the appearance of his subjects: they have hereto been only meanly attired, were easily contented with the commodities they received; and so far from wishing to continue in this country, were never happy until they could complete their lading, and return. Now I remark a strange difference. A great number richly dressed are anxious to be allowed to build houses, and to continue among us. Men of such eminence, conducted by a commander who from his own account seems to

have descended from the God who made day and night, can never bring themselves to endure the hardships of this climate; nor would they here be able to procure any of the luxuries that abound in their own country. The passions that are common to us all men will therefore inevitably bring on disputes; and it is far preferable that both our nations should continue on the same footing they have hitherto done, allowing your ships to come and go as usual; the desires of seeing each other occasionally will preserve peace between us.[3]

Chief Ansa's eloquence and skill with words enabled him to forestall the immediate invasion of the Portuguese as they sought another tactic to accomplish their end.

ENDNOTES

1.   Although *The Signifying Monkey* is described with the written word in such works as Roger D. Abrahams, *Deep Down in the Jungle*, 1st revised ed. (Chicago: Aldine, 1970), 113-119, 142-146, 153-156; and Langston Hughes and Arna Bontemps, ed., *Book of Negro Folklore* (New York: Dodd, Mead and Company, 1958), 363-366, audio recordings provide a superior source for gaining insight into this oral form of presentation. Abrahams mentions several recordings on 145-146.

2.   Abrahams, 100-103, 120-129; and Hughes and Bontemps, 366-367.

3.   J. C. deGraft-Johnson, *African Glory* (Baltimore: Black Classic Press, 1986), 129.

Chapter Eight

AFROCENTRIC HEROES

The subtle ironies of being Black and living in the U.S.A. are often missed by White theatregoers and White theatre critics when they witness a great deal of the African-American theatre that is most meaningful to African-American theatregoers. Although Whites miss subtle ironies, we do not suggest a lack of perceptual acuity or intelligence on their part. Instead, the missed perceptions occur because Afrocentric values are significantly different from Eurocentric values. The differences in values cause differences to exist between African-American heroes and European-American heroes. Many of the differences between Afrocentric and Eurocentric heroes grow out of differences in values that promote or reject notions about inherent superiority because of aristocratic birth and male gender.

Being Black and living in the U.S.A. is an experience saturated with incongruities and ironies and, not surprisingly, African-American heroes often expose incongruities and ironies. Apparently some of the ironies that African-American heroes expose in African-American theatre are clarified and intensified by an experiential frame of reference that includes being Black and living in the U.S.A. Much of the negative reaction to Melvin Van Peebles' motion picture *Sweet Sweetback's Badass Song* has been attributed by Van Peebles to a failure of the film's detractors to perceive any difference between a Black exploitation film and a film about Black exploitation. An appreciation of Afrocentric heroes frequently depends upon the audience's ability to

182

perceive subtle differences such as those required to distinguish between a film that exploits African-American people and a film that presents the exploitation of African-American people.

An African-American audience is often able to appreciate subtleties and ironies that seem to require an Afrocentric point of view. For example, a respected White drama critic who attended the opening of an African-American play entitled *Dr. B. S. Black* perceived that, "It uses all the broad earthy cliches that banished such performers as Stepin Fetchit and Rochester from a [White] liberal's respectability list." The White critic further observed that ". . . this play actually is a throwback to the playlets of Bert Williams and the days when sly, shiftless blacks and their womenfolk were figures of fun." The White critic was apparently puzzled by the fact that the nearly all African-American ". . . first night audience seemed to find humor in the characters."[1] The White critic was especially puzzled by the audience's enthusiastic acceptance of the production because Black cultural nationalism dominated the behavior patterns on the Howard University campus in 1970--the time and place of this opening night. Had *Dr. B. S. Black* been perceived by the African-American audience as a "throwback" to sly, shiftless, stereotypical Black characters, there would undoubtedly have been an enthusiastically negative response.

This deservedly respected critic of Eurocentric drama was undoubtedly well-versed in both Eurocentric dramaturgy and in the history of African-American people who have performed before White theatre audiences in the U.S.A. Nevertheless, the African-American audience members laughed unreservedly at the performance because they were able to differentiate between a play that exploits African-American stereotypes for comic effect and a play that presents the exploitation of African-American comic stereotypes. The Stepin Fetchit and Rochester characters to which the White critic refers are scripted in a manner that African-American audiences find demeaning. The dominant trait of such characters as these is their total inability (or unwillingness) to control circumstances for their own betterment. Because they are never in control of anything important, these characters are perpetual victims. Stepin Fetchit, for example, could have exhibited all of his usual cliches of language, superstition, and mannerism and still remained an acceptable Afrocentric characterization; but that was not the case. African-American audiences that found the Stepin Fetchit characterization unacceptable did so primarily because he was controlled, even manipulated, by one or more White characters, often to the obvious disadvantage of Stepin Fetchit.

Rochester, the character that Eddie Anderson played on radio and in motion pictures, was relatively more acceptable (or less unacceptable) to many Blacks. But Rochester was never really in control either. The Rochester character often created the illusion of outsmarting Jack Benny and thereby controlling his situation, which represented an improvement over the usual Stepin Fetchit character. Nevertheless, the Rochester character was always portrayed as Jack Benny's servant. As such, Jack Benny controlled the situation in all the important aspects. Whenever Rochester seemed to outsmart "Mr. Jack," Rochester was in control of some situation which had no real significance. No matter how smart Rochester may have appeared to be in some situations, the audience was never allowed to forget that Jack Benny was always the boss.

On the other hand, characters who are victims differ from characters that generate laughter of recognition and identification from African-American audiences. The title character in *Dr. B. S. Black* is a man of less than modest means who manages to rise above the oppressiveness of his environment. He not only survives, but he also prevails. His ability to control his own fate through the use of imagination and verbal skill enables him to survive with panache. Whenever an African-American comic hero succeeds in controlling his destiny while exhibiting wit and comic irony, African-American audiences seem to be willing to accept some accompanying racial cliches. So, as heroes in plays by African-American playwrights are encountered, a key question must constantly be raised: Who is really in control?

Many important comic heroes are in plays by African-American playwrights. Some of the most memorable characters are Joe Smothers, in *Strivers Row* by Abram Hill; Jesse B. Semple, in *Simply Heavenly* by Langston Hughes; Mrs. Grace Love, in *Contribution* and Charlene, in *Idabelle's Fortune* both by Ted Shine; Rev. Purlie Victorious Judson, in *Purlie Victorious* by Ossie Davis; Tommy in *Wine in the Wilderness* by Alice Childress. Tommy is an African-American woman, as are Grace Love and Charlene. An important point to note is a significant number of the heroes in plays by African-American playwrights are female. This female presence is true not only of the plays that grow out of a sense of comic irony, but is also true of serious plays as well.

The comic and the serious in African-American drama are not always clearly and sharply separated. Comic heroes sometimes provoke tears and serious heroes sometimes provoke laughter. Comedies, as well as serious dramas, have important characteristics that have evolved out of African-American mythology and out of the values that African-American mythology has instilled in us. African-American mythology projects heroic ideals that influence the behavior of Black people in American society. Some of these heroic ideals are vividly presented in a comedy called *Strivers Row* that was first presented in 1940 in Harlem. Since its premiere, productions of *Strivers Row* have been staged in several cities

across the U.S.A. Through the 1980's *Strivers Row* continued
to provide one of the most popular comic characters of the
African-American theatre. This contention is based on the
attendance and the responses of African-American
theatregoers for more than forty years. Mr. Joe Smothers,
better known as Joe the Jiver, makes the following speech as
he enters the Van Striven home where a debutante ball is in
progress.

> [To the cab driver]" Scram Joe meter, you an' that gas
> eater can't beat me for no change, I'm no Sam from
> Alabam'. [To the young African-American man who
> has answered the door] Twist that slammer,
> Gatemouth. That cat may be from the deep south.
> That nickel-snatching taxi driver. [To the guests at the
> Van Striven's] What's happening folks, I'm Joe, the
> Jiver!"

When Mrs. Dolly Van Striven objects to his presence at her
daughter's debutante ball, Joe responds with:

> "Don't play me cheap, I ain't no Bo Peep. Let me get
> you straight, 'fore it is too late. I'm here to stay, so on
> your way. [To the audience] That chick comes on like
> an Eskimo."[2]

Joe the Jiver uses many of the tactics that are exemplary of
traditional African-American comic heroes. Joe has the
requisite verbal skills to be a comic hero. He uses his verbal
skills and his flair for comic irony to express his monumental
contempt for the Eurocentric middle-class values and status
symbols of the African-American inhabitants of Strivers Row.
Verbal skill alone does not make a comic hero. However, Joe
the Jiver's verbal skills also function to encourage African-
American people who see the play to be less concerned with
the creation of artificial barriers of social status and their

symbols and to focus instead on relationships with other individuals by using traditional Afrocentric standards of human worth as the basis for those relationships. Joe's visual and verbal style as well as the magnitude of his usefulness as an advocate of Afrocentric values contribute to the enthusiastic attachment of audience identities to the character of Joe the Jiver. Joe also exhibits sufficient imperfection to avoid the general reluctance of an audience to identify with one who exhibits perfection. Even though he causes identity bonding and exhibits magnitude and verbal skill, a conclusive determination as to whether or not Joe Smothers is a legitimate African-American comic hero remains a function of whether or not he is in control. Joe Smothers finds himself in a situation in which social status is regarded as necessary to survive. Joe has no social status. Nevertheless, he manages to accomplish his goals and establish his personal worth on his own terms. Joe Smothers establishes control in an environment that is structured to insure his inferiority.

Strivers Row exhibits another characteristic that is important to a thorough understanding of the concept of control as it relates to African-American heroes. The play has no White characters to provide a White frame of reference or point of view. The issues that are addressed in the play are viewed by the playwright as issues that Blacks must address for themselves and that Blacks can and must solve for themselves. An African-American character cannot be a hero if his behavior never rises above the level of reacting to the behavior of Whites. African-American heroes must exhibit initiative as well as control. Although some of the other plays mentioned hereafter have White characters, the African-American heroes in these plays act on their own initiative in order to control their own destinies.

The character Purlie Victorious Judson, in *Purlie Victorious* by Ossie Davis, is a hero that is similar to Joe the Jiver in many ways. Although his verbal skills are more characteristic of an African-American preacher than of a secular African-American hero, he, too, has the ability to use his verbal skills to control a situation that is designed to victimize him. Purlie Victorious Judson succeeds in accomplishing his goals on his own terms in an environment that is designed to make him a victim. Further, he does so with wit and with panache.

Also, some African-American women characters succeed in accomplishing their goals, on their own terms, in an environment that is designed to make them victims. Examples of such heroines are Ted Shine's characters Charlene, in *Idabelle's fortune* and Mrs. Grace Love in *Contribution*, and Tommy in Alice Childress' *Wine in the Wilderness*. These female characters differ from the males who have been discussed with regard to the way wit and panache are exhibited. The exhibition of wit and panache by these heroines is more subtle. In the case of Tommy, her wit is disarmingly natural. Charlene and Mrs. Love carefully contrive their wit to disarm people. Charlene, who is a maid, and Mrs. Love, who is a cook, deliberately create the illusion that they are old-fashioned, stereotypical, "mammy" types for the benefit of the White characters who observe them. This subterfuge enables each of these women to accomplish their goals in an extremely hostile environment. Moreover, these women exhibit the same type of stereotypical characteristics that African-American people often find unacceptable in such characters as Beulah of radio drama and Mammy and Prissy in the film *Gone with the Wind*. However, the characters of Shine and Childress differ in that they possess the key factors of initiative and control. Despite their circumstances having placed them in a status that makes them extremely vulnerable to the control of others, Tommy, Charlene, and Mrs. Love control their respective situations.

AFROCENTRIC HEROES

An additional important example of an African-American comic hero is the leading character in the play *Simply Heavenly* by Langston Hughes. Langston Hughes published several books and many articles in the *Chicago Defender* that featured the character Jesse B. Semple (Simple) prior to the creation of the play, *Simply Heavenly*. The play is reminiscent of Langston Hughes' newspaper column and subsequent books in the same serialistic style. The play has an episodic story line held together by the Simple character and the music of David Martin, which grows spontaneously from the action and the locale of the play.

Simple is the prototypical Harlemite. His most extraordinary quality is his ordinariness. Relationships with women, the cost of living, landladies, taxes, alcoholic beverages, and the U.S. Army are Simple's catastrophes and the subjects of his frequent barroom oratory. But the thing about Simple that strengthens his identity bonding to heroic proportions is that he can trace the ultimate cause of all his problems to the fact that he is African-American. As Simple explains it, ". . . something's always happening to a colored man!"[3] Simple is not a gangster or a sports or show-business personality, or a super-successful professional man. He does not drive a Cadillac and wear flashy clothes. Neither is he a pathetic victim of external circumstances. These are stereotypes that are well known in the White world. Simple is concerned with the ordinary things of life. He is disturbed by the fact that Blacks were never mentioned in the newspapers in connection with any non-sensational, positive, or beneficial activity. "Unless we commit murder, robbery or rape, or are being chased by a mob, do we get on the front page, or hardly the back?" Simple asks. He points out that he has read about Karl Krubelowski and Giovanni Battini and Heinrich Armpriester all seeing flying saucers, but never about Roosevelt Johnson or Henry Washington, or anyone that even "sounds like a Negro," seeing one.[4]

Much of the humor in *Simply Heavenly* is comprised of "inside" jokes. Many of the lines that satirize the predicament of African-American people in a society dominated by White people are missed by a significant portion of the White members of the audience. Or, if they are not missed, they do not cause laughter. An example of this phenomenon occurs in the song "Let Me Take You For a Ride." Zarita invites Simple to go riding in a friend's convertible. She sings, "Let me take you for a ride!" and Simple answers, "Let the breeze blow through my hair!"[5]

African-American people laugh first at the things that make them different from Whites in order to eliminate or reduce the hurt and embarrassment that results from ridicule of those differences by the dominant group. When African-American people experience this hurt in response to negative institutional recognition of racial differences, African-American people do not feel that the differences are indicative of their racial inferiority. Rather, the frequency, force, and magnitude of negative assertions by White people and White institutions becomes overwhelming. Simple frequently makes statements that may appear on the surface to suggest that African-American people are inferior. For example, he says, ". . . I been caught in some kind of a riffle ever since I been Black."[6] But Simple is articulating an irony that functions very effectively in the identity bonding process. The irony is that the victim of the act of oppression, rather than the perpetrator, gets the blame. The "fault" that causes the victim to get the blame is that the victim is Black. No African American is completely able to escape this irony. Therefore, African Americans can readily identify with Simple in this respect. But the most important thing about Simple is that he seeks to control his own destiny. And, in his own very ordinary way, he succeeds.

AFROCENTRIC HEROES

Although *Simply Heavenly* was first produced as a play in 1957, it is based upon *Simple Takes A Wife*, a book published in 1953. So the social issues that are treated with such comic effectiveness are issues of the early 1950's. Within that context, Simple expresses both pride in his Blackness and confidence in himself. He asserts that, in the newly integrated Army, he would ". . . rise right to the top today and be a general." Further, he insists that he wants to command a White regiment from Mississippi. He goes on to explain that he would " . . . do like all the other generals do, and stand way back on a hill somewhere and look through my spy-glasses and say, 'Charge on! Mens, charge on!'" After his imaginary White troops have succeeded in battle under his leadership, he will assemble them to forgive them for their past racial transgressions and present them with medals for bravery. He concludes his speech by asking his White troops to stop fighting him and join him in a drink to celebrate their victory.[7] As with all Afrocentric comic heroes, Simple provides an illustration of how African-American people can come to terms with hostile environments, control their circumstances, and achieve their goals. Comic heroes recognize the incongruities and ironies of their environment and are able to laugh at them. A true comic hero causes the audience to recognize not only the foibles of others but their own foibles as well.

Sometimes in dramatic literature we are confronted with a heroic character whose struggle to overcome a hostile environment demands the endurance of pain and suffering. These heroes are usually referred to as tragic heroes. There may be moments of comic irony and the character may exhibit wit, but the route to the achievement of his goals leads to a confrontation with the forces that are preventing the achievement of his goals. The essential differences between comic and tragic heroes are seen in the way they deal with efforts to prevent them from accomplishing their goals. Tragic

191

heroes confront the forces that stand in their way, whereas comic heroes navigate a route to their goals that seeks to avoid the struggle and suffering that usually accompanies confrontation.

A recurring phenomenon among African-American people in the U.S.A. has generated a type of African-American hero in theatre and other art forms. This African-American hero is an individual who has faced American racism all of his or her life and who suddenly and sometimes without apparent overt provocation gets tired of trying to cope with the overwhelming effects of racism. This African-American hero makes a decision and takes a stand. He or she makes this commitment with the full realization that to take a stand against racism usually results in death or some barbaric form of punishment, such as castration for males or rape for females. But this hero says, "I don't mind dying," and means it. In real life, such a hero may or may not actually die as a result of taking a stand against racism. Mrs. Rosa Parks must have fully expected if not to die, at least to be thrown in jail and subjected to physical abuse when she refused to give up her seat to a White passenger on a bus in Montgomery, Alabama, in 1955 and thereby initiated a series of events that precipitated the Montgomery Bus Boycott.

Most African Americans in the U.S.A. with some sanity and dignity remaining have said, on some occasion, to themselves, "I don't mind dying," and really meant it. But the sincere expression of the phrase "I don't mind dying" does not make one a tragic hero. A decision to confront the forces that stand in one's way does not, in and of itself, generate dignity. Dignity does not automatically result from pain and suffering, even when the pain and suffering is totally unjustified. However, dignity is undoubtedly easier to recognize when pain and suffering has been unjustly inflicted. One does not have to have much strength of character in order to maintain one's dignity in an environment of comfort and convenience. On the other hand, one whose dignity prevails while enduring pain and suffering evidences a strength of character that may be regarded as heroic when it is accompanied by other elements that a hero must exhibit. Members of the audience must identify with a hero in a manner that is dictated by their values and to an extent that causes them to regard themselves as connected to the hero. A hero must have one or more characteristics that are of sufficient magnitude for his or her achievements to rise above the personal. A hero makes a decision to overcome an obstacle in an effort to control his or her destiny and to survive.

African-American people in the U.S.A. exist in an environment of institutional racism that is not generally recognized as such by those who do not have to suffer its consequences on a continual basis. Institutional racism in the U.S.A. provides an environment of pain and suffering that demands considerable strength of character in order to simply survive with one's dignity intact. Appropriately, we reiterate that in the tradition of African-American culture, finding a way to survive is an important element of heroism. When an African-American hero says, "I don't mind dying," he is not seeking to achieve martyrdom. He does not wish to die or to suffer for a cause. He simply recognizes the inevitability of his pain and suffering within the context of a society that systematically oppresses African-American people. His strongest impulse is always to survive. But his survival includes a strong desire to achieve some reasonable degree of human dignity, not only for himself but for his group as well. Sometimes the struggle for human dignity for self and for group overrides the impulse for individual biological survival.

This kind of African-American hero does not want to provoke a violent reaction that causes pain and suffering. He simply recognizes that he exists within a societal structure that is programmed to inflict pain and suffering and possibly to cause a violent death to any member of his group who overtly refuses to accept sub-human status. In this context, suffering is not inflicted by the gods or as a result of some internal character flaw. The suffering is inflicted by institutional racism through White oppressors or the non-White agents of those oppressors. The African-American hero's choice, then, is whether or not to assert his human dignity in an environment that has been structured to overwhelm him with denials of his human dignity. When such an African-American hero is presented as a character in a play, he must reflect some important priorities and values of African-American culture through his actions. The simple assertion of self worth in the face of White oppression is not enough.

Some important African-American heroes are in serious plays by African-American playwrights. A few of these heroes are well known by a broader American public--the Younger family in *A Raisin in the Sun*, for example. An African-American play that has achieved some success before White audiences may still be an important and worthwhile play by African-American standards. The mere fact that White audiences find a play with African-American characters acceptable does not guarantee that the play is or should be unacceptable to African-American audiences. On the other hand, on numerous occasions African-American audiences overwhelmingly found a character to be demeaning while White audiences found the same character to be quite acceptable. As a result, some African-American people may be suspicious of any play with African-American characters that acquires the enthusiastic support of White audiences.

In the case of *A Raisin in the Sun*, African-American audiences generally see a positive image of an African-American family dealing with issues that are important to African-American people. The central issue is the continuation of the family as a unit within an environment that is structured to oppress and exploit them. This central issue raises several specific questions. The playwright, Lorraine Hansberry, raises the question of abortion as it relates to African-American values. The question of who should handle the family finances is discussed. But who owns the insurance money is different from the question of who is head of the household. The quest for higher education is another issue that is important to African-American audiences who often find validation for their own decisions in the Younger family's decision to sacrifice for Beneatha to become a medical doctor. Implicit in the play is the idea that both of the adult generations of the Younger family regard higher education as an important mechanism, not only for the financial rewards that accrue to the recipient of the education, but especially for the non-financial rewards associated with the delivery of desperately needed professional services to African-American people. Another issue that affects the continuation of the family as a unit is security for the family. The generations differ as to the details of what constitutes security. However, all members of the household are working to achieve it. The broader theme that brings all of the issues together into a significant whole is the concern of all for the progress of the race. Strategies may differ from one member of the Younger household to the next member, but they all desire to see the race progress.

Walter Younger grapples with the issues facing the Younger family and, in doing so, emerges as a hero. Walter is the only character in the play who changes as a result of self realization. He is able to rise above his personal strivings and relate to larger issues. Walter has not been generally regarded as a hero by White theatre critics. The principal difficulty they have in recognizing Walter as both the central character of the play and as a hero seems to be that Walter, a virile

Black male, poses a threat; whereas Lena does not. Lena is usually played by a woman who is visually reminiscent of the mammy stereotype, although the character is not a stereotypical mammy character. White audiences and critics seem to obtain comfort from seeing her as a mammy figure. In contrast, Walter is a young Black man who is both angry and virile. White audiences and white critics seem to assuage themselves by diminishing Walter's role in the overall scheme of things. By their viewing Lena as a bossy old woman, they are relieved of the disquieting prospect of recognizing Walter Lee Younger as a force with which to be reckoned. This avoidance of Walter as a representative of angry and virile Black males is accomplished by focusing upon the "scientific discovery" by White sociologists that African-American families, especially poor ones, are inevitably ruled by matriarchal figures. The tradition of matrilineal succession and the respect and power women enjoy as a result is very definitely a significant part of our African cultural heritage. But, to see this play from the White sociologists' point of view of "the poor Black matriarchal family" is to miss the essence of the play. Although the play is undisputedly about the entire Younger family, the central character in the play and the head of the Younger household is Walter Younger.

Two important factors in *A Raisin in the Sun* seem to go unnoticed by those who regard this as a play about Lena. First, Walter's father and Lena's husband, the head of the Younger household for more than 35 years, has recently died. Most families require a period of adjustment following such a trauma. Second, Walter respects his mother both as mother and as the elder of the family. Consequently, Walter's behavior is comparable to that of an African chief who must listen to the elders before important decisions are made. The African chief does not have to follow the elders' advice, but he must listen to it. Likewise, Walter must listen to his mother's advice, although he is not obliged to follow it. Even

AFROCENTRIC HEROES

Lena Younger herself states, at the end of Act II, scene 2, "I'm telling you to be the head of this family from now on like you supposed to be." Somehow the respect Lena receives from Walter and his wife Ruth and demands from her daughter, Beneatha, as mother and elder is misconstrued by Whites to be matriarchal rule.

The concept that Lena Younger's rule prevails in the Younger household has little to do with the content of the play and a great deal to do with prior assumptions, sometimes known as prejudices. As we have already mentioned, Walter is the only character in this play who changes as a result of self-realization. In addition, a consensus among White Americans asserts they have conclusive scientific proof that the controlling force in virtually every African-American household is a Black woman. Therefore, when an African-American woman is portrayed as strong of body, mind, and opinion, Whites males immediately conclude that she is the head of the household and has emasculated any and all males in said household. Any suggestion of respect by an adult male family member is assumed to be indicative of subservience. Just as White males seem to regard any assertion of strength or independence by an African-American male as an implicit assertion of White male weakness, any indication of strength or independence by a woman seems to be regarded by White males as a threat to their own strength or independence.

The economic and social forces of White male oppression have caused an unfortunately large percentage of African-American households in which there is no regularly employed adult male in residence. The absence of a male breadwinner in many African-American homes has resulted in the inaccurate assumption that African-American values generate households dominated solely by women. Although this lack of male presence is a terrible social problem rooted in the economic exploitation of African-American males, it has very little to do with the content of *A Raisin in the Sun*, because the Younger household does have an employed, adult male in residence. Any connection between the play *A Raisin in the Sun* and the phenomenon of African-American households without an adult, male wage-earner is a connection that is largely created by the prejudice of the observer.

Joseph Walker's statement of dedication of his play *The River Niger*, suggests his concern about the stereotypical dismissal of the role of African-American men in the family. He says, "The play is dedicated to my mother and father and to highly underrated black daddies everywhere."[8] *The River Niger* is another serious play with an African-American hero who communicates positive values for African-American people. The hero of the play, Johnny Williams, comes to the realization that he has accomplished just about as much as he can reasonably expect to accomplish. Further, he knows that he does not have much longer to live; therefore, he sacrifices himself to save his son. Survival of the family and progress of the race represent higher priorities for African-American heroes than the "save your own skin no matter what" concept of survival. The ideal of freedom that is sometimes expressed by African artists suggests that a man does not have the "freedom" to let his brother go without food and shelter when he has enough of both to share.

A play by William Branch entitled *A Medal for Willie* presents an African-American woman who embodies the characteristics of heroism. The play was written in 1951 and centers around the posthumous awarding of the Distinguished Service Cross to Corporal Willie D. Jackson. The act of bravery that earned Willie the medal also cost him his life. His mother goes to the Booker T. Washington High School Auditorium to accept the medal. Mrs. Jackson is a quiet, hard-working African-American woman who raised a son and a daughter in a small southern town. But Mrs. Jackson's son went off to fight in

198

Korea because he could not get a job in his hometown. Now Willie is dead and a General has come to town to present her with Willie's medal. The Mayor and the Superintendent of Schools have come to the Black high school, too. Mrs. Jackson is clearly in an environment that is structured to place her in a subservient role. She is expected to behave exactly as these White male figures of authority tell her to behave. They have even written an acceptance speech for her. However, as Mrs. Jackson begins to read the speech, she chokes on the hypocrisy of the words, and she refuses to read the prepared speech. Instead, she eloquently expresses her anger over the injustices suffered by her son Willie at the hands of the White establishment. To show her contempt for the military symbol she rejects the medal. She tells the General to take the medal back to Washington to ". . . give it to the ones who send boys like my Willie all over the world to die for some kinda freedom and democracy they always gets the leavin's of!"[9]

Mrs. Jackson exemplifies many of the heroic characteristics often found in African-American mythology. Her acceptance speech shows the process of soul searching that serious heroes undergo. Her actions exhibit those values and ideals that African-American people regard as heroic. Mrs. Jackson, like other African-American heroes, maintains a sense of self in the midst of a hostile environment. Those African-American playwrights who create Afrocentric heroes, both comic and serious, create Afrocentric characters whose self knowledge enables them to perceive the irony in the circumstances, not only of others, but of themselves as well. The values and ideals of heroes in Afrocentric plays reflect the heroic ideals of African people in America.

ENDNOTES

1. Richard Coe, "'Soul' Plays," *Washington Post*, 30 Oct. 1970, Sec.D, 8.

2. Abram Hill, *Strivers Row*, TS, p.I-2-67. The playscript of this African-American classic, first performed in 1940, was first published in 1991.

3. Langston Hughes, *Simply Heavenly* (New York: Dramatists Play Service, Inc., 1959), 62.

4. Hughes, 30-31.

5. Hughes, pp. 20-21 for dialogue leading to the song. Langston Hughes, book and lyrics, *Simply Heavenly*, music and orchestration by David Martin, with Claudia McNeil, Melvin Stewart, and Anna English, Columbia, OL 5240, n.d.

6. Hughes, 62.

7. Hughes, 72.

8. Joseph A. Walker, *The River Niger* (New York: Hill and Wang, 1973), dedication page.

9. William Branch, "A Medal for Willie," in *Black Drama*, ed. Woodie King and Ron Milner (New York: New American Library, 1971), 470-471.

Chapter Nine

AFROCENTRIC CHARACTERIZATION

Afrocentric theatre, like most other successful theatrical genres, is intended for a relatively homogeneous audience. Therefore, the communication of messages that might be necessary for a White audience could prove trite and boring for the intended African-American audience. Afrocentric American playwrights seek to spare their intended audience the ordeal of sitting through expository messages that are descriptive of experiences that are generally well known. When such expository messages are included, many African-American people presume that the primary goal of the play is to inform or persuade White people about African-American people. The sense of African-American community that is necessary to the success of an African-American dramatic event is diminished when a play by an African-American playwright is thought by its African-American audience to be aimed at a White audience. On the other hand, when African-American playwrights do not include such expository material, White audience members often feel that the characters were insufficiently explained, inadequately motivated, or two-dimensional.

Following the opening performance of *Strivers Row* in Atlanta, a deservedly respected White critic who enthusiastically sought to encourage African-American theatre in that city posed some questions, in conversation, that he said were sincere concerns of his. He expressed concern over what he regarded as flaws in the character delineation of Joe Smothers. He asked whether Joe Smothers was a pimp, a thief, or an honest wage earner. The critic also questioned the depth and sincerity of Joe's possible romantic relationships with several of the female characters in the play.[1] These are questions that never seem to occur to African-American people who have seen the play. Instead, those who are motivated to say anything at all about Joe Smothers assert that "I know someone who is just like Joe Smothers." The character of Joe Smothers has proved to be not only enjoyable but easily recognizable and well understood by African-American audiences from the early 1940's through the 1980's. When combined with what African-American audiences already know, the play communicates as much information as they need to know about Joe Smothers.

Modern Eurocentric playwrights have traditionally assumed that they needed to tell the audience about a character's past, possibly going into considerable detail about seemingly unrelated events that occurred many years earlier than that of the action of the play. These earlier events provide insight into the causes of the character's present behavior through the use of oversimplified Freudian psychoanalysis. The assumption is that past events mold a person's character. Therefore, if we want to know why a person behaves the way he does today, we must discover what happened to him yesterday. Usually this alleged insight is dependent upon some specific knowledge about his sexual behavior. If a man's dominant traits are negative, we discover that his mother did not love him as a child. Modern European-American dramatists still seem to be caught up in the religious fervor of Freudian psychoanalysis as a means of explaining human behavior. These so-called character insights are seemingly a necessary part of anything in the modern Euro-American experience that is regarded as legitimate theatre.

These kinds of so-called character insights occupy a significant portion of the performance time of most legitimate modern Eurocentric drama. If all of the Freudian inferences were removed, such drama would certainly take less time to perform. In contrast, many African-American plays are described as short rather than full-length, largely because of a difference in opinion as to what the audience needs to be told about the characters. The terms "short" and "full-length" do not simply describe the time it takes to perform a play. European-American critics make value judgements about the lack of competency and maturity of playwrights who write only short plays. They assume a lesser status is deserved for playwrights who have not exhibited the ability to sustain characters in a full length play. In Afrocentric drama, plot does not necessarily have to grow out of characterization but can grow, instead, out of other environmental and experiential forces. But more importantly, characters may simply be presented without historical explanation based upon Freudian assumptions.

Eurocentric values are often used by White audiences to explain why characters in plays by Afrocentric playwrights behave as they do. The thematic intentions of an African-American playwright may be reversed through the imposition of Eurocentric values to explain Afrocentric character motivations. White audience members, who have observed *Happy Ending* by Douglas Turner Ward, have often expressed the conclusion that all of the characters in the play are behaving in a manner that is morally wrong. More specifically, Eurocentric concepts of morality lead to the conclusion that all of the characters in this play are thieves. Many White audience members further assume that, if *Happy Ending* is to be regarded as a well written play, the audience must be able to discover what motivates such apparently wrongful behavior and what effect this behavior must have upon the characters involved. The Eurocentric assumption is that stealing ought to ultimately result in some sort of negative effect, some punishment, or at least some strong feelings of guilt that imply a form of punishment within the framework of Freudian psychology. But the characters in *Happy Ending* suffer no such negative outcome. On the contrary, when they learn that they will probably be able to continue their activities, they celebrate the news as a happy ending--hence, the title of the play.

The characters in *Happy Ending* are very well conceived and described, if they are examined from within a context of African-American values. The only explanation that is necessary, with regard to the fact that these characters perform acts that Whites regard as stealing, is that they only take things that would otherwise be wasted by their extremely wealthy White employers. The concept is referred to, by most African-American people who engage in the practice, as "totin' privileges." The only character exposition that needs to be communicated to an African-American audience is that the African-American characters have White employers who squander their wealth. Several facts are communicated about the characters in *Happy Ending* that let us know that they possess high moral standards. They never take more than they need so, they are not greedy. They all work hard, so they are not lazy. And they all exhibit a willingness to help other members of their family. They are not selfish. No Freudian explanation for their behavior is necessary.

Another play that deals with "totin' privileges" on a slightly different level is *Livin' Fat* by Judi Mason. David Lee, the central character in the play, has a college degree but is unable to find employment except as a janitor in a bank. When the bank is robbed, he finds over $50,000 in an envelope that the robbers dropped in their hasty departure. When David Lee attempts to call attention to the money immediately after the robbery, he is unable to get the attention of the bank authorities or the police. He takes the money home and decides that the money is payment for the hard times that his mother and father and grandmother have suffered. No explanation is necessary for the African-American audience to understand why David Lee would go to jail if he tried to be "honest" by returning the money to the bank authorities. African-American people in the audience know that David's explanation would not be believed by the White law enforcement establishment. Therefore, the only sagacious decision for David Lee's father to make is to allow the family to keep the money that David Lee found. The characters certainly have no subsequent feelings of guilt, since their standards of morality and justice conclude that no wrong has been done. An important item to note is that David's parents are God-fearing, church-going folks. Prior to arriving at the decision to permit David to keep the money, David's father insists upon "praying over" the moral issues that are presented by David's acquisition. Why do some people find it difficult to accept the notion that an ideal of ethical behavior is presented in *Livin' Fat* and in *Happy Ending* while continuing to idolize Robin Hood?

Even those White critics who have not objected to the concept of "totin' privileges" have dealt with these plays, and others like them, as something they call "social protest." Apparently, a play can be discredited as a work of art by labeling it as social protest. *Day of Absence*, a longer companion piece to *Happy Ending*, has also been labeled "social protest" in an apparent attempt to imply that its usefulness in the perpetuation of African-American values among African-American people somehow reduces its aesthetic worth. Inherent in the message of *Day of Absence* is the premise that, in the time and place of the action of the play, African Americans know a great deal more about Whites than Whites know about African Americans. This phenomenon is the result of the accumulated knowledge of several generations of African-American people who cook and serve the food, take care of the children, clean the filth, and haul away the garbage of their White employers.

White people seldom have such an intimate awareness of the behavior of African-American people, since Whites have traditionally regarded their African-American domestic servants as little more than pieces of furniture. These White people have expanded the way they regard their African-American servants to include African-American people in general. We see evidence of White people's disregard of African Americans in the willingness of White people to discuss, with relative unconcern, their most intimate private affairs before African Americans. On the other hand, African-American domestic servants have traditionally told their White employers only what their White employers wanted to hear. African-American people have seldom allowed their honest feelings and opinions to intrude upon this tradition. *Day of Absence* dramatizes a basic truth that African-American audience members recognize. This truth is probably most impressively articulated by Ralph Ellison in his seminal novel *Invisible Man*. In the prologue, the protagonist says, "I am invisible, understand, simply because people refuse to see me."[2]

To explain, in a concise manner, the full implications of the concept of African Americans as invisible people is difficult. Sensibilities may be heightened through exposure to some of the major works of art that focus upon this theme. *Invisible Man* is undoubtedly an excellent initiation to the concept. *Day of Absence* is a play that focuses upon the idea that White people simply refuse to see African-American people, from a comic point of view. The farcical premise of *Day of Absence* is that all the African-American people in a small southern town just disappear without a trace. The result of this transformation from figurative to literal invisibility is that all of the essential human needs of the town's White population go unmet. Three of the leading citizens of the hypothetical southern city go to the Mayor's office to complain:

> INDUSTRIALIST: Half of the day is gone already, Henry. On behalf of the factory owners of this town, you've got to bail us out! Seventy-five percent of all production is paralyzed. With the Nigra absent, men are waiting for machines to be cleaned, floors to be swept, crates lifted, equipment delivered and bathrooms to be deodorized. Why, rest rooms and toilets are so filthy until they not only cannot be sat in, but it's virtually impossible to get within hailing distance because of the stench!

> BUSINESSMAN: Business is even in worse condition, Henry. The volume of goods moving 'cross counters has slowed down to a trickle--almost negligible. Customers are not only not purchasing--but the absence of handymen, porters, sweepers, stockmovers, deliverers and miscellaneous dirty-work doers is disrupting the smooth harmony of marketing.

> CLUB WOMAN: Food poisoning, severe indigestitis, chronic diarrhea, advanced diaper chafings and a plethora of unsanitary household disasters dangerous to life, limb, and property! ... As a representative of the Federation of Ladies' Clubs, I must sadly report that unless the trend is reversed, a complete breakdown in family unity is imminent. ... Just as homosexuality and debauchery signalled the fall of Greece and Rome, the downgrading of Southern Bellesdom might very well prophesy the collapse of our indigenous institutions.

BLACK THEATRE

> . . . Remember--it has always been pure, delicate,
> lilywhite images of Dixie femininity which provided
> backbone, inspiration and idealogy for our male
> warriors in their defense against the on-rushing black
> horde. If our gallant men are drained of this worship
> and idolatry--God knows! The cause won't be worth a
> Confederate nickel![3]

The situation in the play continues to get worse. A few
citizens previously thought to be one-hundred percent pure
White are discovered missing with the rest of the Negroes.
The Mayor's brother-in-law, two city council members, the
chairman of the Junior Chamber of Commerce, the City
College All-Southern half-back, the chairlady of the
Daughters of the Confederate Rebellion, Miss Cotton-Sack
Festival and "numerous other miscellaneous nobodies" are
missing. The wife of one of the missing persons is seen
carrying a placard which reads "Why Didn't You Tell Us--
Your Defiled Wife and Two Absent Mongrels."

The characters in the play are deliberately two dimensional.
Most are not even given names, but are simply referred to by
occupation, such as Supervisor, Mayor, Industrialist,
Businessman, and Clubwoman. The play is intended to be
performed as a minstrel show in reverse--an all Black cast
performing in whiteface. The two exceptions to this are the
Northern, White television announcer to be played as a
straight role by a White man, and Rastus to be played by a
Black man with straight makeup.

Other plays have used African-American actors with
whiteface makeup. The technique has been used for reasons
other than to convey the idea of a minstrel show-in-reverse.
Carlton and Barbara Molette's *Rosalee Pritchett* is a serious
play that uses African-American actors in whiteface makeup

208

to portray all of the White characters in the play. The playwrights' notes to the director state that:

> We are opposed to the idea of having the Guards played by whites. They should be played by Black men in white-face makeup. It's not that we have anything against white actors in the Goodoleusofa, but they just ain't capable of the kind of objectivity that is necessary in the portrayal of these roles.[4]

Although the assertion that White actors are incapable of objectivity is made with sarcasm, the request that African-American actors portray the White characters in this play is a sincere request. Further, the request suggests that some African-American playwrights are doubtful that White actors can and will portray the truth that African-American playwrights perceive to be the behavior of White people.

Frequently the meaning of a character in an African-American play is not communicated through European rules of character exposition but is communicated through experiences held in common among the African-American members of the audience. These common experiences create attitudes and values that are shared by African-American people. Whites are often oblivious to these attitudes and values and have difficulty accepting the truth of African-American reality. One such truth that underlies African-American character behavior is that Whites, in general, are frequently held in contempt by African-American people. Contempt and hatred are not synonymous, however; most African Americans who hold Whites in contempt do not hate Whites. Consequently, African-American heroes frequently have contempt for Whites in heroic, that is larger than life, proportions.

BLACK THEATRE

An African-American mythological hero whose heroism is closely connected to his contempt for Whites is Shine in *The Titanic*. Even though it is presented from a comic perspective, Shine's monumental contempt is, in large part, the reason that the Shine character conveys a sense of truth to an African-American audience. But there is an apparent reluctance, on the part of Whites, to regard the kind of contempt that is exhibited by Shine as having a ring of truth. After all, nobody wants to think of himself or herself as being worthy of contempt.

Whites expect African-American drama to exhibit what they regard as authenticity of external detail. This usually means having African-American character types who fit easily into preconceived Eurocentric notions about who and what African-American people are. Therefore, pimps, prostitutes, dope addicts, and petty thieves are regarded as authentically African American. Such characters also lend themselves to stereotypical exaggeration and simplification. Conversely, doctors, lawyers, bankers, college professors, businessmen and even professional athletes are not regarded as authentically African American. Further, such characters present difficulties in stereotypical exaggeration and simplification that the former group of characters does not present. On the other hand, when Whites analyze the so-called universality of characterization in an African-American play, they seem to be obliged to ask: "Do the characters rise above their Africanness?" In addition, they usually inquire: "Are the characters motivated by the same stimuli and in the same ways that White characters are?" A more Afrocentric way to phrase the query is: "Are these characters oreos?" "Oreo" is a term of disparagement used by African-American people to describe a person who is Black on the outside and White on the inside.

AFROCENTRIC CHARACTERIZATION

No Place to be Somebody by Charles Gordone contains characters that are regarded by most White critics as well conceived and well drawn. Highly praised as the first African-American play to win the Pulitzer Prize, this play received more critical acclaim from the American literary establishment than any other play by an African-American playwright in the two decades between *A Raisin in the Sun* and *A Soldier's Play*. Ironically, *No Place to be Somebody* is an extremely effective argument in favor of the myth of White racial superiority. The play attempts to make heroes of African-Americans who compulsively seek not just to enter White society but to establish their most intimate relationship with a White person. *No Place to be Somebody* is dangerously deceptive because Charles Gordone is effectively colorful in his use of African-American urban street language and in his portrayal of some of the most negative characters to inhabit the African-American experience, while subtly presenting his messages of White supremacy.

The play is so well constructed and the characters are so authentic in their external detail that African-American audience members are often beguiled by those attributes into ignoring the play's dominant thematic element. The characters that the play presents in a negative light are all seeking their self-actualization within the African-American experience. These characters not only fail to achieve self actualization, they even fail to survive. On the other hand, those who do appear to achieve some success relentlessly seek vicarious self actualization through intimate association with some White character who is permitted by the society to be somebody. The flaw in the theme that Gordone communicates is that human beings do not self-actualize vicariously. The play succeeds in communicating its theme of White supremacy to the extent that the audience believes that the best African-American people can hope to achieve is vicarious self-actualization.

211

BLACK THEATRE

No Place to be Somebody is reminiscent of *Uncle Tom's Cabin* by Harriet Beecher Stowe. Both Stowe and Gordone suggest that African-American people need to connect their self-actualization to the goals and aspirations of a White person. Every African-American character in *No Place to be Somebody* who still has a reasonable opportunity to "be somebody" as the play ends, owes the opportunity to an intimate relationship with a White person. Each of those African-American characters will "be somebody" only to the extent that they are able to connect their own goals and aspirations to the goals and aspirations of their particular White person.

The character Uncle Tom, as delineated by Harriet Beecher Stowe and by numerous theatrical adaptations of her novel, is never in control of his own destiny. For this reason, many White people find the character both dignified and lovable, while the overwhelming majority of African Americans find Uncle Tom pathetic or disgusting or worse. The character Uncle Tom has been the symbol of a cause since Harriet Beecher Stowe's novel *Uncle Tom's Cabin* was first published. The nineteenth-century Eurocentric cause for which Uncle Tom stood was the abolition of slavery as an American institution. Ironically, from an Afrocentric perspective, an "Uncle Tom" is one who is willing to accept a subservient role with outward complacency or even happiness. *Uncle Tom's Cabin* was an important piece of abolitionist rhetoric when first written. The original intent was to show White people the inequities, the cruelty, the un-Christian nature of slavery. Uncle Tom was assumed by Mrs. Stowe to be an effective character because he is lovable. But the White people in Mrs. Stowe's novel, and those who read it who claim to love Uncle Tom, love him not as an equal but as they would an obedient old pet dog. For African-American people, the term "Uncle Tom" symbolizes the degradation that can result from placing complete trust and faith in White people and thereby being controlled by them.

AFROCENTRIC CHARACTERIZATION

The stated source of Uncle Tom's subservience is his recently acquired Christianity. Uncle Tom is the quintessence of all that the Black Muslims in America claim that Christianity has done to degrade African-American people. When Uncle Tom's African-American friends tell him to run away because he is to be sold, he refuses. He refuses because he is loyal to his master and because he has faith in "de Lawd." He wants to be free; but since he has accepted the White man's religion, Uncle Tom sits around singing spirituals and waiting for "de Lawd" to free him. He has been so completely emasculated by the system he has been taught to call Christianity that he allows Eva, a little girl who is no more than eight or ten years old, to order him about and use him as a plaything. When Eva stamps her foot, Uncle Tom jumps. Even though he finally stands up to Simon Legree, the brutal White overseer, Tom does so in a way that is totally without strength and dignity. He makes no effort to survive and no effort to control his own destiny. Uncle Tom passively permits himself to be beaten to death by Simon Legree. Even in the self-realization that comes with his death, Uncle Tom fails to "be somebody." Uncle Tom is not capable of even thinking about what is in his own best interest. He sincerely believes that what is best for "his White folks" is best for him. He has no identity except through "his White folks."

One must note that *Uncle Tom's Cabin* was written by a White woman; and White women are also indoctrinated to believe that they can only achieve "somebodiness" through obedience and subservience to a White male. Ms. Stowe's position is not surprising, then, as she sincerely regarded Uncle Tom's behavior as exemplary. In a "stage Negro" tradition that has lasted to the present time, only the African-American woman (Cassy) has the strength to take overt action against Simon Legree. The only other characters in the play that seem to have a positive impact upon African Americans are George and Eliza Harris. The Harrises always aspire to "be somebody" and work at controlling their own destinies. However, even in the case of the Harrises, African Americans have some negative reaction. The Harrises consider their human aspirations and stronger wills to result from their partial European ancestry which is easily recognizable in their skin color and hair texture. The Harrises imply that to be "almost White" is to almost "be somebody."

A character who is comparable to Uncle Tom appears in a nineteenth century play by an African-American playwright. But, in *The Escape*, by William Wells Brown, the comparable character, Cato appears only on the surface to be an "Uncle Tom." Cato is regarded as a true and acceptable character by African-American audiences because he pretends to be an "Uncle Tom" in order to seize control of his own destiny. Even though the Cato character has more of the traditional stereotypical attributes than does the Uncle Tom character of Ms. Stowe, Cato strives to control his own destiny and eventually succeeds. As a result, contemporary African-American audiences find Cato an acceptable humorous character.[5] On the other hand, Uncle Tom not only does not control his own destiny, but he is also philosophically opposed to the notion of attempting to control his own destiny. White Christians have taught him that God intended for African-American people to be inferior to White people; therefore, African-American people are rightfully the slaves of White people. Because Uncle Tom has accepted this allegedly Christian doctrine, he will take no action that might cause his freedom or disturb "his White folks." Uncle Tom is convinced that he must wait for God and "his White folks" to set him free.

The phenomenon of the "Uncle Tom" stereotype obviously did not end with Emancipation. One may find many contemporary examples of such characters. *Purlie Victorious* by Ossie Davis is a play of the 1960's. An important character in the play is Gitlow, the brother of Reverend Purlie Victorious Judson. Gitlow is a character who appears to be an "Uncle Tom," but is not. Gitlow Judson appears to be an "Uncle Tom" for tactical reasons. He is convinced that he can get more for less work from Ol' Cap'n by being an "Uncle Tom" than he could get through protest. Ol' Cap'n calls upon Gitlow to testify about the way Negroes really feel about integration.

> OL' CAP'N: Gitlow Judson, as God is your Judge and maker, do you believe in your heart that God intended white folks and Negra children to go to school together?

> GITLOW: Nawsuh, I do not!

> OL' CAP'N: Do you, so help you God, think that white folks and black should mix and 'sociate in street cars, buses, and railroad stations, in any way, shape, form or fashion?

> GITLOW: Absolutely not!

> OL' CAP'N: And is it not your considered opinion, God strike you dead if you lie, that all my Negras are happy with things in the southland just the way they are?

> GITLOW: Indeed I do!

> OL' CAP'N: Do you think ary single darky on my place would ever think of changing a single thing about the South, and to hell with the Supreme Court as God is your judge and maker?

GITLOW: As God is my judge and maker and you are my boss, I do not![6]

Later, Gitlow makes a concise statement of his attitude toward standing up to fight like a man. He states that running ". . . emancipated more people than Abe Lincoln ever did." Gitlow says he is an "Uncle Tom." However, he is quite a different character from his namesake of *Uncle Tom's Cabin.* Gitlow creates the impression that he is an "Uncle Tom" as a means of controlling situations and achieving his goals in an environment that is set up to victimize and oppress him. So Gitlow, in spite of all his broad, earthy cliches, is a character that African-American audiences find funny, acceptable, and true. The "Uncle Tom" characters that are created by African-American playwrights generally seem to behave the way they do in order to exert some control over their own destiny. On the other hand, the "Uncle Tom" characters created by White playwrights generally appear to be motivated by the belief the characters are better off under the total control of "their White folks" than if they seek some control over their own lives. These differences in characterization grow out of different presuppositions about what constitutes truth.

Important African-American characters have been reduced to something bordering on the Uncle Tom stereotype by the introduction of a White character who seems to initiate an important action. The African-American character would be regarded as heroic if this action had been internally motivated and initiated. The specific African-American character and African-American people in general are thereby portrayed as unable to initiate actions on their own behalf or to think or speak effectively for themselves. The important action, then, appears to be conceived by Whites and either initiated or articulated by Whites. Two of the most widely seen examples of this phenomenon are the television miniseries *King,* starring Paul Winfield and the made for television motion picture *The Autobiography of Miss Jane Pittman*, starring Cicely Tyson. In both cases the presence of a White character seems to be necessary in order to initiate an action that is required for the character to consummate a key act of confrontation. The ubiquitous White liberal labor leader from New York in *King* suggests a lack of initiative and control on the part of Martin Luther King, Jr. that those people who are known to have been present during the events portrayed in that television miniseries do not recall.

In the novel by African-American writer Ernest J. Gaines, Ms. Pittman tells her own story.[7] In the screenplay by Tracy Keenan Wynn, the story appears to be told to us not by Ms. Pittman but by Quentin Lerner, the White male reporter. The nice Northern White reporter who seems to be so necessary to the telling of Miss Jane Pittman's story diminishes her status. Even the climactic moment--when Ms. Pittman drinks from the "White" water fountain at the county courthouse--is shared with Quentin Lerner. Ms. Pittman's story seems to emerge onto the screen as a result of Quentin Lerner's desire to make Ms. Pittman's story known. Her story becomes his story. The climactic scene is edited in a manner that divides the focus of attention and the suspense between two different plot elements. The dominant focus is upon whether or not Quentin Lerner will salvage his job by reaching Cape Canaveral in time to cover a space shot that his editor has told him to cover and still complete his story about Ms. Pittman. Lerner wants to provide his story about Ms. Pittman with an exciting climax. Ms. Pittman has been asked to provide a symbolic impetus to the local civil rights movement by drinking from the "White" water fountain at the county courthouse. Whether or not Ms. Pittman drinks from the "White" water fountain is diminished in importance because of the dramatic emphasis upon Lerner's petty concerns. Even when there is a character who is "known" by African Americans to have behaved heroically, the stature of the character can be significantly reduced by simply inserting a White male character who becomes the focus of an important action, or initiates it, or tells the story from his point of view. Then, the African-American character can only "be somebody" through his or her White man's identity and seems to act only because some action is required or desired by that White male.

A traditional Eurocentric point of view for the presentation of interracial marriage in English-language drama was established, no doubt inadvertently, by William Shakespeare in *Othello*. The difficulties faced by Othello in his tragic attempt to assimilate into White society established a tone that has continued to permeate the work of subsequent White playwrights who treat interracial marriage or persons with mixed-race parentage as subject matter. Out of this tradition has emerged a character genre, appearing in serious plays by both African-American and White playwrights, that has come to be labeled the "tragic mulatto" type. Such characters, of mixed-race parentage, are usually of light complexion. But they differ from other African-Americans of light complexion in that "tragic mulatto" types have a strong urge to join the White world. This urge is generally associated with a desire to identify strongly with the White parent. Inevitably, the mulatto character is rejected by White society, and pain and suffering follow. The dramatic conflict is usually triggered by a White lover or a White parent.

African-American playwrights who have written about tragic mulattoes have focused upon the negative impact of the mulatto character on other African-American people. The mulatto character who wants to be accepted by Whites is not regarded as a hero in an Afrocentric play. Instead, the hero is the African-American mother, brother, or sister who recognizes his or her African-American identity and survives by refusing to identify too strongly with the White parent or lover, while the tragic mulatto character does not. Two examples of such plays are *Mulatto* by Langston Hughes and *Ti Yette* by John Matheus. What happens to these tragic mulatto types is not a genetic accident. They are regarded as human beings with problems and their problems usually include other people's reactions to their color and their mixed parentage. They simply deal with their problems, as best they can, from within the context of their values.

On the other hand, plays by White authors with mulatto characters communicate, by implication, that the so-called mixed blood creates conflicts in and of itself. A sort of genetic dissonance controls their lives. Within one human body, the White playwrights seem to say, are two different natures in conflict with each other--the primitive nature of the mulatto's African ancestry and the civilized nature of his White ancestry. The tragedy of these mulatto characters seems to grow out of their inability to overcome their primitive side. Or, in some of the more sophisticated treatments, their tragedy grows out of White society's assumptions about their "African blood", coupled with their unswerving desire to assimilate into White society.

White plays about mulattoes fail to recognize that African Americans have not systematically ostracized people who were culturally African American and of mixed parentage. Further, when non-African-American individuals have sought to assimilate into African-American society, the African-American societal response has generally been one of guarded acceptance. African-American aesthetic values dictate that the tragic mulatto type is neither tragic nor heroic. Since European-American society eventually confronts African-American people who seek to assimilate with violent rejectior African-American people who feel a compulsive urge to en White society are regarded by most African Americar pathetic, as sick, as victims of the myth of White superiority, but certainly not as a heroes.

BLACK THEATRE

The presentation of an African-American hero who achieves his goals usually makes a legitimate positive statement to an African-American audience. But an Afrocentric play may also make a legitimate positive statement to an African-American audience by portraying one or more African-American characters who fail. *Ceremonies in Dark Old Men* by Lonnie Elder is a sensitively detailed character study of an African-American family. But none of the characters can be regarded as heroic because the characters in *Ceremonies in Dark Old Men* fail to exert any real control over their own destinies. Instead, they succumb to the oppressiveness of their environment, even though the characters possess the requisites to emerge as captains of their own fate. They own and operate their own barber shop. They are all reasonably intelligent and they all exhibit some momentary indication of survival capability. Despite these occasional glimmers of potential, they all manage to fail beyond any hope of redemption.

Ceremonies in Dark Old Men achieves a positive goal by focusing upon the negative. Since these characters could have succeeded, the audience must be concerned with what happened to cause such a monumental failure. To the extent that the audience gains insights into the forces that generate the downfall of the entire Parker family, the play is successful. Some plays portray negative examples of African-American characters in an effort to cause African-American audience members to gain the insight to avoid similar negative circumstances.

For some people, both Black and White, plays with heroes are unrealistic. Many actual situations are not populated with heroes but are worthy, nevertheless, of presentation. Some plays without heroes seem to suggest that the human spirit seldom if ever rises above the level of the situation being dramatized. Other plays without heroes seem to suggest that

AFROCENTRIC CHARACTERIZATION

"here is a negative situation that could be made more positive," but the audience is expected to supply the link to the positive. In truth, all situations do not work themselves out so that everyone lives happily ever after. Moreover, in real life, we are at least as likely to learn from our negative experiences as from our positive ones. In order to determine the difference between positive and negative presentations from an Afrocentric point of view, one must address issues that are more complex than whether or not the African-American protagonist prevails before the play ends or whether or not an important African-American character causes laughter.

Black people in America exist in an environment of institutional racism. Those who are not compelled to suffer the consequences of institutional racism on a continual basis generally fail to recognize the severity of its impact. When a character in an African-American play decides to risk pain and suffering or death for what White critics regard as no apparent reason, those White critics may be exhibiting a lack of awareness of African-American existence. When they say "the character is not properly motivated," Eurocentric critics do not appreciate that being Black and living in the U.S.A. can provide motivation enough.

James Baldwin's *Blues for Mr. Charlie* provides an example of an African-American character who chooses to confront the forces that seek to take away his human dignity. Although Richard Henry may not possess all of the requisite characteristics for status as a hero, he provides an excellent example of how institutional racism can collide with an actual occurrence. Both the actual character, Emmitt Till, and Baldwin's fictional character, Richard Henry, undoubtedly appear to some to lack sufficient motivation to decide to collide with institutional racism in a manner that will lead to pain, suffering and probably death. James Baldwin says that his play *Blues for Mr. Charlie* ". . . is based, very distantly indeed, on the case of Emmitt Till--the Negro youth who was murdered in Mississippi in 1955."[8] After the man who was indicted for Till's murder was acquitted, he claimed, as best we can recall, that after confronting Till for whistling at a White woman, Till's behavior was so "uppity" that his death was necessary in order to maintain the honor of White folks. He insisted that he did not want to kill Till, but that Till left him no choice. Emmitt Till was murdered because he challenged institutional racism in his own very small and personal way. But his small personal confrontation with oppression and the exploration of this phenomenon by James Baldwin may shed some light on larger issues.

James Baldwin explores a larger picture than the individual African-American youth who challenged the racist traditions of a specific time and place. Baldwin explores the picture of institutional racism from a variety of points of view. He examines the incident not only from several African-American points of view and a White liberal point of view, but from the point of view of the White racist who murders Richard Henry, as well. James Baldwin has sought to illuminate the concept that White people who commit demonic deeds within the context of institutional racism are not necessarily demonic individuals. Baldwin has said "No man is a villain in his own eyes."[9] More importantly, Whites who commit violent acts against African Americans do not do so because they have chosen to do wrong. They are doing what seems to them to be the right thing to do at the time, no matter how misguided their actions may be. Their behavior reflects their values. The evil, Baldwin suggests, is the system that instills racist values, not the individual who reacts to perpetuate and defend them.

The audience is more receptive to the thematic elements of a play when the characterizations reveal values that are in

222

concert with the audience's values. When members of an audience recognize traits in the behavior of the characters that reveal values that are similar to their own, the feelings and concepts that are presented are more readily accepted as truth. Afrocentric perceptions about what constitutes truth determine the truth that an Afrocentric dramatist reveals through the characters in a particular play. These perceptions are often different from those that grow out of a Eurocentric cultural perspective. Since the differences exist, assertions will no doubt continue to be made about the superiority of both Afrocentric and Eurocentric perceptions of what constitutes truth. Possibly both perceptions will come to be regarded as valid, legitimate, and appropriate for their own situations.

ENDNOTES

1.   Personal interview with the newspaper critic whose identity will not be revealed since confidentiality was requested at the time, November 8, 1971.

2.   Ralph Ellison, *Invisible Man* (New York: The New American Library, 1952), 7.

3.   Douglas Turner Ward, *Day of Absence* (New York: Dramatists Play Service, 1966), 41.

4.   Carlton and Barbara Molette, *Rosalee Pritchett* (New York: Dramatists Play Service, 1972), 4.

5.   This statement is based upon our observation of actual audience reactions to a 1976 production of *The Escape* at Texas Southern University, presented by the Theater/Cinema Area of the School of Communications.

6.   Ossie Davis, *Purlie Victorious* (New York: Samuel French, Inc., 1961), 37 and 63.

7.   Compare Ernest J. Gaines, *The Autobiography of Miss Jane Pittman* (1971; rpt. New York: Bantam, 1979); to the made for TV motion picture based on the Gaines novel, with the same title, starring Cicely Tyson, screenplay by Tracy Keenan Wynn, produced by Robert W. Christiansen and Rick Rosenberg, directed by John Korty, CBS-TV Special, 1974, video disc rpt.

8.   James Baldwin, *Blues for Mister Charlie* (New York: Dell Publishing Co., Inc., 1964), 5.

9.   Baldwin, 6.

Chapter Ten

IMAGES IN THEATRE AND MEDIA

Within the context of theatrical presentation, visual images communicate messages to the audience. Much of the traditional Eurocentric analysis of theatre art has focused upon the words of the script. But theatre art is at least as visual as it is verbal. Messages are communicated visually as well as verbally in theatre and media drama. Audiences see facial expressions, gestures, and bodily movement, as well as the clothing, jewelry, and makeup that adorn the performers and the objects that create the performance environment. These visual elements are at least as important an aspect of creating theatre as the words that are spoken. The apparent emphasis upon words as opposed to the visual elements of theatre, in an analysis of a play, grows out of the traditional European-American approach to the classification of theatre as a sub-category of literature. Thus, persons who are trained in the analysis of literature, more often than not, have been regarded as the appropriate specialists for the analysis of theatre. Literature specialists are usually astute enough to analyze those elements of theatre that they are best prepared to analyze while ignoring those elements of theatre (the visual ones) in which they have less interest or are less well equipped to analyze, or both.

The adage "seeing is believing" is as true as it is trite. Whereas words may be powerfully persuasive, visual perception of an occurrence is regarded as proof. Widespread use of the term "eye witness," rather than "ear witness," exemplifies the importance of visual messages. Theatre audiences are not significantly different from people in general with respect to the relative value of "eye witness" and "ear witness" perceptions in ascertaining a sense of truth or at least plausibility.

What we see is at least as dependent upon psychological factors as upon physical ones. One such psychological factor is that individuals acquire a set of visual cues that allow them to categorize what they see quickly and easily. One use of this psychological phenomenon is the creation of the illusion of three dimensions in a two dimensional painting or photograph or stage setting. The laws of perspective describe the basic visual cues that people employ to determine relative distance in the third dimension. Experience with these visual cues teaches that parallel lines appear to converge at a point on the horizon. A person knows that, as he looks down a highway, the highway does not actually get narrower in the distance and the telegraph poles do not actually get shorter as the distance increases. Instead, the illusion of diminishing size is interpreted to mean increasing distance. This visual cue is a learned one. A person who has not had sufficient visual experience to establish the illusion of linear perspective might assume that the road actually narrowed and the telegraph poles actually got shorter. Instead, the illusion of diminishing size is interpreted to signify increasing distance. Further, one who has had no previous experience with these visual cues or with color, would, no doubt, assume that the apparently purple mountains in the distance are actually purple.

Another example of visual cues in operation is the notion that all African-American people look alike. African-American people do not think that all African-American people look alike, just as Asians do not think that all Asians look alike. On the other hand, some African-American people and some Asian people believe that all Caucasian people look alike.

Such notions have a logical explanation. Experience develops a perceptual shorthand that enables a person to distinguish the characteristics that make one individual look different from others of similar appearance. Since this perceptual shorthand is learned, it functions badly or not at all when one sees characteristics that are foreign to one's experience. In spite of the greater amount of attention that is paid to persons with unfamiliar visual characteristics, subtle differences between such persons are more difficult to perceive and describe. For example, White Americans are usually able to describe variations in skin color among White Americans. When a White American uses the word "dark" to describe a person's complexion, he usually means dark for a White person. "Olive" and "swarthy" are two other words that might be used to describe the same complexion. On the other hand, a Black American would normally describe the same complexion as "light" or "bright" or "high yellow." Within the realm of normative experience, each describes the complexion accurately, although one calls it a light complexion and the other calls it a dark complexion.

In the early 1960's, photographs on identification cards had not yet become commonplace. Identification cards then often contained verbal descriptions instead of photographs. One of the standard verbal descriptors was "complexion." At least one very liberal midwestern university inserted the word "light" in the space on their student identification cards reserved for a description of the complexion of all students then called Negroes. This rather bizarre policy probably resulted from a scenario in which one or more African-American students of light complexion by Afrocentric standards were officially proclaimed to be dark by the White staff members making the decisions and entering the information on the students' identification cards. One or more African-American students undoubtedly objected. In those days, "dark" was not regarded as a complimentary designation. An informal comparison of

227

a brown-skinned student's complexion with the verbal description "light" on his official student identification card suggests that, at least at the operational level, the university avoided potential objections by calling "Negro" students "light," regardless of their skin color. This anecdote suggests that the White staff persons either could not or would not perceive and describe significant differences in skin color among African Americans.

An individual whose visual experience is limited to persons whose skin is lighter than most African Americans, will probably encounter some difficulty in perceiving subtle variations in the complexions of most African Americans. Many White Americans have insufficient experience to see subtle variations in skin color and hair texture among African Americans. Further White Americans with this experiential deficiency exhibit little, if any, interest in increasing their visual awareness of African Americans. In order to differentiate among dark complexioned actors, these persons require more obvious visual cues than those required by persons whose experiences allow them to make more subtle distinctions. Therefore, when Whites are in control of a presentation in which more than one African-American actor appears, visual cues are frequently employed that assure distinctiveness.

The most commonly used tactic to assure distinctiveness is to exaggerate the controllable factors of the visual image of individuals. The most difficult set of factors to exaggerate is facial appearance. Clothes and personal adornments may be exaggerated with considerably less difficulty. Manners--that is visually observed behavior--may be exaggerated even more easily than clothes and personal adornments. Thus, a tradition has evolved in mainstream American theatre and media drama that allows an audience with limited visual experience to distinguish several African-American characters in a production. The behavior, clothing, and personal adornments of the African-American characters in these productions are exaggerated.

Theatrical presentations are created events that are at least as visual as they are verbal; therefore, visual elements of these presentations ought to be created with as much concern for truth as the verbal elements. Playwrights may envision an environment with rather specific visual characteristics. The specific visual details that are realized in production are normally characteristics planned collaboratively by the director and designer with the stated goal of carrying out the intent of the playwright. When the visual details of a production are "right," knowledgeable observers derive a sense of truth from the visual messages they receive. Moreover, visual messages that convey a sense of truth enhance the observer's understanding of the structure--the characters, their behavior, and the resultant thematic ideas. Visual messages that are not in harmony with other elements of the production have a negative impact upon the audience's understanding and appreciation of the whole.

Cognitive dissonance is created when other elements of the play (plot, character, theme, mood and rhythm, and language) are accompanied by visual messages that seem to be inappropriate to those who come to the production with accurate prior information about the surface details of the subject matter of the play. Cognitive harmony is especially difficult to create in mainstream theatre and media presentations with African-American characters since those Eurocentric people who are in control or in the "majority" often believe that dissonant elements are actually in harmony because of the constant repetition of exaggerated stereotypical African-American images over an extended period of time.

BLACK THEATRE

Stereotypical characters are different from the African-American actors who portray those characters. At least one organization that claims to represent African Americans has blamed some African-American actors for portraying characters that generated negative or stereotypical notions about Black people. African-American actors rarely have advance knowledge of the final editing of a feature film or television episode. Therefore, African-American actors cannot always determine what images will be presented ultimately to the audience or how those images will interrelate or how those images will be interpreted. For example, Cecily Tyson undoubtedly did not know the film *The Autobiography of Miss Jane Pittman* (discussed in Chapter nine) was going to be edited in a way that would make her appear to some viewers to be a pawn in the chess game between the White newspaper reporter and his editor. To blame African-American actors for negative images is to blame the victim for the crime.

The "Buckwheat" character that Eddie Murphy created on the television program *Saturday Night Live* has a certain comic potential if you KNOW the characterization is "wrong." This knowledge allows one to see beneath the surface of the outrageously negative stereotype and recognize that Murphy is lampooning the stereotypical portrayal of the "Buckwheat" character of *The Little Rascals* and *Our Gang* series of motion pictures. For example, a White person who has not been exposed to real visual images of African-American people but who has been regularly exposed to the stereotypical visual images of African-American people presented in dramas via television, motion pictures and live theatre is likely to fail to appreciate the comic irony of Murphy's portrayal of "Buckwheat." In order to appreciate this comic irony, one must know that the visual images being lampooned by Murphy only existed in the minds of the White people who were in control of the series of motion pictures and the White audiences for such motion pictures. This knowledge allows one to recognize that Eddie Murphy is not making fun of an African-American child or of African-American children in general. This recognition then makes it possible to find humor in Eddy Murphy's lampoon of the monumental ignorance and prejudice of the White folks who created and perpetuated this aberration named "Buckwheat" as well as the other numerous pickaninny characters and the White audiences who love these pickaninnies and believe them to be a true representation of African-American children.

A Gallup poll conducted to determine the winners of the *Tenth Annual People's Choice Awards*, a CBS-TV Special presented on March 15, 1984, indicates that Michael Jackson, Emmanuel Lewis, and Mr. T. were mainstream America's favorite African-American characters at that time. This poll was the last such Gallup Poll not to be influenced by the phenomenon of *The Cosby Show*, which premiered the following September. The poll further indicates that White America's favorite television programs included several with major continuing characters who are Black. In addition to *Webster* with Emmanuel Lewis and *The A-Team* with Mr. T., the other television program in the top three in the "Favorite Overall New Television Program" category was *Hotel*, with a continuing African-American character who plays the hotel's security officer. This character is remarkably similar to the major African-American continuing characters in *Hill Street Blues*. Among the top three "Favorite Comedy" and "Favorite Dramatic" categories, the only television program with major continuing characters who are Black is *Hill Street Blues*. One African-American person is included in the top three in the "Favorite All Around Male Entertainer" category--Michael Jackson. In addition, all three of the top three "Favorite Music Video" titles are by Michael Jackson. No African-American females were in any of the "Favorite" categories.[1]

The results of this Gallup poll suggest that the aberrant African-American character that Whites seem to have the greatest desire to see and is most often seen on prime time television is the male who appears to be completely asexual, dominated by a White person, or both. Mammy stereotypes are also asexual but are expected to be assertive. African-American female character stereotypes who are maids are not totally submissive in the way that similar African-American male character stereotypes are. Coincidentally, African-American female characters were not as likely to be regarded as "favorite" among the cross section of "mainstream" Americans who named the previously mentioned African-American males as their "favorites." Traditional Uncle Tom stereotypes are both submissive and asexual. The organized objections of African-American people to the old stereotypical images of African-American people, along with the growing sophistication of White audiences, demanded the emergence of a new Uncle Tom character in the 1980's. This new Uncle Tom was new only with respect to a few surface features. His pattern of behavior and motivation did not change. New visual features were added to avoid the objections to the old Uncle Tom stereotype. The new visual image is not that of an elderly man, but a male child. This African-American male child, as a result of some bizarre set of circumstances, lives in the house of a White male. The African-American child is almost totally divorced from close personal contact with other African-American people.

Incidentally, some evidence must be present in the plot to dispel any thoughts that the White male is homosexual. This relationship is sharply portrayed as that of father and son-- White father, Black son. This classic "big me, little you" relationship permits a degree of White domination to which the well-known Uncle Tom stereotypes of earlier eras seldom descended. The potential for visual reinforcement of the "big me, little you" relationship was exploited through the use of

232

such techniques as positioning the camera and the actors to emphasize the contrast in size on the television screen. Optical illusions were created by selecting a longer focal length for the camera lens, thereby causing a character standing in the foreground to appear larger in comparison to a character standing farther away from the lens. In addition, unusually small African-American children were presented with White males who were larger than average. This visual contrast, along with such other characteristics as the relatively high soft voice that is usually present in diminutive male children, created a basis for comparing African-American and White male images that proved to be exceedingly popular among the masses of White Americans. In the Gallup poll that preceded the March 1986 People's Choice Awards television program, the dominance of *The Cosby Show* was evident. However, Emmanuel Lewis remained a solid favorite in the "Favorite Young Television Performer" category. Of course, the child actors in *Webster* and *Diff'rent Strokes* were cute and talented; they also portrayed characters who were fundamentally subservient to a White male.

Other variations of this Uncle Tom of the 1980's stereotype were evident. One such variation is the jive genie of the short-lived *Just Our Luck* television series. The jive genie did not have to be diminutive in size, age, or vocal quality. This Black genie, like other such mythological creatures, exists only to fulfill his master's fantasies. Total domination, again, is visually reinforced by the behavior that the genie exhibits as he bows, scrapes, and scurries about seeking to carry out his master's wishes. Further, since genies are spirits, they are sexually safe in the sense that the kind of stable relationship that leads to marriage, child rearing, and the perpetuation of values is unthinkable. The jive genie belongs to another major variation of the Uncle Tom of the 1980's stereotype, the Black eunuch.

BLACK THEATRE

A eunuch is a male with the physical attributes and the combat skills to guard a harem as well as the asexuality to be trusted to guard a harem. Eunuchs are highly reliable and loyal as well, because they have no families of their own to provide a basis for personal ambitions that might conflict with the goals of the man whose orders they execute. All Uncle Tom stereotypes may be totally trusted to avoid even the appearance of sexuality in the presence of White people. In addition, the Uncle Tom of the 1980's who is a eunuch is usually big, strong, and muscular to the extreme. Feats of strength, loyalty and even technocratic skill were frequently exhibited by the Black eunuch stereotype. But these visually virile African-American males perform their feats of strength, loyalty and skill on orders from their particular White male leader. The White man's orders are never questioned by the eunuch. The television series *The A Team* provided the most popular example of the Black eunuch stereotype during the 1980's.

The award-winning *Hill Street Blues* television series presents a much more sophisticated approach to the eunuch stereotype. The African-American male continuing characters on *Hill Street Blues* were undoubtedly among the most fully drawn African-American characterizations created prior to September, 1984, in a series that has survived on network television for a season or more. Ordinary observation suggests legitimate, mature, masculine male images of African-American policemen. They have the physical attributes and the combat skills to be competent policemen. Their characterizations as policemen are as three-dimensional as the others on this series. But some Whites on the police force on *Hill Street Blues* reveal relationships with parents, with children, and with spouses or lovers through visual images as well as through dialogue. Although the White relationships are not ideal, the Blacks on the series reveal no such relationships. An African-American policeman does not have,

234

for example, a continuing mature relationship with a woman. The African-American policemen on *Hill Street Blues* have exotic, picturesque affairs to provide evidence for the audience that they are heterosexual. The audience needs to know that the African-American policemen are not homosexual, only because their close friendship and loyalty to some White policemen might cause the audience to doubt the masculinity of the White policemen. The African-American policemen have exotic, picturesque affairs with African-American women who are the tragic mulatto stereotypes of the 1980's. They are prostitutes and drug addicts who die within a few episodes. The African-American men and women on *Hill Street Blues* were not shown in familial situations that provide models for ensuring cultural stability or perpetuating a set of traditions that will promote their spiritual and physical survival. The only memorable African-American mother character in the series was a drug addict who was clearly unable to care for her child. Of course the boy's father was noticeably absent and unmentioned. The boy's only hope for survival seemed to be his foster parent--a single White policewoman.

The Cosby Show premiered in the fall of 1984. The series was ranked number three in the 1984-85 season by the A. C. Nielsen Company. In the four consecutive seasons that followed, *The Cosby Show* was ranked number one in the Nielsen Ratings with a larger percentage share of the television viewing audience than any other show in the history of television. In the 1989-90 season, the show held a strong number two spot and finished in fifth place for the 1990-91 season. An additional indication of the popularity of *The Cosby Show* is its ability to retain viewers for the time slot that follows. In the time slot following *The Cosby Show*, the show's spinoff, *A Different World*, was ranked number two in 1987-88, its premiere season and number four in the 1989-90 season. In the history of television, *All in the Family* and *I*

Love Lucy are the only comedies to achieve a similar degree of commercial success to *The Cosby Show*. The only non-comedy programs to achieve a similar level of success have been *Gunsmoke*, *Bonanza*, and *Dallas*. Thus, since the 1985-86 season, *The Cosby Show* has been the standard by which success in television programming is measured.[2]

Prior to the emergence of *The Cosby Show* as arguably the most popular series in television history, there seems to have been no successful (long running) television series with African-American characters unless there was at least one Black stereotype among the major characters. Many people have asserted that *The Cosby Show*, in addition to its other accolades, is the first successful television series that portrays African-American characters who are free of the old stereotypes. Further, *The Cosby Show* lists in its credits a consultant whose job is to insure that the African-American images that are presented are positive ones. Whereas Bill Cosby has gone to great lengths to portray positive images of African Americans, issues with which we are concerned here do not hinge on the producer's intentions but on the perceptions of the millions of White television viewers who have regularly watched *The Cosby Show*, and who have made the show the most phenomenal financial success in television history. The show's continued popularity is evident by its designation as favorite in the Comedy Series category of the People's Choice Awards in 1992. Further, Bill Cosby was named the favorite in the Male Performer category for 1992.[3]

Prior to the 1984-85 season, large numbers of White television viewers have been consistent in their support of television drama with African-Americans as major continuing characters only when at least one such character has conformed to some variation of a traditional African-American stereotype. Why then is there such spectacular support for *The Cosby Show*? It is because millions of White viewers are receiving a message that producer Bill Cosby did not intentionally send. Millions of White viewers are receiving a message that fits within their comfort level. To obtain this level of comfort with African-American characters for millions of White viewers has previously required that a television series focus significant attention upon at least one stereotypical character. The existence of this comfort level for White viewers is further complicated because significant numbers of African-American viewers have generally objected to the presence of stereotypes in other television programs; yet there has been no such widespread objection to *The Cosby Show.*

One must understand the Eurocentric tradition of the fool as a dramatic device in order to understand how millions of White viewers manage to receive a message that differs from the message that *The Cosby Show* seeks to send, and apparently differs from the one that many African Americans receive. The fool or court jester in Medieval Europe was a person with a special relationship to a king or other lord of a Medieval manor. By dressing and acting the part of the fool, a court jester was able to speak bluntly and frankly to the lord of the manor. Thus, a person of lower rank, who developed a relationship with a king or other lord of a manor that tolerated blunt and frank remarks within a context of humor, might be called the king's fool even if the person was not a court jester by trade.

The Eurocentric tradition of the fool as a dramatic device is exemplified by the character Falstaff in Shakespeare's *The Merry Wives of Windsor* and *King Henry IV, part Two.* Falstaff was the "sidekick" for Prince Hal, functioning as his fool. As a Eurocentric hero, Prince Hal was never hungry or sleepy or afraid. As Hal's alter ego, Falstaff experienced all of the human frailties that Eurocentric heroes must not exhibit. This convention allows the dramatist to indicate that the hero is in danger or tired or hungry without forcing the hero to exhibit these frailties himself. In the twentieth century, motion picture Westerns have made extensive use of the fool as a character type and have conveyed the concept to a much larger audience than the one that saw Shakespeare's plays. Gabby Hays was a sidekick to Roy Rogers; Pat Buttram was with Gene Autry; Edgar Buchanan, as Red Connors, rode with Hopalong Cassidy; Tonto, played by Jay Silverheels, had a "kimosabe" called The Lone Ranger; and Leo Carillo, as Poncho, was the sidekick of the Cisco Kid. These sidekicks provided comic relief in the roles of the fool.

In addition to the fool character type, a stereotype of the African-American fool character or the coon has also evolved in the U.S.A. This stereotypical fool is often said to have been originated by Thomas "Jim Crow" Rice. Rice was a White vaudeville performer who impersonated an African-American character who danced and sang a song called "Jump Jim Crow." Rice was said to have based his impersonation on a Black youngster he once saw singing and dancing. Rice had not been very successful as a performer until he began doing this stereotypical imitation of an African-American youth by wearing rags and blackening his face with burnt cork. Subsequently, "Jim Crow" Rice was an enormous success in the U.S.A. and England in the 1830's and 1840's.

Numerous examples of the coon stereotype appeared in motion pictures and in live performances from the mid-1830's through the first half of the twentieth century. Nearly all of the early coon stereotypes were played by White actors in blackface. While the 1950's saw a few White actors continuing to perform their coon routines in blackface, most of these roles were played by African Americans by the advent of network television. Some of these coon stereotypes were used as dramatic devices to provide a context for contrast with the hero in the manner of the traditional Eurocentric fool character type, while other coon stereotypical characters were presented solely to make fun of persons of African descent.

One of the best known examples of the coon stereotype as a contrasting device for the hero is Mantan Moreland as Birmingham Brown in the *Charlie Chan* motion picture series. And we have already mentioned Eddie Anderson as Rochester, Jack Benny's servant on radio, television, and motion pictures. Examples of the coon stereotype in which no dramatic purpose is served other than to make fun of African Americans include Lightning in the *Amos 'n Andy* show on radio and television. Lawyer Calhoun on the same show did not have the literacy to pass a high school English course; yet he was alleged to be a practicing attorney. The Calhoun character eventually became a businessman after years of protest from the National Bar Association. Traditionally, the coon stereotype has tended to be fearful, docile, and lazy whereas Toms have tended to be endowed with an abundance of loyalty and obedience that allows them to defend "their" White folks if necessary.

Since the 1950's the adventure-drama sidekicks have become more sophisticated; their "foolish" antics now tend to be more verbal and less physical. The television series *McCloud* was about a White Western marshall who was assigned to the New York Police Department. Marshall McCloud had a Black sidekick whose function within the dramatic structure was the function traditionally assigned to the fool. McCloud's sidekick worried about him when he was in great danger or violated police procedures or performed some outrageous feat in order to save someone (usually a "fair maiden") in distress or capture the bad guys. Marshall McCloud's sidekick was a competent, slightly conservative, highly professional police detective who also happened to be African American. This character did not exhibit any of the overt characteristics that African Americans had complained about in pre-1960's characters. He spoke with good diction. Neither his behavior nor his clothing was exaggerated. He appeared to have the intelligence and the competence to do his job. Thus, his function was structurally that of the fool, but he was not a fool in the contemporary sense of the word. The television audience laughed at Joe Broadhurst because he was the opposite of the hero. McCloud was relaxed, dressed casually, spoke with a regional dialect, and was unconventional in every possible way. Joe Broadhurst never relaxed, always wore a coat and tie, did not speak with a dialect, and was conventional in every possible way. McCloud's total disregard for the conventional values that Broadhurst held in such high esteem worried and embarrassed Broadhurst.

Hawk in *Spencer for Hire* also functioned structurally as a fool, but with reverse English. Although Spencer's uniqueness as a TV series detective was his cultivated interior beneath the "blue collar" exterior, his fool was still required to provide the contrast to the hero that fools traditionally provide. Since Spencer's character was the opposite of most television series detectives in that he showed his feelings and his vulnerability, then Hawk was required to do the opposite of what most fools do and not show his feelings. Once this traditional structural function of the fool in Eurocentric drama is understood, then a number of factors about images of African Americans in television drama become clearer. For example, the use of extraordinary costumes is in keeping with the tradition of the court jester. Hawk, in contrast to Spencer, wore costumes that called attention to themselves--expensive Italian silk suits worn with silk turtleneck shirts, a white leather full-length coat, a hat, leather gloves, and the ever present sunglasses. B. A. Barracus, the sidekick of Hannibal on *The A-Team*, was even more bizarre in his appearance. His haircut, clothes, and excessive gold jewelry provided an even clearer contemporary parallel to the traditional court jester.

IMAGES IN THEATRE AND MEDIA

In television situation comedies about a family, the role of the fool is traditionally portrayed by the father. This tradition goes back to the pre-television era when the most popular comedies about a family were *Dagwood* of the newspaper comic strips, and *The Life of Riley* and *The Adventures Ozzie and Harriet* on the radio. The prototype television family, *The Adventures of Ozzie and Harriet*, began as a radio program in 1944, moved to television in 1952, and continued on ABC television until 1966. Although the father character appeared to be enthusiastically stupid in many television situation comedies, such shows as *The Adventures of Ozzie and Harriet* and *Father Knows Best* portrayed fathers as intelligent and competent while still making the humor grow out of the manner in which the father contrasts with one or more other members of the family. In general, the father in such American television situation comedies is portrayed as rigid and a bit pompous while other members of the family are more flexible and down-to-earth in their approach to the various situations that the family confronts. Thus, a large part of the humor in such television programs grows out of the father's inflexibility and pomposity.

Continuing in the tradition of the father functioning in the dramatic structure as the contrasting element out of which the humor grows, emerged *The Cosby Show* in 1984. However, Bill Cosby was not the first African-American father character to elicit humor in this manner. Redd Foxx in *Sanford and Son* first appeared on NBC in 1972 solidly in the tradition of the father character functioning structurally as the fool. *Sanford and Son* provided a father character who was a junk dealer; whereas, the father on *The Cosby Show* is a medical doctor. Further, Fred Sanford was more exaggerated than Heathcliff Huxtable in his rigidity and his pomposity as well as his other character traits from which humor was derived. Nevertheless, both Fred Sanford and Dr. Huxtable are clearly a part of the tradition of the father functioning as the fool within the structure of the American television situation comedy. Both Fred Sanford and Dr. Huxtable have established a high level of acceptability among both Black and White television viewers. The acceptability of Fred Sanford among Whites seemed to center on Sanford's occupation. He operated a junk yard. Thus, his socio-economic status did not threaten White television viewers. Further, Fred Sanford's age rendered him non-threatening insofar as his male sexuality was concerned. Dr. Cliff Huxtable on the other hand appears to be a virile Black male as evidenced by both the size of his family and his relationship with his wife. In addition, his occupation renders him both intellectually and economically capable of making choices in his own best interest and in the best interest of his family without help or advice from any White person. Thus, Dr. Huxtable is not an Uncle Tom. Hence, his popularity among Black audiences.

One cannot exclude the immense talent of Bill Cosby as at least a part of the explanation for the tremendous success of *The Cosby Show* among both Black and White television viewers. On the other hand, several notable African-American male characters have not survived on network television because they provided a strong virile African-American male image. The leading African-American male characters on such shows as *Bay City Blues*, played by Bernie Casey; *Frank's Place*, played by Tim Reid; and *Good Times*, played by John Amos come to mind. In the case of *Good Times*, the show survived but the father character did not. The Eurocentric tradition of the fool as a dramatic device may explain why Dr. Huxtable is acceptable to Whites and yet the fact that he is clearly not an Uncle Tom also makes him more acceptable to many Blacks than most of the available alternatives. Dr. Huxtable is acceptable to Whites because they can laugh at him--no matter how successful he is. He therefore poses no threat. Instead, the comfort level of Whites is increased because Dr. Huxtable is seen by Whites in a role that they associate with the tradition of family situation comedy in which the father functions structurally as the fool.

Dr. Heathcliff Huxtable is acceptable (comparatively speaking) to Blacks because he exists in a Black environment. We see him with Black friends and family. His relationship with his wife provided the first such image to sustain in a television series. He is not made to look inferior to Whites either socioeconomically or as the butt of their jokes. He is not a pathetic character in the sense that he is unable to cope with the larger society in some significant way. Dr. Huxtable is only the butt of the jokes of his own family and friends and in a manner that does not cause him to seem inferior in order to derive humor. Nevertheless, the Cosby show provides "ordinary" Whites with sustenance for their stereotypical and racist views of Blacks by providing an opportunity to laugh at a Black man--even when the Black male character is portrayed as making more money and having more influence and status than they do.

The immense popularity of *The Cosby Show* seems to have provided opportunities for other African-American characters to appear in a prime time television network series. Buoyed by the success of *The Cosby Show* in 1984, the networks introduced several prime time series programs with predominately African-American casts. *Charlie & Co.*, starring Flip Wilson, premiered on CBS in the fall of 1985. Jaleel White who later achieved stardom as Steve Urkel on *Family Matters* played Flip Wilson's son on this series. Although Flip Wilson had hosted a very successful comedy-variety hour, *The Flip Wilson Show*, for four years (number two in the Nielsen Ratings for the 1970-71 and 1971-72 seasons), *Charlie & Co.* had difficulty sustaining the entire 1985-86 season and the series was not renewed for a second season.

Frank's Place premiered in the fall of 1987. This series was set in New Orleans and starred Tim Reid and Daphne Maxwell Reid. African-American playwright Samm-Art Williams was employed as story editor for this series. The restaurant setting provided an opportunity for presenting characters from a variety of walks of life who are among the most fascinating array of humanity, African American or otherwise, ever congregated into a television series. While the plots were entertaining and humorous, the strength of the series was the engrossing conglomeration of characters who inhabited Frank's recently inherited restaurant. *Frank's Place* is without a doubt our favorite network television series ever.

Despite its critical acclamation as one of the best shows of the 1987-88 season, the show was canceled following its first and only season in which the time slot for the series was changed four times.[4] The poor ratings that prompted canceling *Frank's Place* could have been due to the difficulty the show's audience had in adjusting to its erratic schedule or to the discomfort White viewers had in accepting a broad array of well defined African-American characters or both. Although *Charlie & Co.*, *Frank's Place*, and other shows with an array of well defined non-stereotypical African-American characters premiered in the years following the first year of *The Cosby Show*, none of these shows were able to sustain a sufficiently large audience to compel renewal for a second season.

Family Matters premiered in the fall of 1989. In the first season the emphasis of *Family Matters* was centered on the domestic activities of the Winslow family--father, mother, their three children, grandmother, and the recently widowed sister of the mother and her young son. At first, *Family Matters* seemed destined to travel the road of *Charlie & Co.* and *Frank's Place*. However, by the beginning of the second season the focus of the show had changed significantly. The obnoxious next door neighbor, Steve Urkel, a Black teenaged male, became the center of attention. The character of Steve Urkel emerged as an update of the traditional coon stereotype. Donald Bogle describes the traditional coon stereotype as ". . . those unreliable, crazy, lazy, subhuman creatures good for nothing more than eating watermelons, stealing chickens, shooting crap, or butchering the English language."[5]

One of the traditional plot devices of the early coons was to have them pursue and be rebuffed by a woman who was obviously deserving of something better than a coon. Steve Urkel began as the intellectual nerd next door pursuing Laura Winslow, the teenage daughter of the Winslows. Naturally, Laura rebuffed Steve at every opportunity. Response from White viewers during the first season of *Family Matters* revealed a potential gold mine for the series. Thus, the change in focus from the Winslow family to the buffoonery of Steve Urkel in much the same manner as the shift in focus in 1974 and 1975 on the *Good Times* series from the parents played by John Amos and Esther Rolle to their son, J.J., a coon stereotype played by Jimmy Walker.

The 1990's variation of the coon stereotype as seen in the Steve Urkel character has greater negative potential than the more traditional coon stereotype. The potential for greater negative impact comes from the shift from a character whose laziness and ignorance generates laughter to a character who generates laughter because he is smart, dedicated, and exhibits considerable initiative. Thus, the Steve Urkel character reinforces the message that America sends to young Black males: Black males are not expected to excel in intellectual pursuits; further, those young Black males who do excel in intellectual pursuits are destined to be objects of ridicule by the society as a whole and especially by young Black females.

This Black male character who excels in school presents a thoroughly laughable visual and auditory image. He speaks in a high-pitched nasal voice while most African-American males cultivate a low resonant vocal tone as soon as they are physiologically able to do so. He also needs very thick glasses, wears his trousers several inches above the level that would be considered normal and acceptable, and carries his body in a manner that is exactly the opposite posture that young Black males generally have sought to achieve. Whereas Steve Urkel's typical mode of dress and body movement could reasonably be characterized as contrary to the desired visual image of most Black teenagers, his appearance frequently becomes far more ludicrous. For example, the episode that aired on Valentine's Day, 1992, presented Steve Urkel as cupid clad in a skin-tight pink body suit over which he wore white boxer shorts with large red hearts. Atop his head was a curly blonde wig. In spite of the excellent character portrayals by the other cast members, White viewers do not see a domestic situation comedy; White viewers see a coon show. Further, White viewers are comforted by the image of Black manhood that Steve Urkel presents.

Ironically, the most popular African-American characters on a prime time network television series, other than the obviously stereotypical characters and those on *The Cosby Show* and its spin-off *A Different World*, seem to appear in a context in which most of the principal characters are White. Thus, these African-American characters are not generally presented in an environment in which complex relationships with other African Americans are portrayed. Further, the importance of each of these African-American characters is diminished for White viewers by presenting the African-American character and his or her goals in an environment in which White characters and their goals clearly prevail. For example, the television series *In the Heat of the Night* is based upon a group of characters and a locale created in several feature films that starred Sidney Potier as Virgil Tibbs, a successful big-city policeman and Rod Steiger as the chief of police in the small Mississippi town of Sparta in which Virgil Tibbs was born and reared.

In the television series, Virgil Tibbs and his wife Althea provide a view of a mature African-American marriage in which both husband and wife have jobs that, while less affluent than the Huxtables, require intelligence, initiative, and a college education. Further, each character is portrayed as dedicated and caring both in the workplace and in their relationship with each other. However, the episodes do not focus on Virgil and Althea Tibbs; they are a small part of a much larger picture. The series focuses on the entire town of Sparta, Mississippi, its police department, and the sundry murders and other crimes that are requisite to a prime time television detective series. Thus, Virgil and Althea Tibbs are seen in a context in which White characters prevail in numbers and in power.

When African Americans receive a positive message in terms of the portrayal of an African-American character on television, they tend to presume that White people who see the same television program receive the same message they receive. This presumption may be in error. Thus, African Americans may see a program in which an African-American husband and wife are portrayed in a manner that is acceptable from an African American point of view, while millions of White viewers are able to enjoy this television series without having their stereotypical views about African Americans disturbed in any significant way. Despite the portrayal of several African-American characters who apparently break the tradition of African-American dramatic stereotypes, *In the Heat of the Night* was selected as one of the top three programs in the People's Choice awards favorite television Dramatic Series category.[6]

Further, the winner in that category, *L.A. Law*, presents an African-American male attorney, Jonathan Rollins, as a continuing character who seems not to be a stereotypical character but upon closer examination is a continuation of the "supernegro" tradition of African-American stereotypes. This "supernegro" tradition is a modernization of the noble savage stereotype and is most notably exemplified by Sidney Potier in such films as *Guess Who's Coming to Dinner?* and *Brother John*. *L.A. Law*'s massive popularity among White television viewers appears to continue the pattern of earlier decades in which White audiences demanded African-American characters who did not disturb their established stereotypical views of African Americans. We have occasionally seen Jonathan Rollins in relationships with his parents and with African-American women. However, these other African Americans are not continuing characters; thus, their impact upon the popularity of the series is minimal. What initially appeared to be a romantic relationship between the African-American attorney and an attractive African-American woman who was enrolled in law school turned out to be a presentation of two additional contemporary African-American stereotypes. She was in the process of divorcing her husband, making her a single parent stereotype. More significantly, her soon-to-be ex-husband was portrayed as a violent anti-intellectual who did not want his wife to go to law school because it heightened his awareness of his own failure as a breadwinner.

While Jonathan Rollins' relationship with other African Americans seems fleeting at best, *L.A. Law* has exploited still another contemporary stereotypical image of African-American males by placing this handsome, successful, affluent Black man in a torrid romance with a White woman. Thus, America's favorite law firm has hired one Hispanic man and one African-American man and each of these super-successful men of color has eventually found love and happiness with a

White woman. The theme of these two plot threads in the *L.A. Law* series suggests that connection to a White lover allows persons of color to achieve personhood in the White world. In *L.A. Law*, this thematic thread reminiscent of *No Place to Be Somebody* is not the main focus of the series. The characters of Jonathan Rollins and his Hispanic counterpart, Victor Sifuentes, are diminished by being placed in a context in which White characters prevail in numbers and in power.

In contrast, the beginning of the 1990's provided a look at an interracial "love affair" from the point of view of an African-American male. In Spike Lee's film *Jungle Fever*, the Black male/White female relationship is one that is more of the hormones than of the heart. The thematic element of the film that focuses on the "love affair" takes a position that is essentially opposite to the theme of *No Place to be Somebody*. The audience is definitely not left with the impression that the successful young architect in *Jungle Fever* enhances his sense that he is somebody as a result of his sexual encounter with the young White secretary in the architectural firm where he is employed. Instead, the audience is left with the idea that this successful young architect achieves his personhood as a husband, father, son, brother, and friend in his totally African American "pre-jungle fever" environment. His interracial "love affair" destroys rather than enhances his personhood.

In *L.A. Law*, *In the Heat of the Night*, and several other successful television dramatic series of the early 1990's, the African-American characters are shown in an environment in which they are in the minority. Whereas, many of these characters seem less stereotypical than earlier African-American characters in prime time television dramatic series, their significance as characters is reduced in the eyes of White television viewers through the use of variations of a dramatic device that places an African-American character in a context that makes his or her goals subservient to the goals of some White person. This contextual device creates an illusion of an Uncle Tom stereotype to the extent that masses of White Americans are comfortable enough with these African-American characters to regard the television series in which they appear as among their favorite.

European-American values inspired the saying, "DOG BITES MAN is not news; but MAN BITES DOG is news." Awareness of such values may aid in understanding the non-White stereotypes that are created and perpetuated by White Americans, and superimposed by White Americans on legitimate non-White images. Portrayals of non-Whites by White Americans generally follow the trend of ignoring the normative, ignoring those things that the non-White group itself regards as better than normative, and focusing instead upon those things that are unusual and picturesque in a sub-normative direction. For example, photographs of Africans whose clothing and personal adornment is bizarre from a European-American perspective seem to have been published in *National Geographic* magazine down through the years to the virtual exclusion of the more frequent, easier to locate, and less "picturesque" peoples of Africa.

Deviant behavior is regarded as more dramatic by those who control the European-American theatre and as more newsworthy by those European Americans who control the dissemination of the news. Although this fascination with deviant behavior is likely to affect decisions about White subject matter as well as Black, the impact upon the projection of African-American images is more negative. Visual images of contemporary African Americans in stage, television, and motion picture dramas focus upon such deviant stereotypes as pimps and prostitutes, and members of street gangs with overwhelming frequency. African-American businessmen and professionals are not picturesque. Ordinary, working class

African-American people are even less picturesque. They "look White," meaning they do not blatantly deviate from the European-American norm to the extent that they may be readily and effortlessly ridiculed by virtually all White people. Joseph Papp undoubtedly produced more plays by African-American playwrights in New York than any other White producer. In contrast to this seemingly laudable accomplishment, Papp has been quoted as saying, "Whenever the black realizes that he's as fucked up as anybody else, then I say, 'Okay, I'll do the play.'"[7]

The presentation of African-American stereotypes in White controlled theatre, television, and film must be considered because of its potential impact upon African-American theatre. American society increasingly regards television images as real and true. African Americans are not immune to this phenomenon. African Americans, like White Americans and others, are controlled by television to the extent that people generally allow television to significantly influence their concepts of reality. To decide what appears on television and what does not is to decide, to a significant degree, what is real and what is not. Thus, the rest of the world is shifting its sense of what is real toward a concept of what is real according to the values of upper middle class White American and European males over the age of fifty. The members of this demographic group decide what programs all of us must watch, if we elect to watch network television, and produce most of the nationally publicized plays and motion pictures with African-American characters as well.

As time passes, the need becomes greater for presenters of Afrocentric theatre to understand the European-American stereotypical view of African Americans. Although a conscious desire to avoid the negative influences of White stereotyping seems, on the surface, to be a laudatory goal, the need to present theatre that is plausible to African-American audiences cannot be escaped. But the overwhelming impact of film and television may cause African-American audiences to regard Afrocentric truth as implausible and White mass media reality as truth. Consequently, to the degree that African-American people allow their view of what is real to be affected by White stereotyping, as expressed in mass media reality, African-American theatre may be forced, out of necessity, to shift its reality.

The familiar visual image of Mr. T. as B. A. Barracus is so obviously bizarre that it does not pose a serious threat to mature African-American people in this regard. Although the image he projects cannot help but reinforce White stereotypical notions of African-American people, there is little likelihood that even relatively unsophisticated African-American adult television viewers will regard the image of B. A. Barracus as plausible in any context other than a television action adventure fantasy. On the other hand, television also presents African-American images that are sufficiently plausible in appearance to cause Eurocentric stereotypical notions of African-American life to influence both White and Black adults' expectations of how African-American people ought to appear, both on television and in reality. Further, since media reality seems to be capable of supplanting truth, the more plausible stereotypical images of African-American people can be especially insidious in their negative impact upon African-American people's attitudes toward African-American people.

Because White America continues to be the dominant source of television programs for the Third World, this phenomenon is not restricted to Black people in the U.S.A. In the worst of scenarios for the future, Whites avoid blatant physical oppression of African Americans and provide a constant supply of the kind of African-American images regularly seen on prime time entertainment television. In this scenario, Whites have created the most effective technique for the enslavement of African-American people yet devised--Black acceptance of images of African-American people who prefer to be controlled by White people.

ENDNOTES

1.   Ann Hodges, "People make their choices," *Houston Chronicle*, 15 March 1984, Sec.5, p.6, cols. 1-3; and the display advertisement "People's Choice Awards" on the same page cols. 4-5. This material can probably be verified in the March 15, 1984, issue of any major metropolitan newspaper in the U.S.A.

2.   Alex McNeil, *Total Television* (New York: Penguin Books, 1991), 1060-1062. Data after 1989-1990 season was obtained by telephone from the research director of the NBC affiliate station in Baltimore, Maryland.

3.   "Country Singers are People's Choice," Baltimore *Sun* 19 March 1992: D1. We focus on the People's Choice Awards to the exclusion of other television awards such as the Emmy awards because the People's Choice Awards are determined by a poll conducted by the Gallup organization; whereas, most other award winners are selected by either critics, industry colleagues, or some other effort to generate what will be regarded by the general public as "expert opinion." We are interested in discovering and commenting upon the opinion of the general public rather than the opinions of industry colleagues, newspaper critics, or any other form of expert opinion.

4.   McNeil, 276.

5.   Donald Bogle, *Toms, Coons, Mulattoes, Mammies, & Bucks* (New York: The Viking Press, Inc., 1973), 8.

6.   "Country Singers . . . ," D1.

7.   Faye Levine, *The Culture Barons* (New York: Thomas Y. Crowell, 1976), 102.

BIBLIOGRAPHY

WORKS CITED

Books and Articles

Abrahams, Roger D. *Deep Down in the Jungle.* 1st rev. ed. Chicago: Aldine Publishing Company, 1970.

Abramson, Doris E. *Negro Playwrights in the American Theatre, 1925-59.* New York: Columbia University Press, 1969.

Asante, Molefi Kete. *Afrocentricity: The Theory of Social Change.* Buffalo: Amulefi Publishing Co., 1980.

_____. "Intercultural Communication: An Afrocentric Inquiry into Encounter." In *International Conference on Black Communication*, Bellagio, Italy, 1979. Ed. Bruce E. Williams and Orlando L. Taylor. New York: The Rockefeller Foundation, 1980.

Bailey, Peter A. "The Contemporary Black Theatre Movement." *Crisis* 90, No.2 (1983), pp. 22-25.

Barashango, Ishakamusa. *Afrikan Genesis.* Silver Spring: Fourth Dynasty Publishing Company, 1991.

Belcher, Fannin S., Jr. *The Place of the Negro in the Evolution of the American Theatre, 1767-1940*, Diss. Yale 1945. Ann Arbor: University Microfilms International, 1969.

Bentley, Eric. "Must I Side With Blacks or Whites." *New York Times*, Arts and Leisure, 23 January 1972, pp. 1 and .

Bogle, Donald. *Toms, Coons, Mulattoes, Mammies, and Bucks: An Interpretive History of Blacks in American Films.* New York: Viking Press, 1973.

Bowman, Ned A. "A Roundup of Recent Theatre Buildings." *Theatre Design and Technology.* No. 5 (1968), pp. 10-23.

BLACK THEATRE

Brawley, Benjamin. *The Negro Genius.* New York: Dodd, Mead and Company, 1937.

Brockett, Oscar G. *The Essential Theatre.* New York: Holt, Rinehart and Winston, 1980.

_____. *History of the Theatre.* 2nd ed. Boston: Allyn and Bacon, 1974.

_____. *History of the Theatre.* 6th ed. Boston: Allyn and Bacon, 1991.

Cockerham, William. "One of the Biggest Frauds in History?" *Houston Chronicle.* 23 August 1981, *Zest,* pp. 8 and 39.

Coe, Richard. "'Soul' Plays." Rev. of *Dr. B. S. Black* by Carlton Molette. *Washington Post,* 30 October 1970, Sec. D, p. 8.

DeGraft-Johnson, J. C. *African Glory.* Baltimore: Black Classic Press, 1986.

DewBerry, Johnathan. "The African Grove Theatre and Company." *Black American Literature Forum.* 16, No. 4 (1982), pp.128-131.

Diop, Cheikh Anta. *The African Origin of Civilization: Myth or Reality.* Translated by Mercer Cook. Westport: Lawrence Hill and Company, 1974.

_____. *Civilization or Barbarism: An Authentic Anthropology.* Translated by Yaa-Lengi Meema Ngemi. Edited by Harold J. Salemson and Marjolijn de Jager. Brooklyn: Lawrence Hill Books, 1991.

_____. *The Cultural Unity of Black Africa.* London: Karnak House, 1989.

_____. *Precolonial Black Africa: A Comparative Study of the Political and Social Systems of Europe and Black Africa, from Antiquity to the Formation of Modern States.* Translated by Harold Salemson. Westport: Lawrence Hill and Company, 1987.

DuBois, [W.E.B.] "Krigwa Players Little Negro Theatre: The Story of a Little Theatre Movement." *The Crisis.* July 1926, pp.134-136.

BIBLIOGRAPHY

_____. *The Souls of Black Folk*. 1903; rpt. New York: New American Library, 1969.

Ellison, Ralph. *Invisible Man*. New York: New American Library, 1952.

Fields, Cheryl M. "Controversial Book Spurs Scholars' Defense of the Legacy of Margaret Mead." *Chronicle of Higher Education*. 11 May 1983, pp.28-29.

Fletcher, Sir Banister. *A History of Architecture on the Comparative Method*. Seventeenth Edition. New York: Charles Scribner's Sons, 1963.

Franklin, John Hope. *From Slavery to Freedom*. New York: Vintage Books, 1969.

Gaines, Ernest J. *The Autobiography of Miss Jane Pittman*. 1971; rpt. New York: Bantam, 1979.

Gordone, Charles. "Yes, I am a Black Playwright, But . . .," *New York Times*, Arts and Leisure, 25 January 1970, pp. 1 and 11.

Hatch, James V., and Omanii Abdullah. *Black Playwrights, 1823-1977: An Annotated Bibliography of Plays*. New York: R. R. Bowker Company, 1977.

Hodges, Ann. "People make their choices." *Houston Chronicle*, 15 March 1984, Sec. 5, p. 6, cols. 1-3.

Hughes, Langston, and Arna Bontemps, ed. *Book of Negro Folklore*. New York: Dodd, Mead and Company, 1958.

Hutton, Laurence. "The Negro on the Stage." *Harper's*. June 1889, p. 133.

Karenga, Maulana, Selected and Retranslated. *Selections from The Husia: Sacred Wisdom of Ancient Egypt*. Los Angeles: The University of Sankore Press, 1984.

Kerr, Walter. "We Are Left With Only the Nightmares." *New York Times*, Arts and Leisure, 6 December 1970, pp. 5 and 7.

Kernodle, George, and Portia Kernodle. *Invitation to the Theatre*. New York: Harcourt Brace Jovanovich, Inc., 1971.

BLACK THEATRE

Kramer, Hilton. "Black Art and Expedient Politics." *New York Times*, Arts and Leisure, 7 June 1970, p. 19.

Levine, Faye. *The Culture Barons.* New York: Thomas Y. Crowell, 1976.

Marshall, Herbert and Mildred Stock. *Ira Aldridge: The Negro Tragedian.* New York: Macmillan Company, 1958.

Mbiti, John S. *African Religion and Philosophy.* New York: Praeger, 1969.

McNeil, Alex. *Total Television.* New York: Penguin, 1991.

Mitchell, Loften. *Black Drama.* New York: Hawthorn Books, Inc., 1967.

Molette, Barbara, and Carlton Molette. "The Ripoff King." *The Informer and Texas Freeman* (Houston). 15 October, 1977, p. 6.

Molette, Carlton. "Artistotle's Union of Rhetoric and Dramatic Theory." *The Southern Speech Journal.* 34, No. 1 (1968), pp.47-51.

Moore, Mavor. Address to the International Council of Fine Arts Deans, Washington, D. C. 24 October 1982.

Nkosi, Lewis. *Home and Exile.* London: Longmans, Green and Company, Ltd., 1965.

Odell, George C. D. *Annals of the New York Stage.* New York: Columbia University Press, 1928. Vol. III.

"Psyches different between races, psychologists say." *Houston Chronicle*, 22 May 1983, Sec. 3, p. 4, col. 1.

Schlesinger, Arthur M., Jr. *The Age of Jackson.* Boston: Little, Brown and Company, 1945.

Sutherland, Efua. "The Drama-Theatre Argument: A Clash of Concepts." *Encore*, 1970, pp. 3-8.

Thompson, Robert Farris. "African Influence on the Art of the United States." In *Black Studies in the University.* Ed. Armstead L. Robinson, Craig C. Foster, and Donald H. Ogilvie. New Haven: Yale University Press, 1969, pp.122-170.

BIBLIOGRAPHY

Van Sertima, Ivan. ed. *Egypt Revisited*. Vol. 10, *Journal of African Civilizations*. New Brunswick: Transaction Publishers, 1989.

——————————. *They Came Before Columbus*. New York: Random House, 1976.

Veblen, Thorsten. *The Theory of the Leisure Class*. 1899; rpt. New York: New American Library, 1953.

Woodson, Carter G. *The Mis-Education of the Negro*. Washington, D. C.: The Associated Publishers, Inc., 1933.

The World Book Dictionary. 1979 ed.

Film, Video, and Audio Recordings

Autobiography of Miss Jane Pittman. Writ. Ernest J. Gaines. Screenplay by Tracy Keenan Wynn. Prod. Robert W. Christiansen and Rick Rosenberg. Dir. John Korty. CBS-TV Special, 1974. Video disc rpt.

Ethnic Dance: Roundtrip to Trinidad. Writ. Martha Hyer. With Geoffrey Holder and Carmen deLavallade. Prod. National Educational Television and Radio Center by the Lowell Institute Cooperative Broadcasting Council, WGBH, Boston, 1960. Black and white film. 29 minutes.

Franklin, C. L., Rev. *The Twenty-Third Psalm*. Chess, 9309, n.d.

Griffith, D. W., dir. *The Birth of a Nation*. Mutual, 1915.

King. Writ. and dir. Abby Mann. Prod. Paul Maslansky. NBC. February 1978.

Massy, Morris. *What You Are Is Where You Were When*. Farmington, Michigan: Magnetic Video Corporation, 1976.

BLACK THEATRE

Plays by Black Playwrights

Baldwin, James. *The Amen Corner.* New York: Dial Press, 1968. 1st prod. 1954.

──────────────. *Blues for Mister Charlie.* New York: Dell Publishing Co., Inc.,, 1964. 1st prod. 1964.

Branch, William. "A Medal for Willie." In *Black Drama.* Ed. Woodie King and Ron Milner. New York: New American Library, 1971. 1st prod. 1951.

Brown, [James]. *King Shotaway.* Script not extant. 1st documented prod. 1823.

──────────────. *Tom and Jerry, or Life in London.* Adapted from play by Pierce Egan. Script not extant. 1st prod. c. 1822.

Brown, William Wells. *The Escape; or, A Leap for Freedom.* 1858; rpt. Philadelphia: Rhistoric Publication, n.d. Date of 1st production unknown.

Childress, Alice. *Wedding Band.* New York: Samuel French, 1973. 1st prod. 1967.

──────────────. *Wine in the Wilderness.* New York: Dramatists Play Service, 1969. 1st prod. 1969.

Cotter, Joseph S. *Caleb, the Degenerate: A Study of the Types, Customs, and Needs of the American Negro.* 1901; rpt. in *Black Theatre USA.* Ed. James V. Hatch. New York: Free Press, 1974. 1st production unknown.

Davis, Ossie. *Purlie Victorious.* New York: Samuel French, 1961. 1st prod. 1961.

Elder, Lonnie. *Ceremonies in Dark Old Men.* New York: Samuel French, 1965. 1969.

Fuller, Charles. *A Soldiers' Play.* New York: Samuel French, 1982. 1st prod. 1981.

Gordone, Charles. *No Place to be Somebody.* New York: Bobbs-Merrill Company, 1969. 1st prod. 1969.

Hansberry, Lorraine. *A Raisin in the Sun.* New York: Random House, 1959. 1st prod. 1959.

Hill Abram, *Strivers Row.* TS. 1st production 1939.

BIBLIOGRAPHY

Hughes, Langston. *Mulatto.* 1931; rpt. in FIVE PLAYS BY LANGSTON HUGHES. Ed. Webster Smalley. Bloomington: Indiana University Press, 1963. 1st prod. 1935.

——————. *Simply Heavenly.* New York: Dramatists Play Service, Inc., 1959. 1st prod. 1957.

Lee, Leslie. *First Breeze of Summer.* New York: Samuel French, 1975. 1st prod. 1975.

Mason, Judi Ann. *Livin' Fat.* New York: Samuel French, 1974. 1st prod. 1976.

Matheus, John. *Ti Yette.* In *Plays and Pageants from the Life of the Negro.* Ed. Willis Richardson. Washington, D. C.: The Associated Publishers, 1930. 1st production unknown.

Mitchell, Loften. *Star of the Morning.* In *Black Theatre USA.* Ed. James V. Hatch. New York: Free Press, 1974. 1st prod. 1955.

——————. *Tell Pharoah.* In *The Black Teacher and the Dramatic Arts.* Ed. William R. Reardon and Thomas D. Pawley. Westport: Negro Universities Press, 1970. 1st prod. 1968.

Molette, Carlton. *Dr. B. S. Black.* In *Encore*, 14 (1970), Tallahassee. 1st prod. 1969.

Molette, Carlton and Barbara. *Rosalee Pritchett.* New York: Dramatists Play Service, 1972. 1st prod. 1970.

Shine, Ted. *Contribution.* New York: Dramatists Play Service, 1970. 1st prod. 1969.

——————. *Idabelle's Fortune.* TS. 1st prod. 1969.

Walker, Joseph. *The River Niger.* New York: Hill and Wang, 1973. 1st prod. 1972.

Ward, Douglas Turner. *Day of Absence and Happy Ending.* New York: Dramatists Play Service, 1966. 1st prod. 1965.

Williams, Samm-Art. *Home.* New York: Dramatists Play Service, 1979. 1st prod. 1979.

Young, Clarence. *Perry's Mission.* TS. 1st prod. 1971.

ADDITIONAL WORKS RECOMMENDED

Anthologies of Plays by Black Playwrights

Barksdale, Richard, and Keneth Kinnamon, ed. *Black Writers of America*. New York: The Macmillan Company, 1972.

Branch, William B., ed. *Black Thunder: An Anthology of Contemporary African American Drama*. New York: Mentor, 1992.

Hamalian, Leo and James V. Hatch, ed. *The Roots of African American Drama: An Anthology of Early Plays, 1858-1938*. Detroit: Wayne State University Press, 1991.

Hatch, James V., ed. *Black Theatre USA: Forty-Five Plays by Black Americans, 1847-1974*. New York: The Free Press, 1974.

King, Woodie, and Ron Milner, ed. *Black Drama*. New York: New American Library, 1971.

Ostrow, Eileen Joyce, ed. *Center Stage: An Anthology of 21 Contemporary Black American Plays*. Oakland: Sea Urchin Press, 1981; reprint, Urbana-Champaign: University of Illinois Press, 1991.

Patterson, Lindsay, ed. *Black Theatre*. New York: Dodd, Mead and Company, 1971.

Perkins, Kathy A., ed. *Black Female Playwrights: An Anthology of Plays before 1950*. Bloomington: Indiana University Press, 1990.

Richardson, Willis, ed. *Plays and Pageants from the Life of the Negro*. Wash., D.C.: The Associated Publishers, 1930.

Turner, Darwin, ed. *Black Drama in America: An Anthology*. Greenwich, CT: Fawcett, 1971.

Wilkerson, Margaret B., ed. *Nine Plays by Black Women*. New York: Mentor, 1986.

BIBLIOGRAPHY

Books

ben-Jochannan, Yosef A.A. *Africa: Mother of Western Civilization.* Baltimore: Black Classic Press, 1988.

Bernal, Martin. *Black Athena: The Afroasiatic Roots of* Classical Civilization. Vol 1, *The Fabrication of Ancient Greece 1785-1985.* New Brunswick: Rutgers University Press, 1987.

_____. *Black Athena: The Afroasiatic Roots of Classical Civilization.* Vol 2, *The Archaeological and Documentary Evidence.* Brunswick: Rutgers University Press, 1991.

Berger, John, et al. *Ways of Seeing.* London: British Broadcasting Corporation and Pelican Books, 1972.

Brisbane, Robert H. *Black Activism: Racial Revolution in the United States 1954-1970.* Valley Forge: Judson Press, 1974.

Craig, E. Quita. *Black Drama of the Federal Theatre Era: Beyond the Formal Horizons.* Amherst: The University of Massachusetts Press, 1980.

Gayle, Addison, Jr., ed. *The Black Aesthetic.* Garden City, NY: Anchor Books, 1971.

Hill, Errol, ed. *The Theatre of Black Americans.* 2 vols. Englewood Cliffs: Prentice Hall, 1980.

James, George G. M. *Stolen Legacy.* New York: Philosophical Library, 1954; reprint, Newport News: United Brothers Communications Systems, 1989.

Kamalu, Chukwunyere. *Foundations of African Thought.* London: Karnak House, 1990.

Karenga, Maulana. *Kawaida Theory: An Introductory Outline.* Inglewood: Kawaida Publications, 1980.

Kent, George E. *Blackness and the Adventure of Western Culture.* Chicago: Third World Press, 1972.

MacDonald, J. Fred. *Blacks and White TV: Afro-Americans in Television Since 1948.* Chicago: Nelson-Hall, 1983.

BLACK THEATRE

Mitchell, Loften. *Voices of the Black Theatre.* Clifton, NJ: James T. White and Company, 1975.

Sampson, Henry T. *Blacks in Black and White: A Source Book on Black Films.* Metuchen, NJ: Scarecrow Press, 1977.

Smith, Arthur L. a.k.a. Molefi Asante. *Rhetoric of Black Revolution.* Boston: Allyn and Bacon, 1969.

Van Sertima, Ivan and Larry Williams, ed. *Great African Thinkers : Vol 1, Cheikh Anta Diop.* Incorporating *Journal of African Civilizations*, Vol. 8, No. 1. New Brunswick: Transaction Books, 1989.

Williams, Chancellor. *The Destruction of Black Civilization: Great Issues of a Race from 4500 B.C. to 2000 A.D.* Chicago: Third World Press, 1976.

Woll, Allen. *Dictionary of the Black Theatre: Broadway, Off-Broadway, and Selected Harlem Theatre.* Westport, CT: Greenwood Press, 1983.

ABOUT THE AUTHORS

Barbara and Carlton Molette have amassed a myriad of artistic and scholarly credits and collaborated as scholars, playwrights, and designers. As a result of their research on issues associated with theatre, culture, and values in the African diaspora, the Molettes have presented papers for international and U.S. professional organizations, published articles and the first edition of *Black Theatre: Premise and Presentation.*

As playwrights, the Molettes have collaborated on several productions including *Rosalee Pritchett*, produced by the Negro Ensemble Company, the Free Southern Theatre, and several colleges and universities; and published by Dramatists Play Service and in *Black Writers of America*, edited by Richard Barksdale and Kenneth Kinnamon, Macmillan Press. Their other plays include *Dr. B.S.Black*, a musical in collaboration with Charles Mann, first performed by the Atlanta University Summer Theatre; *Booji*, first produced by The Morehouse-Spelman Players and later by Texas Southern University as a video drama and aired over KPRC-TV, Houston; and *Noah's Ark*, published in *Center Stage* by Sea Urchin Press and reprinted by the University of Illinois Press. The Molettes are members of the Dramatists Guild.

Barbara Molette was born in Los Angeles and attended public school there. She earned a B.A. from Florida A. & M. University, an M.F.A. from Florida State University, and a Ph.D. from the University of Missouri. She has taught theatre, mass communication, and humanities at Spelman College and Texas Southern University. She was an administrative fellow for the Mid-Missouri Associated Colleges and Universities and

265

director of Arts-in-Education programs for the Mayor's Advisory Committee on Art and Culture in Baltimore. She has conducted workshops on writing, scriptwrighting, staff development, humanities, costuming, and makeup design for teachers and theatre artists; and served as consultant to government agencies and businesses. Her play, *Perfect Fifth*, won third place in the WMAR-TV television competition and was produced by Arena Players of Baltimore. Barbara is past president of the National Conference on African-American Theatre. She is a research consultant for the Maryland Writing Project's Urban Sites Program, Coordinator for Writing Across the Curriculum and Associate Professor at Baltimore City Community College.

Carlton Molette was born in Pine Bluff, Arkansas and attended public school in Kansas City, Missouri. He earned a B.A. degree from Morehouse College, an M.A. from the University of Iowa, and a Ph.D. from Florida State University. His theatrical credits include over 100 productions as playwright, producer, director, designer, publicist, stage manager, actor, and technician. He has served on the faculties of Spelman College, and Atlanta, Howard, and Florida A. & M. Universities. As an administrator, Carlton has served as Director of the Atlanta University Summer Theatre, Chair of the Division of Fine Arts at Spelman College, founding Dean of the School of Communications at Texas Southern University, Dean of Arts and Sciences at Lincoln (MO) University, and Vice President for Academic Affairs at Coppin State College. He has also served as guest director at the University of Michigan; seminar leader at the University of Iowa Afro-American Summer Drama Institute; consultant for universities, colleges, theatre companies, government agencies and businesses; and on the boards of arts organizations in Atlanta, Baltimore and Houston.